HOW TO GROW YOUR BUSINESS

From the UK's most popular magazine for entrepreneurs

crimson

This edition first published in Great Britain 2009 by
Crimson Publishing, a division of Crimson Business Ltd
Westminster House
Kew Road
Richmond
Surrey
TW9 2ND

A catalogue record for this book is available from the British Library.

ISBN 978 1 85458 411 3

Printed and bound by MPG Books Ltd, Bodmin, Cornwall

CONTENTS

IV

INTRODUCTION

Growing a business is exciting, and can be immensely satisfying and financially rewarding. It is also often treacherous and stressful, and is likely to involve considerable personal sacrifice. Yet surprisingly, many people in charge of businesses merely fall into it rather than choosing to go for it. For some it seems inevitable and is accepted as if it were one of life's unwritten laws: businesses must grow to be successful. Yet that is not so. Businesses can and should choose whether or not to grow, and to what extent and at what rate. If you have never thought about that before, it might be worth thinking about it now.

I have grown three businesses of my own, and been strongly involved in the growth of a fourth. I have loved much of it, but not all. Along the way I have run into all kinds of hurdles that my businesses have needed to get past (sometimes neatly jumping, other times running round the side...). And I have had the privilege of speaking to thousands of CEOs, including most of the UK's 'Celebrity Entrepreneurs'. I have found that most of the problems I came across are the same as those encountered by other growing businesses.

The growth phase of a business, from small to substantial or even large, usually involves several challenges that established large businesses or small and static businesses don't face. Yet many CEOs feel as though their problems are unique, and that advisers probably won't understand or be able to help them.

I sought help and guidance from all manner of people and books, yet have never found what I presumed must exist – a handbook to assist those steering their businesses through growth's rapid, dangerous waters. There are a few books written specifically on the subject, but none that I have come across combine real-world examples with practical help in the way I believe growing businesses need it. And of course there are thousands of business books which feature growth, and within this mass there are most certainly some real gems – yet many of those steering their business will have a small fraction of the time needed to read all that.

Some years ago I set up the magazine *Growing Business* to cover the same area. I am immensely proud of what the magazine has become, but have realised that a magazine is a different product than the handbook I mentioned above.

So we set out to create the book you are now reading, which I hope very much will support you with the answers and guidance you are after. It has turned into a larger project than originally hoped, involving the collaboration of many people, all experts in their field. It mixes some business school theory with plenty of examples from businesses you will probably know, and lots of tips and details of how to do all these things, all written in a way that can be read and understood quickly and easily – it's this combination which I believe makes this book so valuable, and which marks it out as unique.

Growing businesses matter. They matter, of course, to their staff and shareholders. But much, much more than that, they matter to the economy. Research in America suggests that almost all the new jobs created in the economy came from fast growth companies – not from the large corporate giants most people presume provide all the jobs, or indeed from the vast numbers of startups. No doubt you are not running your business in order to provide new jobs (a great result, but not a great reason to grow your business!) but it is worth pausing to pat yourself on the back for all your business is doing for the economy. And at the time of writing, March 2009, the economy surely needs all the help it can get. Part of my motivation for creating this book and putting far more time and effort into trying to get it right than is probably wise, is to do my own little bit to help our economy.

There are various business school answers to the questions you may have about how to grow your business, and these are discussed within this book. But fundamentally, it breaks down into: launching and growing your own products or services, or buying and growing existing businesses. Part Two of this book covers the first option and Part Three covers the second approach. Part Four deals with your organisation's structure and its resources, and how they might change as your business grows.

The foundation stone of every growth business should be a vision of where it's heading. To put you in the mood, Part One includes accounts of how four businesses grew. Each of their stories are inspiring, and each of the businesses are highly successful. I would love to include the story of how your business grew in a future edition of this book.

Enjoy the journey.

David Lester

BUSINESS GROWTH

UNDERSTANDING THE ROLE OF GROWTH IN BUSINESS

THIS CHAPTER WILL DISCUSS:

- Growing your business: why rise to the challenge?
- The typical stages of growth companies
- Disadvantages of growth in business
- To grow or not to grow: growth is a choice
- Is growth right for your business?

Growing your business: why rise to the challenge?

Running a successful, fast-growing business can be an exhilarating experience. As an CEO, you may find blowing past targets and leading a growing organisation hugely satisfying.

It is great to have more products in the top sales charts, to have a bigger stand at your industry trade show every year, or to be asked to speak at trade conferences as the exciting business in your space. And, of course, it feels good to be worth more money as your shares in the business gain in value. Such feelings are important and valid if your business is growing. And they are important for the wider national economy too: the UK needs those with drive to push their businesses on to further growth, specially now more than ever, since the recent economic downturn. Growing a business is challenging and hard work, but it can be immensely rewarding.

Interestingly, most growth companies, regardless of industry sector, share certain key characteristics and experiences.

> **Growing a business is challenging and hard work, but it can be immensely rewarding**

The typical stages of growth companies

The character of a business will inevitably change as it grows because of the increase in the number of staff, in particular, in the number of staff at head office. This change often shows clear patterns.

Characteristics of smaller companies

A team of between five and 10 will often consider itself a family, and will work together efficiently and closely. Everyone knows what their role is and what the company mission is. As the CEO, you can speak to everyone from time to time and get to know them well. It's easy to go to the pub with the whole company when you have up to about 15 staff.

Characteristics of larger companies

An organisation that has grown to 25 staff will usually be different from that described above. It now needs a layer of management, which changes the way the organisation needs to communicate. And many of the people who were great in a general role within the smaller business will not be right for the more specialist management roles the larger business needs.

Changing roles of long-term staff

Your role, as founder or CEO, will change considerably. Your business will probably have grown to where it is now on the back of cheap labour – your own labour, and that of your early staff, who will probably have worked long hours for lower pay than they could have got elsewhere.

People are often willing to work far harder for less pay for very small organisations where they feel connected and fiercely loyal to the young small business and its founder. Sometimes this is helped by talent which at first lacks experience. But as every business grows, that cheap labour is harder to maintain. Your early stalwarts get tired, and their market value rises; worse still, inevitably and importantly, it is not possible for you to spend as much time with them as when the business was smaller. You have more people to manage, more clients to look after, more complex business issues to solve. You cannot escape this. Some of these early heroes may well then become disillusioned.

Disadvantages of growth in business

So, are you sure you want to grow your business? That might sound like a strange question at the start of a book designed to tell you all about growth. Your answer almost certainly will be yes, of course, which is why you are reading this now. The reason we are asking the question here is that many people assume that growth is automatically good, even essential for a healthy business. Not only is that not true, but you should also be aware that growing a business can be risky and not as much fun as it appears from the outside.

Several things typically happen to fast-growing businesses that go from being small to medium-sized or medium-sized to large.

Investment before profit

Going for growth in business is very much like going out on a tree limb to get something at the end. You need to commit your business to investments in resources and people before you know whether the revenue and profit will come through. The most obvious form of that is premises. You will need to sign up for usually five years or more on some larger space to accommodate your planned expansion. If the growth stutters, is slower than you expect, or, worse still, simply doesn't happen at all, you will still be stuck with the more expensive premises expense for the remainder of the lease. Ultimately, this risk can make businesses which try to grow but fail go bust. American research suggests that most businesses that try to go beyond small don't make it.

> **The single most important aspect of growth in business is risk**

Effect of changing roles

As CEO, one of the people who can become disillusioned with the changes is you!

As your business grows, your role needs to change, and your close team may well have to change, too. You almost certainly won't be able to do what you did when you first set up – the front-line customer-facing work. You will depend on other people to do this, and it might be hard to find someone who can replicate your zeal, energy and passion for quality; after all, you had the business idea in the first place and worked as long as it took to make that dream a reality. Even very good employees are unlikely to have the same level of enthusiasm. The level at which your role becomes different will vary depending on the business type – a retailer can have lots of different shops but still retain the small head office feel, whereas a consultancy will change at lower overall employee numbers.

To grow or not to grow: growth is a choice

> **Businesses can and should choose whether or not to grow, and to what extent and at what rate**

Many CEOs we speak to haven't ever thought about growth as being a choice – they simply assume that their business needs to grow in order to remain viable and successful. In some industry sectors it is possible that 'critical mass', the size a business needs to be in order to be profitable, might grow fast and yet remain committed. Yet surprisingly, many people in charge of businesses merely fall into the notion of growth rather than choosing to go for it. You need to be aware that this isn't necessary.

If you have never thought about growth as a choice before, it might be worth thinking about it now.

KNOW YOUR CHOICES

The key to growing your business is not to be scared, but rather to move forward knowing what to expect. At every level you have several choices – continue to grow, perhaps bringing in new management, stay small, or even sell some or all the business. The point of this chapter is to make sure you take an active decision to choose one of these paths, rather than feeling growth is the only path that's available to you.

Small but perfectly formed

A business can be highly successful even without the objective of all-out growth. American small business journalist Bo Burlingham has written the best book on this subject so far, *Small Giants*, in which he describes the phenomenon of businesses that have chosen the path of excellence while staying small. It's well worth a read, and its core message, backed up by extensive research, is that it is entirely possible to run highly successful non-growth businesses.

Grow or die?

Depending on your business sector and stage, you sometimes might not have a choice.

The software business Impressions was quite happy growing at a very modest rate until it realised that it was falling behind. The rest of the industry was making bigger and better products, which required considerably more investment. Impressions could not afford to invest enough money to bring out products that would compete without more international sales. But if it didn't produce better products, its existing customers would leave. Impressions had no choice – it could either grow or die. So it opened an American sales office, went for it, and succeeded.

Others in the business who had been faced with the same dilemma and had tried the 'get bigger, fast' route failed.

Is growth right for your business?

You will have heard the classic venture capitalist's question: would you rather own 100% of a £5 million business, or 10% of a £50 million business? To put this another way, would you rather continue to run a small, closely knit business where you love your role and your team, or would you rather set out to become a larger business?

Don't try to answer this question now, but try to hold it in your mind as you read through the parts of this book that most interest you. This chapter will have succeeded if you go forward knowing that there is a question to ask.

Of course in the end, you are the only person who can answer the question for yourself. And it's the biggest question you need to address within your business. It's your business and you need to make sure you know where it goes next. But it will almost certainly be better if you talk it through with people who know you, your business and the situation. Ideally, that should be someone removed from the business itself. It could be a non-executive, a mentor, or possibly a business coach.

If you choose to grow: enjoy the ride!

Don't mistake the above cautionary notes as meaning that you shouldn't go for growth. Many of you probably will, and will thrive. The term 'serial entrepreneur' has evolved recently to describe people who keep growing businesses, then selling them, and then doing it again. They keep coming back for more typically not because they need more money but because they love it. For many people, including this book's core authors, growing a business is simply the best thing they can imagine doing with their working week.

The next chapter discusses the impact of the downturn on growing businesses.

! TOP TIPS

! Growing a business can be challenging but very rewarding.

! Most growth companies, regardless of industry sector, share certain key characteristics and experiences.

! Change of roles can cause disillusion if not properly handled.

! The single most important aspect of growth in business is risk.

! In most instances, businesses can and should choose whether or not to grow, and to what extent and at what rate.

THE DOWNTURN:
THREAT OR OPPORTUNITY-IN-WAITING?

THIS CHAPTER WILL DISCUSS:

- Putting the downturn in perspective – doom and gloom?

- Opportunities in the downturn

- Threats in a downturn

- What is in it for your business?

TYPICAL EVENTS IN A DOWNTURN

- Demand falls
- Businesses try to cut costs, especially marketing
- They focus on their core business, to protect their 'home turf'
- Bigger companies try to sell or shut down non-core business units.

You can expect:
- Price pressure from customers (perhaps aided by desperate tactics from some competitors)
- Longer credit terms
- More bad debt
- Difficulties in raising money (bank loans or share capital)
- Some competitors running into financial difficulty.

As we go to press, the world is gripped by possibly the biggest economic downturn it has ever known. At best this is the worst economic climate in several decades. Hence, it would be inexcusable not to discuss this in a book such as this, which is focused on growth. Obviously, any economic downturn can have a major effect on growth opportunities. But what effect?

Putting the downturn in perspective – doom and gloom?

Is it all so grim that we should pack our bags and sit the next few years out? Will all business suffer regardless of sector or approach? It's already clear that the answer to that is a resounding 'No!' There will undoubtedly be major casualties from the current economic climate. But history suggests that there will also be some major winners – those who seize these troubled times as an opportunity to grow.

The Sunday Times published a prominent article in the 1980s showing that Rupert Murdoch's business empire had net negative

Probably the most important question in times like these is how long will your cash last

---

CASH IS KEY

If your business has enough cash to get through the tough times, it should survive until the good times return. In the meantime, you might well be able to take advantage of the climate to grow your business.

---

liabilities of the order of more than £1 billion. His publically quoted companies were deemed by the world's stock markets to be worth less than they had been, because suddenly there was more debt than equity. (These days negative equity is a familiar concept in housing terms, and effectively Murdoch's empire had negative equity, the article explained.) But today Rupert Murdoch is a wealthy man presiding over an impressive business empire. Despite falling into negative equity, he held out and has grown substantially since. He not only held on, but came through and thrived. Probably the most important question in times like these is how long will your cash last.

Every cloud supposedly has a silver lining, and economic gloom certainly has, too. For the bold, the current times represent perhaps a once-in-a-lifetime opportunity to grow substantially, to emerge from the current downturn as a much more significant player in your market. For the growth oriented, ambitious CEO, times like these can be very good news.

Opportunities in the downturn
Marketing

In almost every downturn, all manner of businesses and organisations first tend to cut back on their advertising budgets. If they spend less money, they argue, they can make profit at a lower level of sales, and thus keep shareholders happy. On the other hand, there is plenty of research showing that those companies that continue to promote their brands throughout the downturn are the ones that emerge the strongest.

However, the point for you may be somewhat different. If you spend the same as you did last year, your money will almost certainly go considerably further now than it did then – many media owners will be happy to sell you space at lower prices than before. Even if you pay the same for each advertisement, your advertisement will be considerably more prominent than before, simply because there are many fewer advertisements around, in whatever media.

So the downturn is a great time to aggressively market your business – your money will never go as far again. And naturally, people are drawn towards optimism, and would rather deal with a business giving out positive rather than negative messages. See Chapter 2.2 for more on advertising and promotional activities.

Squeezing competitors

It's likely that your competitors will be affected to some extent – possibly bad debts, lower revenue, resulting poor morale, and so on. Typically, most companies focus inwardly at times like these rather than looking to seize the opportunities that may be out there. So you could hardly imagine a better time to be aggressive and try to poach customers from your competition, with lower prices or some other offer.

Better supplier terms

Many of your suppliers will be affected as well and their revenue will likely be down. For example, car parts suppliers have been significantly affected as all major car manufacturers are cutting back on production.

Understand your competitors before trying to squeeze them. For example, you don't want to start a price war that you are unlikely to win.

So this is a good time to ask your suppliers to sharpen their pencils a little, whether that means better prices or longer credit. Almost certainly they will want to hang on to your business, especially if you are clearly a growing and healthy customer.

New premises

Taking on new premises in a downturn will cost you far less than in a boom, both in terms of initial capital outlay and ongoing expense

Landlords are facing considerable vacancies, each of which costs them money while they sit unused. Again, it's a good time to strike a deal for new premises. There will be landlords offering low rents and even capital to fit out the premises, and possibly also a rent-free period. A retail landlord may also consider letting you space on a percentage of turnover deal, where they share the risk of a new outlet with you. Instead of paying them a set rent per quarter, you pay them an agreed percentage of your turnover from that outlet instead of rent. That takes away much of the risk of opening a new outlet. Taking on new premises in a downturn will cost you far less than in a boom, both in terms of initial capital outlay and ongoing expense.

Hiring able staff

Unsurprisingly staff tend to be rather more loyal in times of recession, and it's usually easier to hire good people. For many people, the opportunities available are shrinking, so you will find high-calibre people willing to take roles during downturns that they would deem too small or too risky to take in better times. So it's an opportunity to hire some wonderful talent, which will help make your growth plans a reality. And you can almost certainly pay them less than you would need to in a boom.

Acquisitions

Typically the market value of all companies tends to fall in a recession. Buyers are willing to pay only smaller multiples of a target business's

EXPERT OPINION

THE IMPORTANCE OF MANAGING SUPPLIERS

The Chartered Institute of Management and Supply (CIPS) offers advice on nurturing buyer-supplier relationships

Managing relationships, especially with suppliers can be difficult, but it's crucial for any business to get it right.

CIPS defines supply relationship management as "the process for managing the interactions between two entities – one of which is supplying things to the other".

This is a two-way process in that it should improve the performance of both the buying organisations, as well as the supply company, and so be mutually beneficial. It involves proactively developing relationships with particular suppliers.

Increasingly, relationship management is being seen as a softer skill, after all it's about dealing with people, communication and interaction.

As a buyer, the purpose of investing time in a relationship with a supplier is to ensure that the supplier always operates to the best of their abilities, or perhaps if it hasn't been performing as

expected, find out the reasons why. Performance management and managing changes are, therefore, integral to the relationship.

Just like any relationship, supplier relationships will vary in intimacy, depending on what is deemed necessary for the relationship to work. A relationship, for example, could be deliberately kept at arms' length, but still remain very cordial. This may be enough for the relationship to work and nothing friendlier is needed.

A more distant relationship may be normal for suppliers offering items of relatively low value, or needed infrequently, or posing little risk if there is a shortage of supply.

Moving to the other extreme is the long-term, close relationships that become a partnership. This will often be the case when items are high risk, high value and integral to organisational operation.

Supplier reliability and high-quality output are crucial to any organisation operating in a competitive environment. Eliminating defects, hitting delivery deadlines, reducing lead times and cutting costs are all elements that will impact on customer satisfaction.

Getting the relationship off the ground in the first place can be a major hurdle. Especially if in the original negotiation the buyers have used an adversarial approach. Keeping the relationship going can also be a challenge and does require time and investment on behalf of the buyer and the supplier. There are certain methods that can be employed to ease the process:

- Supplier support and development programmes – these can stress continuous improvement in the supplier's processes, product and service quality and delivery performance.
- During initial meetings with suppliers, top management should attend, showing commitment to the programme.
- Suppliers must also benefit from the alliance (no relationship works if it's one-sided). The agreed benefits that the suppliers expect from the relationship need to be monitored to ensure they are met or even exceeded.
- Buyers can help suppliers improve their operations, so spend time with your suppliers.
- Cost saving can be shared equally when the supplier meets the buyer's targets.
- Implementing supplier performance reporting will help suppliers analyse and measure their productivity. This can track statistics on quality and delivery.

The difficult part, however, is being flexible. This not a case of one size fits all and each relationship needs to be moulded to suit the situation, the organisation, the people and the product/service being bought/supplied.

Even the best relationship management techniques alone are not enough to survive in a global competitive economy, but they are now an integral part of the professional purchasers' toolkit.

For more information, visit www.cips.org

SNAPPING UP UNTAPPED TALENT

As the number of graduate openings has fallen, thousands more graduates are seeking work than there are appropriate jobs available. An excellent way to take advantage of this is to set up internships, where you take some enthusiastic and able people on in a training role, giving them valuable experience but very little money – usually interns will get living expenses, although a small number of schemes do not pay their interns at all.

profits than they would in better times, owing to the reduced supply of buyers and the increased number of willing sellers. Yet many people decide they would rather sell than fight through the tough times. As long as you can take the long-term view, it can be a good time to buy other businesses.

You may be finding that some of your competitors, suppliers or even customers are failing. There is no doubt that this is painful for those involved in the failing business, but such businesses can present some of the best opportunities for those aiming to survive the downturn. You can buy assets that can greatly improve or grow your business at a very low price. These acquisitions can be fraught, and are almost certainly more risky than a normal acquisition due to the compressed time period that is usually required and a lack of the usual legal protection for the buyer. But if you think any business(es) in your sector might be struggling and at risk of going under, and that your business would improve if you acquired them, it is well worth learning as much about the business in advance, so that when the administrator or receiver is called in you are well placed to act quickly.

Threats in a downturn
Increasing risks

Of course it's unlikely to be all good news. Your business will be impacted in some way by the effect of the recession on your market sector. In the early 1980s recession, for example, the computer

> It is important to have a greater element of contingency in your budgets and cashflows than in better economic times.

boom was just beginning, so many businesses in that sector grew rapidly despite the recession. Even in a hard-hit sector there can be opportunities for an ambitious business to grow, whether by acquisition or organic means. But nonetheless almost every business will face greater risks, such as:

- People and businesses that owe you money may default
- Falling demand
- Key suppliers going out of business.

As mentioned above, one of the keys to getting through economic downturns is having sufficient cash. No matter how profitable you might be, if you can't pay your bills then your business will fail.

Raising capital

> **Seek a medium- or long-term loan rather than an overdraft, so you know you have the funds available for a set time period**

Raising money is usually hard and time consuming, and even more so in down times. If you plan to raise capital, it's wise to start earlier than you might have done otherwise, and if you can, raise slightly more than you think you need. Businesses with plenty of cash don't fail. There is considerably more detail about raising money further on in this book, but briefly, you should expect to have to give away slightly more equity if you raise share capital in the current time, and to pay a higher premium over base rate for any bank debt. However, bank base rates are at an all-time low, which can still mean that a bank loan is exceptionally cheap by historic standards. If you can, seek a medium- or long-term loan rather than an overdraft, so you know you have the funds available for a set time period.

Consider fixing the interest rate for the entire length of the loan if you can. There is much speculation about how much banks are lending to small- and medium-sized businesses. The truth is that they are very much still lending to good businesses, but they are more risk averse than they were a year or two ago, and will probably want a greater level of security from you as a result.

What is in it for your business?

As CEO of a growing business, you need to weigh up the right strategy for your business – which risks to take and which to leave. If you're confident that demand for your business will remain strong and you have the cash to see you through, it's a great time to grow fast. If you're unsure of either demand or your funding, it might be wiser to grow more slowly, or even pause growth altogether if you're particularly concerned about either demand or funding. It is far better to survive the current downturn ready to grow again than to take excessive risks now and fail. Growth always involves risks, whatever the economic conditions.

So – the downturn could present a higher risk, but rare opportunity to make substantial step forward: your call. The next chapter profiles the real-life challenges and successes encountered by four UK growth companies.

Growth always involves risks, whatever the economic conditions

! TOP TIPS

! Offer competitors' customers competitive terms (lower prices, better credit terms).
! Market aggressively – the same budget as you had before the downturn will go far further now: you might get better rates in some media, and your advertisements will stand out far more as there will be considerably less marketing activity in the economy as a whole.
! Buy up ailing competitors – you can either approach them now or wait until they actually fail. Be prepared –know as much about them as you can to give yourself the best chance of buying well.
! Buy customers/suppliers.

HOW THEY GREW:
SOME SECRETS OF SUCCESSFUL GROWTH

THIS CHAPTER DESCRIBES
How four growth companies embraced the challenges of growing their business successfully in a competitive market. the companies are:

- The White Company
- Clapham House
- Lornamead
- Laithwaites

The White Company

A disdainful department store assistant inspired Chrissie Rucker to launch a mail-order luxury goods business based on great service that makes the customer feel valued. The fact that the venture has been a huge success clearly shows she was on to something.

Name: The White Company

Founder: Chrissie Rucker

Proposition: A seller of 'white' luxury goods

Year founded: 1993

Funding sources: Inheritance, plus government grant

Initial aim: To build a successful mail-order business

Current turnover: £60m

In this profile

- Turning an idea into a business
- Early growth
- Expansion – from mail order to retail
- Sustaining a business
- The challenges of growth

Two London hotels are playing host to a team of retail staff on a training weekend. One hotel offers fantastic customer service – lovely bath products, robes and efficient room service. The other provides an experience that can only be described as miserable – no towels, beds not made properly, malfunctioning key cards, no bath products and poor room service. When the store staff arrive at their rooms, neither of the teams knows they are being set up to experience customer service issues at the sharp end. And when the two teams get together, they have a lot to say about customer service.

That is exactly what Chrissie Rucker, founder of The White Company, intended. Since launching in 1993, she has built her rapidly growing retail empire on three pillars: quality products, value and customer service – and she is prepared to go to great lengths to illustrate the importance of those principles to her staff.

Turning an idea into a business

It was a poor customer service experience that inspired Rucker to launch her own business. When a shop assistant at a designer department store doubted her ability to buy from the more expensive range and made her feel distinctly unwelcome, Rucker left the store with a germ of a business idea: why not sell quality products at affordable prices, while making the customer feel valued in the process?

At the time, Rucker's journalism career was flying, having secured the assistant editor role at publishing's paragon of glamour, *Harpers and Queen*. However, she couldn't quell the desire to run her own business, specially since her partner happened to be Nick Wheeler, founder of the Charles Tyrwhitt mail-order clothing company. The only problem was that she wasn't entirely sure what shape her business would take.

The eureka moment came in the form of a chance remark from Wheeler's sister that it was difficult to buy good-quality white sheets anywhere. The comment took Rucker back to her brush with the snobbish shop assistant. 'I realised there was a gap in the market,' she says. 'There were plenty of places selling cheap and nasty white bed linen, but if you wanted quality you had to go to really expensive designer retailers – the very ones who could be very snotty indeed to those who they deemed not quite suitable for their stores. There was nothing in between.'

Testing that theory, Rucker researched the market and concluded there was money to be made. She was cautious at first, retaining her job at *Harpers* while she began to source suppliers. Wheeler, who was already well established in retail, advised her that mail order would be the most cost-effective route to a national market.

Cost effective or not, Rucker still needed cash to launch the business. So at just 24, she sold the shares left to her by her grandmother, pooled some cash, and in 1993 started up The White Company with £20,000.

Early growth

From the outset, Rucker's old job at *Harpers* proved invaluable. As assistant editor, she had organised photo shoots and pages of editorial. This meant that when putting together the all-important mail-order brochure, she was on familiar ground.

However, Rucker didn't rely entirely on her own judgement. From November 1993 onwards she wrote to exhibition centres – the National Exhibition Centre (NEC) in Birmingham and Olympia and Earls Court in London – asking for past trade show catalogues to use as templates. Alongside this research, Rucker set about securing a supply base, using both UK-based people and importers.

'I started with a very small range,' she recalls. 'The brochure was only 12 pages and featured china, towels and bed linen, among a few other things.' The unifying factor was that everything in the catalogue was white and of premium quality.

Having funded the production of the brochure, Rucker found herself left with just £5,000 out of the original £24,000 to market the catalogue or even to buy in a mailing list. Deploying her publishing skills, she put together a business plan and a press release, sending it to all the journalists she knew. Then she scribbled down a mailing list of 800 names, including her mother and her mother's friends.

The week the brochure was printed, *The Financial Times* picked up her story, printing an article on her company. The immediate flurry of interest shows just how effective good public relations can be. 'The phone lines went ballistic, and in the space of three days I had another 1,000 names and addresses,' Rucker recalls.

I started with a very small range. The brochure was only 12 pages and featured china, towels and bed linen, among a few other things

Having outlined the unique selling point of the company, it seems she had struck a chord with journalists, who also loved the idea that every product was white. No one had ever based a company on such a premise before. To build an entire business around a colour and succeed remains unusual. But scarcity or uniqueness, after all, are among the most valuable assets you can have, and luxury white linen was hard to find.

Like many nascent mail-order businesses, Rucker worked from modest accommodation, packing a couple of orders a day from a rented attic room where she had set up a small office. 'It was fine until the boxes started arriving and filling the spare bedroom and bathroom,' says Rucker. 'By the time the kitchen was full, Nick had had enough. I moved all the stock into a warehouse and took a spare room in the back of his office.'

If at this stage it seems like the business lacked any formal strategy, that's because it did – just like many other startups. 'I was incredibly young and naïve,' says Rucker. 'I had an idea and launched on a whim. I had no formal business sense – I was just young and gung-ho.'

Expansion – from mail order to retail

The perception of mail order, even 10 or 15 years ago, was that it was cheap, poor quality and mass marketed. Boden, Racing Green and Wheeler's Charles Tyrwhitt helped change this view. A standard 28-day wait dropped to just two or three days, and the new entrepreneurs on the block aimed for the more affluent market. The White Company rode this wave with spectacular results: the business grew by more than 40% each year for much of its first decade, and as sales volumes escalated, the product range broadened. From bed linen and towels, it became a complete lifestyle brand. Having started out at 12 pages, the company's catalogue now runs to 148.

Seven years in, the business opened its first store – in a prime location opposite the back of John Lewis' Peter Jones department store just off Sloane Square in the well-to-do Kensington and Chelsea borough of London. It was a move born out of necessity. More and more customers were coming to the company's warehouse to look at the products, and in that environment it was difficult to provide a customer experience that was in keeping with the quality of the products.

This shop did well enough for Rucker to open more; there are now 12 stores in the UK, three franchise outlets in Dubai, plus two concessions in Selfridges and one in Allders. In addition, the company diversified in 2004, introducing its first The Little White Company products for children. There are now two stand-alone stores just for this market and plans for more. The White Company stores have been an unqualified success, with sales exceeding targets and representing 20% of total turnover in 2007. The stores have brought a shift in customer profile: the average age has dropped, with The Little White Company inevitably attracting pregnant women and young mothers, opening up a new generation of buyers.

Sustaining the business

Customer service

Diversification has made The White Company more of a cradle-to-grave brand, with products now ranging from clothes and linen to children's toys and furniture. White still dominates, but Rucker has introduced a splash of colour into certain products. All this has paid off, with like-for-like sales continuing to rise steadily, even at times when the retail sector as a whole was experiencing falling volumes.

Multi-channel customers spend more, because you're making it incredibly easy for them

Since the move to retail, the company has worked hard to keep things fresh. The product range changes every three weeks, bar the staple white items. Rucker also recruited her old boss at Clarins to take charge of customer events, at which customers are offered champagne and nibbles, along with product demonstrations and a catwalk-like experience with models showing off the clothes. These events boost interest and loyalty, and support Rucker's ethos of providing a sanctuary for people with stressful lives.

Rucker also believes passionately in looking after the company's best customers, so individuals are segmented according to how they buy and when they last bought. Those who haven't bought for some time are targeted with communications to reactivate their interest, while regular customers are rewarded with special offers under a so-called VIP loyalty scheme. The best customers also get the first look at new catalogues and early notice of sales.

At least 450,000 households receive 10 brochures a year, but, as is often the way with mail order, many of the 600,000 on the full list haven't bought at all. The aim is to convert their enquiries through the smaller, more compact catalogue. The company also rents lists, sending taster brochures and placing inserts in magazines. Inevitably, keeping on top of this is crucial. There is a natural cycle, and if customers haven't bought for a long time, The White Company doesn't mail them so often. Regular buyers get all brochures, and the biggest ones. The key is to send the right size to the right person, otherwise the cost outweighs the benefit.

It's certainly the case that pricier models and photographers equate to more conversions, and just as she did at the outset, Rucker still plays an active part in the process. 'I always sign off the models and shoot locations,' she says. 'I see all mood boards before they're shot, proofread the brochures and write quite a lot of copy.'

Internet sales

The internet has been another key element in the company's success. According to Rucker, The White Company is now a truly multi-channel retailer, where each of the components – mail order, conventional retail and online selling – gets as much attention as the next. And while each channel has its own bespoke marketing strategy, Rucker is adamant that all parts of the business talk to each other, enabling customers to shop via whichever channel is convenient at any particular time. Not only is this good practice in terms of customer service, Rucker believes that it also pushes up sales. 'Multi-channel customers spend more,' she explains, 'because you're making it incredibly easy for them.'

An impressive – and rising – 22% of revenue is generated online. It's a part of the business Rucker is particularly pleased with, and the site now boasts the company's entire range of more than 2,500 products.

Standing out from the crowd on the internet is never easy, but Rucker has been determined to stay ahead of the online retailing curve. She introduced a 'flick-able' brochure, an innovation in UK online retailing, designed to create an online environment that will appeal to mail-order shoppers. 'I saw one on a US website,' she says. 'I think we're the first here to do that. The thing about a website is you can't turn the pages and have to click through everything. It's a very different way of shopping.' So now online shoppers get the choice of flicking or clicking.

Rucker has commissioned research on the psychology of online and mail-order customers, and an in-depth analysis of the effectiveness of marketing activity is also ongoing. Click-throughs from third-party sites (including search engines and advertising banners) are also studied carefully to identify which of the incoming channels deliver the highest sales.

Online marketing

Online marketing is hugely important and, like a great many internet retailers, The White Company has increased spending on search engine optimisation to ensure that it appears high up on the first page on a portal such as Google or Yahoo when a potential customer is searching for a particular product. The company has also introduced an affiliate marketing scheme under which a range of participating websites carry links to The White Company and are rewarded on a pay-per-click basis. The initiative, which was set up by TradeDoubler (a European leader in affiliate management), offers commissions of up to 10%. Blogs are another recent innovation. Regular contributions are made to an online 'The White Company diary' and have also helped to increase traffic to the site since it was re-launched in 2007.

The challenges of growth

Delegation

Rucker admits that in the early days of the company, she was a 'total control freak', but taking charge of everything in a company with 450

> **Handing over responsibility is an important part of job satisfaction**

employees and a turnover of £60m is simply not possibly. Over time, she has learned how to cede operational control of certain areas to others, but not without the help of a delegation course.

'It was life-changing,' she recalls. 'It taught me an enormous amount. Handing over responsibility is an important part of job satisfaction. I had to learn how to brief properly, but the more you hand over the more they enjoy their jobs.'

It's been six years since the delegation course epiphany, and the management structure has evolved accordingly. These days, The White Company's senior team comprises a managing director and financial director, along with merchandising, human resources, retail, marketing, customer services and creative directors. Rucker also employs an unofficial chairman, while husband Nick also sits on the board. To ensure a coordinated and integrated approach, Rucker uses a marketing agency for select projects. 'Until now I have always driven the marketing,' she says.

From a personal point of view, the enlarged management team enables her to juggle family and work, but the structure is designed to compensate for her deficiencies. 'I'm not a figures person and hopeless at operational management,' she admits. 'I'm definitely a product person, though.'

Reinvesting in the business

A key feature of The White Company has been its focus on reinvestment, and Rucker points to a cycle that the company tends to go through. Time and money is spent on improving customer service and the fulfilment infrastructure. Then profit levels go back up to 8% or 10%. After that, the company reinvests to improve service still further.

Much of 2005 was spent moving from a 30,000sq ft warehouse, where a marquee was erected during busy periods, to a new £1.3m 100,000sq ft base, more capable of feeding 30 stores and up to 6,000 orders a day. Moving was a painful experience that threw up unexpected problems, such as a data feed that wasn't quite big enough to meet demand. It should have been an easy matter to fix,

"

We could grow faster, but I'm interested in strong, solid growth 🠚

but the line ran under another business, and putting in a system with more capacity took six months. Throughout that period, the company had the inconvenience and expense of biking despatch notes from the call centre in London to Northampton in order to send the parcels.

The warehouse also had to close for four days for a complete stock-check. For a company that prides itself on fast delivery, this posed a major problem. To avoid disappointing customers, it held stock at stores and fulfilled mail order and internet orders from there. The result was a slight delay of two days in customer dispatches,

SECRETS OF SUCCESS

Have a strong concept
Chrissie Rucker's plan to base a business around the concept of the colour white was unique, a fact that made the company hugely attractive to consumer journalists in search of interesting trends and concepts. Early publicity was instrumental in driving sales.

Identify a market
Rucker saw a clear niche for a company that would offer white linen (initially) to customers who wanted quality at affordable prices.

Focus on customers
Ordering goods by mail order is something of an act of faith. Rucker has continued to insist on excellent customer service as a means to ensure that those who buy once will be have positive experience and thus be more likely to buy again.

Diversify
In a multi-channel world, customers want to interact with brands offline and online. The White Company offers its products through retail stores, the net and mail order.

Delegate
As The White Company has grown, Rucker has delegated key duties to talented new managers, freeing her up to think more strategically and focus on her core product skills, while her staff are move motivated and feel more valued through their extra responsibility.

Reinvest
To move the business forward, Rucker has continued to invest in new products and routes to market.

but nothing that was overly damaging. The company also picked the quietest time – spring – to carry out the work. Upgrades continue on warehouse systems and IT, but the business is now largely geared for growth. 'We re-forecast every quarter, and every pound certainly counts,' Rucker says.

Looking ahead, the company has a top line five-year plan, then a three-year plan 'with a bit more beef'. In five years, depending on whether the company tackles the USA, it expects to hit a turnover of £110m. 'We could grow faster, but I'm interested in strong, solid growth,' says Rucker.

Clapham House

Originally floated on AIM with the express purpose of buying up restaurant chains for expansion, Clapham House has been an object lesson in growth by acquisition.

Company name: Clapham House

Founders: David Page, Paul Campbell

Proposition: Buying up and growing restaurant businesses

Year founded: 2004

Initial funding: £15m flotation on AIM

Initial aim: To grow small restaurant chains to 25 outlets or more

Acquisitions to date: The Real Greek Food Company, purchased 2003; Bombay Bicycle Club, purchased 2004; Gourmet Burger Kitchen, purchased 2004; Tootsies, purchased 2006

Current turnover: £60m

In this profile

- The Pizza Express years – building a track record
- Turning an idea into a business – floating on AIM and selecting acquisition targets
- Early challenges – persuading owners to sell their restaurants
- Sustaining the business – finding an ethos and a structure that works
- The future

Say you are an investor talking to the directors of a newly formed company seeking to raise £15m through a flotation on London's Alternative Investment Market (AIM). Everything seems fine – after all, plenty of companies float on AIM every year – until you find out that this particularly company has no products or services of its own to offer. Instead, it's a vehicle established to buy up small restaurant chains and scale them up into much bigger operations. As yet, no acquisitions have been made. So would you put money into this company?

This was Clapham House's proposition in 2004, and the answer to that question was a resounding 'Yes'. The flotation went ahead as planned and the company launched as a so-called 'cash shell' with £15m in the bank to make acquisitions.

Most new companies start small, grow their sales over a period of years and then begin to think about acquisitions and external investment. A flotation on a stock market – if it happens at all – is usually some way down the line, often following years of successful trading. In contrast, Clapham House's founders, David Page and Paul Campbell, dived in at the deep end. But why did investors back a new company taking such an unusual approach? According to Page, Clapham House's executive chairman, the answer was simple: 'We'd done it all before.'

The idea Page and his co-founder Paul Campbell put to investors was that they would use the £15m to buy three profitable emerging restaurant chains with between three and five branches and expand them. And the partners had form. Investors value market knowledge and a proven track record, and Page had already demonstrated that skill in abundance.

The Pizza Express years

I had a knack for running restaurants, making customers happy and choosing sites

Having both recently exited the Pizza Express chain, Campbell and Page could safely claim to know all about the restaurant industry, while presenting investors with a balanced mix of financial and commercial skills.

Chief executive Campbell was appointed group finance director of the Pizza Express group in 2002, having previously established his entrepreneurial credentials by setting up and running leisure management group Relaxion in the 1990s. Page, meanwhile, had a 25-year association with the restaurant chain behind him, joining the company in the kitchens after having been expelled from school and sacked from his first job as a cartographer. So he had learned the restaurant business from the bottom up.

Working at Pizza Express part-time while training as a teacher, Page's employer had noticed where his true talents lay – even if he, by then, hadn't – and offered him the opportunity to run one of the restaurants. To Page, it meant a 15% share of profits, a decent salary and, perhaps most importantly, an introduction to the rudiments of a small business.

After five years learning his trade, Page decided he wanted to strike out on his own. A second mortgage and a loan of £6,000 secured him a Pizza Express franchise in Chiswick. Over the next decade, Page established a portfolio of restaurants, which included – after buying out his former employer – 14 Pizza Express franchises, under the company name of G&F Holdings. By the end of the 1980s, he had built a turnover of around £5m and cash profits of £1m. 'I had a knack for running restaurants, making customers happy and choosing sites,' explains Page. 'All my restaurants were successful and had 20% profit margins.'

But Page had his eyes on bigger things. When the original founders of Pizza Express decided to sell in 1992, Page saw it as his chance to join the big league. As the major Pizza Express franchisee, Page's G&F Holdings was absorbed into the newly acquired Pizza Express Company and floated on the stock market in February 1993. Page was appointed chief executive of the group by new owners Luke Johnson and Hugh Osmond, and he oversaw a period of spectacular growth, with the issue share price of 40p rocketing to a high of £9.50.

The spectacular rise of the company at the hands of Page was in stark contrast to his personal finances. 'I put every single penny into the business and there was no room for error,' he says. 'When we floated, I was technically a millionaire, but I had negative equity in my house. I didn't own anything other than a lot of paper that said I was a millionaire.' And it was perhaps this that fuelled Page's enthusiasm to reinvest some of the profits he made from the eventual sale of Pizza Express. By that time, its share price had fallen to a less-frenzied figure, but at around £3 a share, Page insists the buyers got a 'very good purchase' – not that he stopped to dwell on it. Page was more interested in putting the years of experience gained to good use in a new venture.

Turning an idea into a business

So with Campbell's financial and entrepreneurial credentials and Page's track record as a developer of restaurant chains, the partners were ideally placed to 'sell' the concept of their investment vehicle to the City. By buying small restaurant chains, Page and Campbell would benefit from the groundwork that had already been done by the original owners. With the building blocks in place, they would be free to use their experience to grow the businesses.

The key was the AIM-listed cash shell, an enterprise which, at least at the outset, doesn't boast any business assets or trading activity. It exists as a repository for investor cash. In the case of Clapham House, that cash would be used to fund acquisitions. Page believed it was the logical way to start a business where the strategy was to grow in this way. 'If you have the cash in the bank, you can buy the businesses more efficiently,' he says. 'If the business you want knows it's essential for you to float, the price will go up – that's only natural.'

As Page later recalled, some investors were a little tentative, fearing the company would simply take their money and put it in the

It is a terrible decision for these people to make. They've got a successful business, so why sell it to us?

bank. But its pledge to make all three acquisitions within the first two years of trading pacified most of the doubters. As a result, institutional investors, such as Schroders, Framlington and Shell Pension Fund, jumped in. 'They were all people that had already made money out of Paul and me, so I suppose you could say they were throwing more good money after good,' says Page.

Early challenges

To make the idea work, Clapham House also had to convince restaurant owners to sell up. Put simply, the problem with buying exciting growing businesses on the crest of exploiting their potential is persuading the owners they should sell to someone else rather than do it themselves. As someone who realised in his twenties that he 'didn't want to be an employee', it's an issue Page was very much aware of. 'It is a terrible decision for these people to make,' he says. 'They've got a successful business, so why sell it to us?'

But Clapham House could offer small restaurateurs the power to grow. Expanding from three or four units can be a huge leap, and although the potential rewards are great, so are the risks. Page and Campbell offered both the financial support and experience necessary for fast and successful expansion. That's why, according to Page, Clapham House Group became an attractive option. The company structured its deals with big earn-outs (additional payments) for the seller based on the future profits that Clapham House would help them to generate. Unlike venture capital, debt finance or private investment (see Part Four), the owners got some money straight away through the sale, as well as the chance to work towards a far bigger pay day.

'We give them big incentives to perform over two or three years in terms of earn-out,' explains Page. 'They sell us the shares for say 20% of what they're worth on day one and then, in two or three years' time, if they make profits, we reward them by buying them out for a formula.' The owners also gained Page's expertise and experience in the field. 'It's quite easy if you're rolling out a retail business to choose the wrong properties in terms of location and rent, and it holds you back,' says Page. 'We know most of the high streets below Inverness; we know where to – and where not to – open.'

Buying right

The first three acquisitions took less time than expected, with the Real Greek Food Company, Indian restaurant chain the Bombay Bicycle Club, and the Gourmet Burger Kitchen (GBK) agreeing to buy-outs within the first two years. All three were established, popular and profitable companies serving quality food with proven business models that demonstrated potential for growth – criteria far more important to Page than the type of food they specialised in. Indeed, Page insists the group will never buy a startup and isn't interested in turnarounds as it 'only wants to be associated with success because anything else is too risky'.

Certainly the chains in question had already carved out their own niches in the food market. The Real Greek Food Company was a small operation, owning the award-winning Hoxton Restaurant and two informal mezze bars, but Clapham House saw significant development potential in what it perceived as an under-developed market. Similarly, when the Bombay Bicycle Club was purchased in 2004, it had already won itself an enviable reputation for selling high-quality food. Over its 20-year life, it had amassed a database of more than 100,000 customers, and this convinced Clapham House that it was a brand that could be grown in the fragmented Indian restaurant market. For its part, GBK already boasted six outlets, catering for a clientele that wanted food that was fast, but good. It had tapped into a zeitgeist of sorts, eschewing the low-cost unique selling point of McDonalds for an offering that put the emphasis on high quality. Page and Campbell saw huge potential at this end of the market.

Clapham House spent its money wisely. The Real Greek deal saw an initial payment of just £263,000, rising to a possible £9m over time, while the Bombay Bicycle Club and GBK cost £2.42m and £2.6m (rising to £7m), respectively. Importantly, Clapham House didn't just dive in, cheque book open, at the first opportunity. It held initial talks with more than 40 different Greek, tapas, noodle, Indian and burger restaurateurs. It wasn't simply a case of picking those that made the most profit – and that's where Page's experience of 'what makes a good restaurant' came in. 'First we chose the ones where we liked the food best, then those where the customers seemed to value the restaurant,' explains Page. 'Finally, the deciding factor was whether the restaurant had a good management team in place. We have to think like a private equity house and there's no point us buying businesses unless we're confident they are well run.' This meant weighing up and mostly ruling out several chains that may have appeared to have had plenty of potential to the untrained eye. 'There are some businesses around that the public think are marvellous, where queues stretch right out of the door, but don't actually make any money,' explained Page. 'They take a lot, but don't make a lot – and we're not interested in that.'

Page believes that, in each case, the companies that interested them were capable of adding something new to an existing market. 'We were looking for businesses with clever propositions, clever management and clever employees, that had got to the four- or five-unit level and were ready to grow to the 25-unit stage if we gave them the money and support,' he says. The acquisition of the first three businesses left Clapham House with £14m in the bank, but Page and Campbell didn't rush into making a further purchase. Initially, the company planned to focus on growing its existing brands rather than splashing out on new chains.

However, in 2006, the company went on the acquisition trail again with the purchase of Urban Dining, owner of the Tootsies chain. It was a smart move, boosting turnover in the year to 21 April 2007 to £46m, compared with just £17.3m 12 months earlier.

Sustaining a business – visions and values

The ethos of Clapham House is to allow each business a degree of freedom rather than insisting that they conform to a single corporate line on all things. 'What happens if you impose a chain culture is that staff wander round like robots and customers become bored,' says Page.

But there are unifying factors. Certainly, customer experience was always central to the company's thinking. For instance, its purchase of GBK was partly borne out of a belief that the UK's current burger restaurant offering was 'appalling'. However, while Page believed that with GBK, Clapham House was investing in a market where there was a growing demand for better quality fastfood served in pleasant surroundings, he wasn't of the view that the big names in the burger business should follow the 'gourmet' model.

Far from it, the Clapham House approach to business is focused on each restaurant chain knowing its own market. For instance, in Page's opinion, McDonalds was losing ground in the fastfood market, because an effort to go up market meant it was losing touch with its audience. 'It's "food for fuel driven by price",' he says. 'All their customers want is somewhere warm to sit for half an hour and eat and drink something really cheap. Because their management presumably went to university, they have aspirations, but their customers are not aspirational.'

Getting the price point right has been an important part of the Clapham House strategy, not least because a business model based on growing the number of restaurants in a chain is best served by maintaining relatively low prices. It's a simple equation: the more upmarket and expensive a restaurant is, the smaller its potential audience. That, in turn, limits the number of outlets that it is possible to own.

> **The Clapham House approach to business is focused on each restaurant chain knowing its own market**

The future

Ironically, perhaps, Clapham House has itself been the subject of takeover speculation. For instance, in January 2008, Capricorn Ventures raised its stake in the company to 25%, fuelling expectations that a bid was on the cards. Meanwhile, the company is looking beyond the UK for growth, with Campbell speaking of the possibility

SECRETS OF SUCCESS

Investors back experience

Clapham House used the AIM to raise cash which could then be used to buy up and develop restaurant chains. Investors needed assurance that the money would be well spent. Fortunately, founders David Page and Paul Campbell could point to years of experience in the trade.

Structure acquisitions wisely

When Clapham House buys a company, it generally structures the deal with an earn-out element to link the ultimate payout to performance. This keeps the initial costs down and motivates the sellers and management teams to stick with the business and work it hard.

Choose acquisition targets carefully

Page and Campbell talked to more than 40 businesses before making their first three acquisitions.

Look for potential

Page and Campbell didn't necessarily choose the business with the highest profits. Instead they looked at factors such as customer satisfaction and the potential of the business to be grown.

Know your customers

Page puts his success at both Pizza Express and Clapham House down to knowing the customers and keeping them happy, while also choosing good sites. Giving the customers what they want and expect from a particular restaurant chain is vitally important.

of extending into Turkey, Ireland and the Middle East through a franchising scheme.

But regardless of the future ownership, Clapham House provides ample evidence that when a company is in experienced hands, acquisition can be a fast track to growth.

Lornamead

Lornamead has thrived on a strategy of buying and improving brands that were being neglected by multinationals.

Name: Lornamead

Founder: George Jatania

Chief executive: Mike Jatania

Proposition: Developing and acquiring personal care brands

Year founded: 1978

Initial funding: Less than $100,000 (£60,000)

Additional funding: Combination of senior and mezzanine finance

Initial aim: To trade goods in West Africa

First year turnover: less than $1m (£0.6m) at retail

Current turnover: More than $600m (£340m) at retail

In this profile

- The early years – forging a business model
- The breakthrough – own-brand development
- Growth by acquisition – becoming a global player
- Sustaining the business – brand development
- Running a family business – everyone's responsibility

After starting life trading 'anything and everything' in West African markets, Lornamead has become a much more focused operation. Today, the company specialises in personal care products and has become a global player in this market by acquiring and developing well-known brands.

The early years

The company was launched by George Jatania in 1978, but it wasn't long before it became a genuine family business, with his brothers

> **Focusing on your strengths is the best way to get ahead in business**

Van and Danny coming on board shortly afterwards. Mike Jatania, the current chief executive, joined the team in 1984, having opted to complete a degree in accountancy beforehand.

With the family team in place, the brothers embarked on a change of strategy. Rather than continuing as a generalist trading company, they decided to focus on four key areas: home and personal care, wines and spirits, food products and generic pharmaceutical goods. The thinking behind the move was simply to concentrate on products that would 'make money'. That, in itself, would have marked an important change in direction, but the company was also beginning to establish much closer ties with its multinational suppliers. Where initially the relationship was simply buyer and seller, over time Lornamead began to play a role in brand management.

'We started to get involved in implementing their strategies in terms of pricing, promotion and above the line support for the brands,' Mike Jatania recalls. 'We did this for Colgate, Gillette, Unilever and Heinz, among others. It became the foundation of the group for three years, providing not only valuable cashflow, but also a hands-on lesson in the vagaries of the fast-moving consumer goods market.'

But if the company's close ties with multinationals formed the basis of early success, these relationships also put limits on the company's ability to grow. Put simply, the company was being held back because its partners didn't require its brand management skills outside Africa. This effectively prevented Lornamead from operating in the lucrative markets in Europe and North America.

The breakthrough

The company decided to strike out with its own brands. But it wasn't a move that was undertaken lightly. Indeed, it went hand in hand with a round of consolidation and rationalisation within the existing company. The pharmaceuticals business was sold, largely because the research and development element demanded more resources than the Jatanias were prepared to dedicate to the operation. This was followed by the sale of their food offering, which consisted of baked goods, a move motivated by very low profit margins, intense competition and because there was 'no room for middlemen'.

The wines and spirits business survived the cut, but was put into 'harvest'. In other words, it was left to turn over without any support from advertising or brand development, while profits were churned into other parts of the business. That left Lornamead's personal care range, which was profitable without demanding too large a share of available resources. And once they began to develop their own products, the Jatania brothers found that they could outsource the production of goods and focus their attention on brand development. 'It meant that the working capital we required to run the business was shared, because the outsourcing partner would invest in raw and packaging materials, make the finished goods and even hold onto them for a certain period,' Mike Jatania explains.

It was a strategy that blended diversification and entrenchment. But stripping the business down enabled Lornamead to both branch out into new territories and to buy up more products within its main area of activity. When asked the awkward question whether, in general, it is better to focus or diversify, Mike Jatania takes the view that the two were not mutually exclusive. 'It's like shining a single ray of light through a prism. The light splits into several beams and lots of different colours,' he says.

Financing and developing brands is risky, according to Mike Jatania. He admits the business had 'varying degrees of success' launching and building up its own product lines. There was a string of triumphs including Similar, a range of fragrances designed to look and smell like more expensive designer product lines, and the Tura skincare range, formulated specifically for darker skin. But the brothers soon found that creating successful brands from scratch was a painstaking and exhaustive process. Moreover, there are no guarantees of success and numerous potential pitfalls. 'Bank money was not enough to finance our brands, so we had to keep reinvesting profits back into new launches and development projects,' says Mike Jatania, listing the challenges the group faced in building a product portfolio:

Bank money was not enough to finance our brands, so we had to keep reinvesting profits back into new launches and development projects

- First there is a degree of risk because you have to spend a considerable amount of money on advertising up front. 'While this will be based on market research, there is no guarantee of a return,' he says.
- Then there is the fact that each brand has to be nurtured and encouraged over a long period, and, as the brothers soon discovered, it takes time for people to pledge their loyalty to a new brand – a big reason why plenty of them fail early on.

Growth by acquisition

Mike Jatania took over as chief executive in 1990 and the company redefined its strategy again. Seeing that the business could leapfrog the difficult launch phase by buying up existing brands and improving them, he embarked on a strategy of acquisition. His targets were 'heritage' brands – those that were successful, but outside the core business plan of their parent companies and thus neglected.

'Corporate orphans were famous brands that were either extremely strong in a local market or in a region, but not from a global viewpoint,' Mike Jatania explains. 'What the multinationals wanted to do was simplify their supply chain and their business processes.' And in targeting these corporate orphans, Lornamead snapped up several that were already market leaders, such as Lypsyl. The company was helped by a trend within the personal care industry. Just as Lornamead was turning its attention to brands that had lost their way, giant companies, such as Unilever and Proctor & Gamble, were shedding peripheral products and targeting billion-dollar brands.

Meanwhile, Lornamead was also reaping huge gains from the emerging, but fast-growing, market in eastern Europe, particularly Poland and Russia. As a comparatively small company, it was nimble and could respond to the burgeoning spirit of consumerism that spread across the region following the Soviet Union's demise. 'Perestroika was very good to us,' says Mike Jatania. 'For once, the business could vie for market share on a level playing field, because the personal care giants were no more entrenched in the area than we were. We were very much in the right place at the right time with the right strategy. And you always need a bit of luck in any business venture.'

He played the situation to his company's advantage by purchasing these well performing yet 'non-core' products and spending money on rebranding and marketing, extending their market share further. The strategy is summed up in the company's slogan: 'Adding value to brands'.

The acquisition trail

The flurry of acquisitions began in earnest in 1998, with the purchase of the Harmony haircare range from Unilever. Mike Jatania believes it was the perfect product to launch the new business model: being a flagship brand it gave them a blueprint for future deals. Agreements followed with Henkel, Sara Lee, Network Health & Beauty, Procter & Gamble and Bristol-Myers Squibb, as well as several more with Unilever.

It's hard to overstate the degree to which acquisitions have been the key to the company's phenomenal growth. In this decade alone, the company completed nearly 40 transactions, which collectively have made it a significant player in the personal care market. Of all the acquisitions, arguably the most astute was the purchase of teeth-whitening company Natural White. Lornamead bought the US-based company in December 2002, with the sale including the manufacturing base, intangible assets and the patent on the formula. Purchasing the copyright meant Lornamead benefited from two revenue streams, making money not only from sales of its own product to retailers but also from its competitors who were banned from replicating the product and therefore had to buy under licence from Lornamead to sell on to consumers. The deal also gave the company a firm foothold in a rapidly expanding market. When Lornamead acquired the company, the teeth-whitening market in the USA was worth about $50m, and was operating well below its potential. Since then it has exploded, sending the figure skywards to around $800m.

In 2003, Mike Jatania and his brothers once again demonstrated considerable business acumen by fighting off 40 rivals to win control of

We altered the brand, the category, the package and the range

Ireland's haircare market through a licensing agreement with Proctor & Gamble. The pharmaceuticals giant wanted to buy Clairol and Wella, but the European Commission ruled that the transaction infringed competition laws and forced the company to sell some of its brands before pressing ahead. 'There were around 40 pitches for its Ireland range, for which it hired advisers to whittle down,' Mike Jatania recalls. 'Lornamead won it and entered into a licensing agreement with the company, although the sale went ahead like an acquisition.'

Lornamead won the right to market and distribute several of Proctor & Gamble's leading haircare brands in Ireland, such as Herbal Essence, Silvikrin, Borne Blonde, Loving Care and Lasting Colour.

Sustaining the business

So once it has acquired a brand, how does Lornamead go about adding value to it? According to Mike Jatania, consumer-led research is essential as you have to know if people like it. Equally, you have to understand consumer behaviour and establish whether there is a desire for the brand.

Lip moisturiser stick Lypsyl is a good example. Its name has become synonymous with the kind of product it is – just like Hoover has with vacuum cleaners – and that was a key strength. However, it was only a small product within the Unilever portfolio and was below the radar of the multinationals. Despite being a market leader, it was being neglected. The product line involved only three flavours along with the standard stick, and market rivals had pretty much done the same. Meanwhile, market research revealed who was using the product and how. It emerged that many people had more than one, so Lornamead created more choice, by introducing new flavours and a medicated version. The brand was shown to be popular among skiers, so the company introduced a dispenser that would enable them to use it without having to take off their gloves. 'We altered the brand, the category, the package and the range,' says Mike Jatania. 'In terms of advertising, we found that it was an impulse purchase product, and didn't require lengthy ad campaigns to get people buying it.' To capitalise on this impulse factor, where people would pop in and buy a stick of Lypsyl off the cuff in cold weather, Lornamead ensured there was a strong presence at the point of purchase in shops to encourage sales, while the quality of the product was also improved. Finally, Lornamead decided to sell Lypsyl to every market in the world, effectively letting the product off the leash in terms of its marketing potential.

In other words, the success of the company wasn't built on simply acquiring success stories and letting them run, but by directing a considerable amount of time and creative energy into understanding the brand and its appeal, its marketplace and its potential for future growth.

Running a family business

Amid all this frenetic deal making, the Jatania brothers also found time to set up a private equity fund, EPIC Brand Investments, which co-invests with the Lornamead group in home and personal care brands. Initially floated on the AIM in December 2002, raising £50m, it was bought back by the brothers late last year so they could regain total control over its activities. Despite such a meteoric mix of organic and inorganic expansion, Lornamead's central focus has remained remarkably steady. Mike Jatania makes sure the company sticks to what it knows best and outsources everything else.

Today, Lornamead employs people in Dubai, London, Jersey, Ireland, Toronto, Lagos, Johannesburg and Cape Town, while boasting a distribution network spanning 50 countries. Despite this, Jatania describes Lornamead as resembling a virtual company, because of its emphasis on marketing over manufacture – although it does operate a substantial research and development base, contract-manufacturing arm, tube-filling operation and turnkey solutions. Ultimately, the company reflects Mike Jatania's belief that focusing on your strengths is the best way to get ahead in business.

Our family are the business' shareholders, but we don't treat them any differently to institutional shareholders

A surprising aspect of Lornamead is that it is still essentially a family business, although lately Jatania prefers the term 'business family'. At one time or another, the four brothers have all occupied senior posts, and all remain advisers and shareholders – the family's combined stake totals 100% of the business. Family is clearly very important to the Jatanias. The brothers live together and Mike admits that shoptalk is not confined to office hours. But the family is careful to not let its closeness cloud its business judgement. 'Our family are the business' shareholders,' Mike Jatania explains, 'but we don't treat them any differently to institutional shareholders. We show them the same respect and objectivity. But family can also be a major weakness. You can't become complacent or lazy just because you're answering to people you know very well. You mustn't take it for granted – if you don't it can be of enormous benefit.'

The sibling core of the business is complemented by a strong management team, of which Mike Jatania is obviously very proud. The family would never rule out selling the business, he says, and it is important to make sure it can build on its impressive track record without the brothers' involvement. 'Family and management are separate – something that will help the business in the long term,' he asserts. 'We've brought in a good board with entrepreneurial flair.'

The new blood includes two non-executive directors, but Mike Jatania is still very much at the helm. Since 2006, the company has been focusing on growing internationally, establishing offices in India and Russia, while entering Thailand and Brazil. The acquisitions keep on coming too, with the most recent being Finesse, Aquanet and Woods of Windsor. Jatania's descriptions of the business are littered with references to drive, ambition, enthusiasm and future growth. And at just 41 years old, it seems there's still plenty of time for him to achieve all his business goals, however heady they may be.

SECRETS OF SUCCESS 1

Partner with larger companies

In the early stages of its evolution, Lornamead undertook brand management work for multinational companies, in addition to pursuing its own industries in the food, home and personal care, drinks and pharmaceuticals industry. These contracts provided the company with predictable cashflow and invaluable insights into the consumer goods market.

Don't accept limitations

While brand management played a hugely important role in the development company, it limited Lornamead's international growth, as the contracts didn't extend to overseas markets. Thus, Lornamead decided to develop its own brands.

Buy rather than launch

Developing and nurturing new brands is expensive and risky. Lornamead opted instead to buy successful ones that were not being fully exploited by parent companies.

Cut away the dead wood

In parallel with its strategy of developing its own brands, Lornamead rationalised its existing business, selling pharmaceuticals and food, cutting back spend on drinks and developing the home and personal care side.

Keep it in the family

Lornamead is run as a family business, although where the company is concerned there is little room for sentiment. When business is discussed, all family members are treated as shareholders rather than relatives.

Research the market

The key to developing the brands is to research the market carefully to understand the customer perception of the product and how it is used. Once the customer–brand relationship is fully understood, improvements can be made both in terms of product quality and marketing strategy.

Stretch the brand

Brands can be stretched geographically – in terms of their market – and by expanding the product. Once a brand has established consumer loyalty for a particular function – say, skincare – new products can be released under that name.

Laithwaites

Tony Laithwaite has turned a passion for France and its wine into a multi-million pound turnover business, with a little help from *The Sunday Times* along the way.

Name: Laithwaites

Founders: Tony Laithwaite

Proposition: Supply quality wine to the UK market

Year founded: 1969

Initial funding: £700 loan

Additional funding: Angel investment 1973

Initial aim: To expand the range of wine available

Current turnover: £300m

In this profile

- The early years – turning an idea into success
- First success – *The Sunday Times* Wine Club takes off
- Growth strategies – going organic
- The challenges of expansion – maintaining core values
- Stepping back – relinquishing day-to-day control
- Rebranding – names matter
- Diversification – don't lose sight of the vision

As a teenager, Tony Laithwaite was captivated by the idea of France. But rather than relocating permanently across the Channel, Laithwaite took the opportunity of bringing a flavour of France over to the UK – primarily, its most famous export, wine.

The early years

Like many entrepreneurs, Laithwaite was resistant to the allure of a 'proper' job. So much so that after university, he packed his bags and returned to the Bordeaux area of France where he'd spent holidays as a child, signing up for a course in wine making. But although he found work in a French vineyard, he wasn't able to secure permanent employment. That left him with a dilemma. While reluctant to leave Bordeaux, he was aware that he needed to go on earning money. It was that necessity that led him to taking his first tentative steps towards running his own business.

Someone at a cellar where Laithwaite was working suggested he become an agent and sell wine directly into the UK. 'He gave me a few sample bottles, so I came back to the UK, did a mailing by very naïvely taking a load of names out of the phonebook and had a couple of people ask me to come round and give them a tasting,' Laithwaite recalls. 'I did and they started buying.'

With a £700 loan from his grandmother, herself an entrepreneur, he bought a van and continued taking orders off the back of mailings until he had enough to justify a savoured trip to Bordeaux. Although these were humble beginnings, Laithwaite built Bordeaux Direct – as his company was then called – into a moderately successful mail-order business with its own shop in Windsor. However, there was a limit to what he could achieve. This was the early 1970s, and although the UK was becoming switched on to wine, the masses were far from connoisseurs. As Laithwaite was selling premium wines, the potential market was still relatively small.

First success

In 1973, *The Sunday Times* ran an exposé of fraudulent wine traders – companies that bottled up indifferent products, re-badging them as fine vintages. Laithwaite wrote a letter congratulating the newspaper, which was printed the following week. It said: 'Thanks very much for

> **We did something like 3,000 cases. Previously I'd been going over to France in my van and bringing back 100**

exposing this as I'm a poor starving wine trader living under a railway arch, when I thought I'd be living in St James' Park wearing a pinstripe suit by now. The reason is that I'm competing against these guys who seem to have learnt their trade bootlegging in America and basically aren't playing straight.'

The letter prompted a big response from readers who clearly had an appetite for genuine high-quality wine. Displaying his own entrepreneurial bent, *The Sunday Times* editor Harry Roberts ran a reader offer, with Laithwaite supplying the wine. The response was overwhelming. 'We did something like 3,000 cases,' recalled Laithwaite. 'Previously, I'd been going over to France in my van and bringing back a 100.'

A second offer proved just as successful and Roberts agreed that Laithwaite could run a permanent wine club for the paper. It's still running today and proved the catalyst for the company to really take off. 'It launched us, and overnight we became the second largest mail-order wine merchants in the UK,' says Laithwaite.

Growth strategies

Bordeaux Direct's promise had always been quality wine straight from the producer – and its growth, until recent years, was by organic means, rather than acquisition. Running the company in conjunction with his wife Barbara, Laithwaite set about expanding both sides of the business – Bordeaux Direct itself and *The Sunday Times* Wine Club. For the most part, expansion was funded through profits. Paying themselves nothing more than a salary, the couple ploughed everything back into the business. According to Laithwaite, it was partly a question of keeping the tax bill low. In the early to mid 1970s, the top tax band was 90%, so it made sense to keep taxable earnings down.

However, it was also a strategy born out of a bitter experience with a business angel at the point when the company first secured *The Sunday Times* deal. The sudden growth in demand had presented cashflow problems, along with the need for new premises, additional staff and some proper entrepreneurial support. The angel investor –

the managing director of a publishing house – came in around the time of the initial publicity. 'We gave him a 23% share and he gave us the confidence to think we could do it as a young company – he could pick up the phone and speak to the right people,' Laithwaite recalls. 'He was genuinely helpful at the time, but we fell out. He seemed to be working towards owning the whole thing and we became very unhappy.' Fortunately, the company was making enough cash to buy him out relatively quickly, but the experience discouraged Laithwaite from dealing with the City again and shaped the way the company was run. The business model was never dependent on large capital investments, simply growing the company on the back of its successes and Laithwaite's desire to break new wines.

His strategy was to go further and further afield to find more and more interesting wines that other people hadn't yet discovered. At that time, most merchants only sold Bordeaux and Burgundy, and Laithwaite's business was the first to take the French country regions seriously. Beyond Bordeaux, the next port of call was Languedoc and the wines of south-west France, such as the Rhone Valley and l'Ardeche. As the company built up its offering, sales rose too. The next step was Spain, where Rioja wasn't particularly well known, and Italy – and then Bulgaria suddenly appeared. 'We were the first to get wine out of that country,' says Laithwaite.

The challenges of expansion

By the end of the 1970s, the turnover of Laithwaite's wine business had topped the million pound mark, and by the late 1980s it had risen to £15m. However, his free-spirited approach to business was beginning to present problems – both for the company and his health. The business had become a substantial operation, but it had no senior management structure other than the Laithwaites. In addition, it was becoming increasingly difficult to find premises for warehouses, packing and dispatch – logistically, the company needed organising.

Then, in 1988, Laithwaite had a heart attack. It brought home to him the desperate need to change the way the company was run. 'We set about turning ourselves into a proper business,' he recalls. In practice, that meant creating a layer of management. As a result, a finance director, marketing director, sales director and IT and logistics director were duly appointed, along with a managing director (MD). Laithwaite credits his first MD Greg Holder with 'polishing this rough diamond of a firm and making it the company it is'. But the transformation wasn't without problems.

Stepping back

> **Enthusiasm for the product is vital**

Letting go of absolute control is a notoriously difficult challenge for most CEOs, let alone one who had been at the helm for more than 20 years. Indeed, the culture shock was so great that the new structure of the company collapsed almost as soon as it had been implemented. 'I'd been advised to cut back my hours, but there was no way I was going to stop doing it all – it's what I do,' says Laithwaite. 'So I carried on doing the travelling trips – I was going to bed a bit earlier, but I wouldn't let go.'

The business was Tony Laithwaite's personal project, and he knew exactly where he wanted it to go and what it should look like. And while Laithwaite saw Holder as a 'clever progressive guy', awareness of his talent didn't make the process of standing back any easier. 'It was very difficult – one of hardest things you can do in business,' Laithwaite admits. Despite his personal dilemma, Laithwaite kept faith with Holder, and the move to bring in a management layer was quickly vindicated by accelerated growth brought about from the added efficiencies. By 1994, turnover had grown to more than £50m and was closing in on £100m. What's more, Laithwaite had found a way manage his urges to interfere.

'We treated it like a marriage and both of us had to give up things,' explains Laithwaite. 'I couldn't just go swanning in and give £80,000 away to charity, and he wasn't to do things that went against my standards – Greg's not a wine man and I simply wouldn't deal with certain suppliers offering cheap deals.' To prevent frustrations lingering, just like a troubled but committed couple, Laithwaite and Holder sought mediation in the shape of a psychologist from the London Business School. He brought the two men together every couple of months to hammer out any problems. It was a way of preventing any pent up feelings from festering.

In retrospect, Holder's arrival marked a transition, and while Laithwaite continues to take an active interest in the running of the company, today it has a much more corporate structure, with the group chief executive making many of the operational decisions.

Rebranding

By 2001, while the company's core business hadn't changed, in practice, it was a far cry from the simple mail order wine trading operation of the 1970s. Indeed, the only thing that hadn't been modernised was the name Bordeaux Direct. 'We decided to rebrand basically because it was a silly name to have had for more than 20 years, when for most of that time we'd sold far more than wines from Bordeaux,' explains Laithwaite. 'We paid a company a serious amount of money and they just came up with "Laithwaites", because first it's our business, second people would continue to know I was connected to it, and third it was defendable and you can protect it.'

Business is littered with rebranding catastrophes, but for Laithwaites, the process was trouble-free and even led to a sharp increase in sales. 'We put a lot of time, money and effort into making sure it went smoothly,' Laithwaite insists.

Retaining the culture

Throughout the evolution of the company, Laithwaite worked hard at teaching staff about the origins of the company and its core values, even taking parties, a coach load at a time, over to Bordeaux to see the vineyards where he started. 'It's a nice weekend for them and provides idea of where this "wine thing" came from,' he explains. 'They see this man who is a top wine maker getting passionate and waving his arms around, and realise what we're about – you couldn't teach that, they've got to see it.'

The trips are documented on the company's website and Laithwaites encourages staff to share their knowledge and experience with customers. Laithwaite himself is convinced that they amount to a lot more than a nice jolly. Indeed, he believes that when staff return from France, activity within the company moves up a notch. And enthusiasm for the product is vital. 'Our business is built on the longevity of customers and all our staff know that,' he says. Laithwaites also has regular parties and barbecues for staff and insists the company has maintained the small-office mentality of its early years.

Diversification

Our business is built on the longevity of customers

Today, Laithwaites has a turnover of £300m and employs 877 people, with headquarters near Reading, a new distribution and warehouse base in Gloucestershire and a call centre capable of handling 21,000 inquiries a day. It now has a large online presence, with a customer hotline manned by experienced wine traders offering practical advice to customers. Meanwhile, its own wine brand, which is produced in the cellars Laithwaite worked in as a teenager, now accounts for 20% of the wine the company sells. What's more, the business runs other wine clubs in addition to *The Sunday Times* through partnerships with many major banks and insurance and other companies, such as British Airways, while there are also plans afoot to open four shops in the near future.

Still very much involved in the strategy of the company, if not the mechanics, Laithwaite's thirst for business appears unquenchable – even at the age of 59. He has rejected the notion of ever selling the business, which he hopes to pass on to his children who are 'doing their own thing in business first'. As well as expressing a desire to see the company do more at the retail level, where customers can 'see, touch and taste' the wines, the company has taken the model abroad and now has operations in Australia, Switzerland and the USA. Laithwaite would even like to export the model to its emotional birthplace, France. 'The French customer has traditionally been trickier. They think they're born with the knowledge and so spoil it for themselves – but that is changing,' he says. 'France is now buying wine from around the world.'

Laithwaite believes people's relationship with wine is still blossoming. 'The beauty of wine,' he concludes, 'is that the more people

SECRETS OF SUCCESS 2

Follow your passion

Tony Laithwaite was besotted by both France itself and French wine, and his knowledge of the latter provided the basis for a hugely successful business.

Seize opportunities

Laithwaite's big break followed a *Sunday Times* exposé of fraud in the wine trade. Laithwaite wrote congratulating the paper on running the story, resulting in editor Harry Roberts suggesting a reader offer of quality wines. *The Sunday Times* Wine Club was born.

Keep developing the business

Laithwaite ploughed profits back into the company and travelled to find new sources of interesting wine that rivals hadn't found.

Energise, enthuse and train the staff

Laithwaites takes new staff to visit wine-producing areas. This is a way of imparting knowledge and generating enthusiasm.

Know when to step back

Although partly prompted by ill-health, Laithwaite's decision to appoint a managing director (along with a new tier of management) and take a less hands-on role in the running of the business, was a key factor in its later success.

Stick with your vision

Over 40 years, Laithwaites hasn't wavered from the original concept of providing top-quality wines from small producers.

drink, the better quality they want. Once you've tried a £20 bottle, it's very difficult to go back to a £3.99 one. There's no snobbery there – people in the wine trade aren't snobs, it's all about professionalism and quality.' And nearly 40 years after its birth, Laithwaites delivers to more than 700,000 customers a year, but the ethos remains the same. The company sells top-quality wines from all over the world, relying on a network of small producers for its stock.

The next chapter is the first in Part Two, which deals with growing your business through the first approach mentioned in the introduction to this book: launching and growing your own products or services.

PART TWO

ORGANIC GROWTH

ASSESSING THE GROWTH POTENTIAL OF YOUR BUSINESS

THIS CHAPTER WILL DISCUSS:

- Defining the best growth strategy for your business

- Increasing your sales volumes

- Improving your productivity

- Effective use of tools to maximise cashflow

Gerard Burke, Director, Business Growth and Development Programme (BGP), Cranfield School of Management

Defining the best growth strategy for your business

Right at the start of this book, we stated that growing a business isn't easy. If you want to grow your business, you need to be:

- Committed and relish challenge
- Ready for organisational upheaval
- Prepared to change how your own, and other people's, time is spent.

After some time in business, many CEOs of small firms experience a 'glass ceiling': they reach a plateau in their sales and/or profits, and feel they can't go beyond it. However, there are several ways in which you can break through this 'glass ceiling', and it should be possible to pursue more than one option at the same time. Just remember that *focus* is probably the single most important characteristic of a successful growth strategy.

> *Focus* is probably the single most important characteristic of a successful growth strategy

Having a clear vision of where your business is going

The answers to the following five essential questions will determine whether you have a competitive strategy.

Do you know:

1. Where you should compete (market segment)?
2. How you can distinguish your products/services from your competitors in the eyes of the customers?
3. What competencies, and what kind of organisation, you require to deliver the strategy?
4. What your organisation looks like now?
5. How can you move from 4 to 3?

In other words, if you know which market segment you are competing in, and can identify a clear set of distinctive value-adding benefits you can define your business to deliver the strategy.

Areas to consider when defining growth strategy

There are two broad options that you need to consider when defining your growth strategy:

- Can you increase *sales volumes*?
- Can you *improve productivity*?

Each of the above can be further broken down as shown in the framework in Figure 2.1.1.

REDEFINING THE GROWTH STRATEGY

Company: Pacific Direct
CEO: Lara Morgan

When Lara Morgan participated in the Business Growth and Development Programme (BGP) in 1999, part of her strategy to revitalise her company Pacific Direct was to redefine her target market. In seven years of virtually non-stop growth, Pacific had built its position selling hotel toiletries to more or less anyone who could buy them. Lara had developed a large and growing portfolio of products, mostly under brands that Pacific had created itself, with some through licensing well-known skincare and cosmetics brands such as Penhaligon's of London.

Lara decided to take stock and refine her growth strategy. Better margins and opportunities lay in the upper end of the market, through focusing on four- and five-star hotel chains and business class airline passengers. This was also the kind of business that Lara and her staff enjoyed doing, and did well. Lara planned to whittle down the existing range, increase the number of licences and concentrate on penetrating the upper segments of the market. Six years later, both sales and profitability were up several hundred per cent.

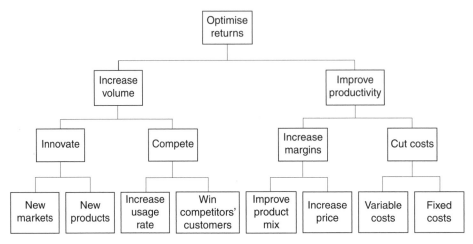

Figure 2.1.1 Organic growth strategic options.

Increasing your sales volumes

In our experience, some of the hardest people to convince of the merits of competing more strongly can be your own salesforce. They think it is unexciting compared with launching new products into new markets. For the smaller growing business, however, improving competitiveness usually ensures better returns. Putting this into practice is usually a two-stage process:

- First, you sell more to existing customers, increasing their usage rate
- Then, you look to capture customers from your competitors.

  To increase sales volumes, you can do two things:

- *Compete* more strongly and win market share from your competitors
- *Innovate* – so you can grow through new products or new markets.

  These strategies are discussed in more detail in the next three chapters, which look at specific ways to grow your current sales, expand overseas and diversify your products. The different strategies have different risks attached to them, popularised over many years by the US business strategist, Igor Ansoff, as illustrated in Figure 2.1.2 and described below.

The maximum risk strategy

The strategy of maximum risk is represented by the box called 'Diversification' in Figure 2.1.2: selling new products to new customers (also described as selling things you don't understand, to people you have never met!). Many CEOs, because they are entrepreneurially minded, find it hard to resist the temptation of conceiving new products and services. This might seem the most dynamic route for driving a business forward, but experience and common sense suggest it's usually the highest risk approach and rarely the most profitable.

The minimum risk strategy

The strategy of minimum risk focuses on 'market penetration': selling more of what you already sell to existing customers and people just like them.

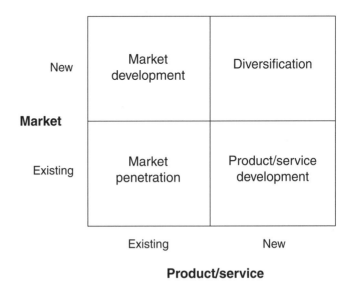

Figure 2.1.2 Product/market growth matrix.

EXPERT OPINION

HOW BARTERING CAN IMPROVE YOUR CASHFLOW

Bartercard explains the benefits of using one of the oldest payment methods for your business today

Preserving cash and improving cashflow are key elements in successful business development and one of the biggest pressures on businesses today. It is especially important for growing companies, where resources are usually stretched and flexibility more limited.

When the economy faces poor economic conditions, this translates to business, and at the very time when resources such as marketing, advertising, increasing selling capacity, training and skilling, etc need to be used to develop the business, funds are often not available to support such expenditure. As a result, the reverse of what is most needed is usually the outcome: retraction and consolidation.

Major brands always increase promotional spend, and hence market awareness, whenever things are tight. If overall spending reduces in any sector, the result is that more companies chase fewer opportunities and it is, therefore, vital that visibility is a key element of growth.

However, if the ability to increase resource is limited or restricted, the only option is to make what is available work harder and go further.

One such solution is to use barter as a core trading tool.

Currently, 85% of the world's Fortune 500 companies have their own in-house barter divisions and more than $1 trillion worth of barter trade is done annually.

While barter is the oldest form of trading, pre-dating formal currencies, it has traditionally been the preserve of multi-national companies that have both the resource and the economies of scale to invest in divisions of their own. However, improvements in technology since the early 1980's have seen the emergence to trade exchanges. These range from village 'swap clubs' to international exchanges spanning the globe.

This development now allows for companies of all sizes, especially growing companies, to be able to participate in this innovative way of doing business.

Principally, a company joins the exchange and then members trade between themselves with the exchange acting as the record keeper and supporting the structure.

How does this help with growth and improve cashflow?

A hotel wanting , say £1,000 worth of printing done traditionally goes to the printer, and when the job is complete has to find £1,000 out of their bank to pay the printer. In the barter sector, both the hotel and the printer would be members of the exchange and when the job was complete £1,000 would be debited to the hotel's account and the same credited to the printer's account. The hotel, therefore, has their printing and has used no cash from the business. It now owes the £1,000 to the exchange members and not to the printer. The exchange promotes them and by bringing them new customers they are able to pay this bill with vacant hotel rooms that would otherwise have remained empty and generated no revenue at all. So they've saved valuable cash and reduced the real cost of the printing as £1,000 worth of hotel rooms does not actually cost the hotel £1,000.

In the case of the printer, he's got a new customer that he wouldn't have got, he's been paid immediately and he now has the £1,000 of trade available that he can spend wherever he wants to. If he then uses those funds for things that he currently buys using cash, he too has saved that valuable cash.

Barter will continue its impressive growth pattern and can be a very useful tool for business owners, generating extra sales and having a significant beneficial effect on cash flow.

For more information, contact Georgina Sparks at Bartercard on 0845 219 7000 or visit www. bartercard.co.uk

The intermediate risk strategy

Selling new products to your existing market and existing products to new markets – the other two boxes in the matrix in Figure 2.1.2 – are strategies of intermediate risk.

What the evidence says

Research for the Business Growth and Development Programme (BGP) at Cranfield School of Management has shown a quite remarkable statistic which is worth bearing in mind when considering your growth strategy. Researchers found that nine out of 10 of the firms showing consistently profitable growth were 'sticking to the knitting': they were selling more of the same thing to their existing customers and people just like them.

The findings shouldn't be totally surprising. By focusing on one well-defined niche, with products/services that have distinctive value-adding benefits for customers in that niche, a growth business can develop close relationships with its customers, in-depth knowledge of the market and its customers' needs, and expertise which is hard to replicate. Sticking to the knitting seems to be a key part of the strategy for most high growth businesses most of the time.

There are some exceptions to these general rules. For example, businesses that are in terminally declining markets must either reinvent themselves or die. For these, the strategy of greatest risk is to continue with what they are currently doing. However, if you are a growth-orientated CEO, you are unlikely to have set up a business in a 'sunset' industry, and the implications of the Ansoff matrix will almost certainly apply.

Improving your productivity

An alternative approach to increasing sales volume is to improve productivity, which should always be on the agenda anyway for a growth-orientated business. Getting more value from what you have

> **Getting more value from what you have is a fundamental part of trying to be better than your competitors and different from them**

FOCUSING ON YOUR BEST CUSTOMERS

Company: Helifix
CEOs: Robert and Fred Paterson

Fred Paterson and his father bought Helifix, a supplier of special fixings and reinforcement systems to the construction industry, in 2005. Prior to the buyout, the company's turnover had remained stagnant for five consecutive years so Paterson and his father were keen to get the business growing.

Paterson worked out that, of their 4,500 customers, 400 were responsible for 90% of turnover. Following this revelation, he and his father spent time getting to know their core market and its needs, and decided to refocus their resources (such as marketing, advertising and technical support) to give more time to, and get more from, their top customers.

'It was really about focusing on the customers who are most important to our business and prioritising how we spend our time,' says Paterson. Now, rather than managing territories, area managers have responsibility for specific customers and for the first time in five years, Helifix posted a 15% increase in revenue in 2007.

is a fundamental part of the constant search to be better than your competitors and different from them.

If a business strategy sees improving productivity only as an activity for periods of economic recession there is a real danger that the business will swing from complacency (and inefficiency) when times are good, to frantic and unrealistic cost-cutting when times are bad. Such a strategy will also have the attendant high risk of unhappy employees and dissatisfied customers.

Cutting costs

In any business, costs need to be controlled and balanced constantly against the needs for quality and service. The starting point for reducing costs is always to separate your *variable* and your *fixed* costs. At the start-up stage canny CEOs strive to be lean and mean, to keep their fixed costs as low as possible. The implication of this strategy is that variable costs are higher. As businesses thrive, fixed costs often start to increase, as the business has the funds to invest in doing things more cheaply in-house. Information technology is a good example of this. Many businesses will create a separate IT department at some stage in their growth. But the benefits of investing in on-site business support should outweigh the costs. The same holds for other business functions, such as purchasing and human resources.

However, there will come a point again, when you need to question whether the emerging fixed cost structure of your business is necessary to run the business effectively and efficiently.

- Would some activities be better outsourced, or bought in only when required?
- Could certain operations be subcontracted to specialists?

Take purchasing as an example. More and more owner-managed businesses are joining buying consortia. These consortia aggregate their members' orders to strike better deals with suppliers, in return for increased volumes. Routine buying and low priority purchasing (such as office stationery) are effectively outsourced at a lower cost, leaving staff to concentrate on activities that are more important to the business.

A strategy for minimising fixed costs

At the chocolates business Hotel Chocolat, joint managing directors Angus Thirlwell and Peter Harris keep their fixed costs under constant review: 'We are all too well aware how easy it is to let the costs run up,' says Harris, a qualified accountant. 'In our case, the supply chain accounts for most of the costs. With each stage of business growth, we ask ourselves: do we need to do this or that activity, or would we be better outsourcing it to someone else?'

Reviewing your cost structure
Do:

- Focus on the big items – it's better to concentrate your energies on attacking areas where the gains will be significant, rather than those where improvements will make a marginal difference

- Remember there are no sacred cows or 'no-go' areas – just because something has always been done in a particular way, doesn't mean it should be done like that forever
- Look for 'easy wins' – in many product-based businesses, for example, there is a strong chance that only a handful of products are really profitable. A second group is marginally profitable or trades at break even, and the rest lose money
- Be ruthless – it's your business and only you can ultimately make it succeed.

Don't:

- Reduce fixed costs by discontinuing investment in technology that brings not only economies but also flexibility for the future
- Outsource a 'core competence' – a set of processes, say, or technical know-how, that is part of what makes you stand out from the competition.

Increasing your margins

There are several ways to increase your margins, including:

- Reducing variable costs
- Enhancing your sales/product mix
- Increasing prices.

Enhancing your sales product mix

If you have a number of different products/services, it's likely that you earn different gross margins on each. Clearly, if you can sell more of the higher margin products, then you will increase overall profitability.

Better margins with greater satisfaction

Raz Khan, founder of market research company Cobalt-Sky, refocused his business on higher value-adding activities for which clients were prepared to pay. This also had the effect of determining the type of client Cobalt-Sky was best suited to serve. Since this change in strategy, the customer base has gradually shifted and, several years down the line, Cobalt-Sky makes better margins doing more rewarding work for satisfied customers.

Enhancing the product mix depends critically on knowing the accurate *gross margins* for each product/service line. *Net margin* is often far more difficult to identify accurately, since the exact allocation of indirect costs is as much an art as a science.

Increasing prices

Increasing your prices may seem the easiest way to improve margins – if you can convince your customers that is. You know instinctively what to do when cutting prices to stimulate demand: you make a lot of noise and publicity. Some people argue that increasing prices should be the opposite: pass the increase silently through to suppliers and customers alike. In some markets, this strategy seems to work: newspapers and magazines heavily publicise reductions to their cover prices, but make no reference to increases.

If your business has been in existence for a number of years, you will know what the industry practice tends to be. That said, a price rise *with no added value* is rarely the way to generate long-term loyalty. If the *perceived* added value is significantly greater, then customers will be prepared to spend considerably more.

Effective use of tools to maximise cashflow

Many businesses find it useful to view growth in the context of cash generation. After all, the long-term value of any business is generally held to consist of its capacity to generate more cash than it absorbs.

Most businesses that have been in existence for around five years will have multiple revenue streams from a mix of products and services. The common term for this is the *product portfolio*. Some products/services in the portfolio will produce cash, whereas others will consume cash. By analysing your portfolio, you can plan how to achieve market share and continue growing while maximising cashflow.

Analysing product portfolios – the Boston matrix

The most widely used tool for analysing the product portfolio is the Boston matrix, a framework first developed by the Boston Consulting Group (BCG) in the late 1970s and early 1980s.

The Boston matrix classifies products based on two dimensions:

- The rate at which their market is growing
- The share of that market relative to competitors.

The analysis creates a two-by-two matrix, in which the business' products/services can be located.

- The *Star* box, on the top left of Figure 2.1.3, reflects a market that is growing strongly and where the business has a strong market position. Typically, in this situation, Star products/services are either cash-neutral or consume cash

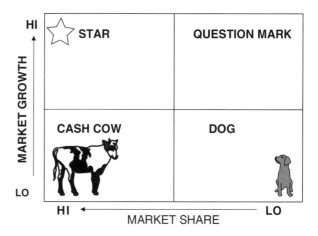

Figure 2.1.3 The Boston matrix.

If you use this analysis when you are still a small growing business, where you may have very small shares of very large markets, it is important to define share in terms of *your market niche versus the direct competition*.

- The *Cash Cow* box, in the bottom left of the figure, shows a market where the firm also has a strong market position, but the rate of growth has slowed, usually because the market is more mature. Products in this box generate the cash that powers the business
- The *Dog* box, on the bottom right of the figure, is occupied by products that have a small share in a declining market. These products tend either to be cash-neutral or to produce smaller amounts of cash
- The *Question Mark* box, on the top right of the figure, is reserved for products that have a low share in a fast-growing market. These products invariably consume cash, because they require considerable financial support but are not yet producing a return. They are Question Marks because it is unclear whether their market share will improve, and so move them into the Star box, or whether they will continue to under-perform and, eventually, as the market matures, become Dogs.

The Boston matrix is a versatile, general-purpose business tool. The analysis can be conducted at the level of an industry, within a group of companies, or for the product/service portfolio of one business.

Active management of product portfolios

The underlying idea of the Boston matrix and similar tools is that businesses (above a certain size) have a portfolio of activities, developed in response to new market opportunities, and sufficiently diversified to spread their commercial risks. The portfolio evolves over time and should be *actively managed*.

ACTIVE MANAGEMENT: KEY POINTS

- Cash Cows fund the investment needed to support the Stars and a selected number of Question Marks
- The business must create action standards for Question Marks, to identify which of those should be encouraged
- Dogs have no long-term future and should receive limited or no investment
- In the longer term, as markets mature and decline, Cash Cows will cease to generate cash and move towards the Dog box. The business needs to have other activities – ideally more Stars – which will become the Cash Cows of the future, as the market rate of growth for the current Cash Cows slows down. At the same time, there should be suitable Question Marks that will then be ready to assume the role of Stars. The direction of investment is shown in Figure 2.1.4.

Advantages of using the Boston matrix

All businesses are viable only insofar as they generate cash

The Boston matrix is used by countless businesses, small and large, across the world, as one of the primary tools for strategic planning. It has certain undoubted advantages:

- The analysis makes you think rigorously and clearly about your business. Many businesses become emotionally attached to activities that can no longer be justified on commercial grounds, and dilute and divert their resources
- Successful businesses need to respond quickly and effectively to changes in their markets. The Boston matrix forces you to think carefully about how your markets are changing, not just today but in the longer term
- This analysis can act as an early warning system to alert senior management to the dangers of spreading resources too thinly or under-investing in the wrong places. In the longer term, no business can support an unlimited number of Question Marks, nor be reliant on too few Cash Cows

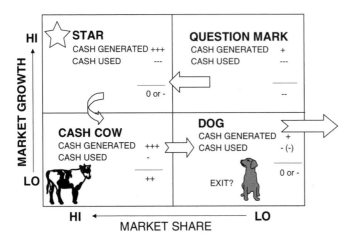

Figure 2.1.4 Boston matrix suggesting the direction of investment.

- All businesses are viable only insofar as they generate cash. The Boston matrix focuses on *cash* as the ultimate business driver, and *not* profit.

   Rod Leefe used the Boston Matrix to plan the development of his executive recruitment firm, Witan Jardine.

Limitations of the Boston matrix tool

There are situations in which the Boston Matrix approach is less useful. The analysis is less relevant for young businesses or businesses that do not have a portfolio of products and services. But it may usefully prompt managers to examine whether they are too dependent on a narrow revenue stream from only one or two areas.

> Don't rely wholly on one way of looking at the world. We recommend using the Boston matrix only if it is appropriate for your type of business, at its stage of maturity. Then, apply your judgement and experience to interpreting the analysis and the conclusions. Discuss this across the management team and with advisers whose opinions you respect.

In addition, like all managerial tools, the conclusions need to be balanced against judgement and experience. In the late 1980s, for example, the big players in the UK tea market were united in their belief that loose teas were Dogs, teabags were Cash Cows and instant tea was the Question Mark ready to become a Star. In fact, things turned out rather differently. The technical challenge of creating an instant tea that catered for the British habit of drinking tea with milk proved too hard: instant tea failed to take off as predicted. The teabag segment still had lots of potential for growth and there were still plenty of niche opportunities to make money in loose packet teas. Those businesses that were dependent on the Boston matrix for their strategic planning were paralysed in their thinking for a while, because the model had not successfully predicted the future.

! TOP TIPS

! A clear focus is the single most important characteristic of a successful growth strategy.
! Know the market segment you are competing in.
! Be absolutely clear about the distinctive benefits your products/services bring to your customers compared with the competition.
! To increase sales volumes stick to what you know and focus on your best customers.
! To improve productivity, look at cutting costs and increasing margins.
! To maximise cashflow, know your product portfolio and plan for the future.

GROWING YOUR SALES EFFECTIVELY

Gerard Burke, Director, Business Growth and Development
Programme (BGP), Cranfield School of Management

Growing your sales is a logical and often low-risk way to expand your business. However, before you start to go down that path, it's important to understand fully the needs of your customers and where you stand in the marketplace:

- What is distinctive about your product/service?
- Why do your customers choose to buy from you?
- How would you describe your relationship with your customers?
- Are you doing business with the right people?

Your customers and your competitors

Your customers

One way of defining your marketplace(s) is through *market segmentation*. This is the name given to the process of organising customers and potential customers into clusters or groups of similar types of customer. For example, a restaurant has regular customers and passing trade. The more passing trade it can convert into regular customers, the better business it's likely to do. Understanding both segments will help the restaurant increase its customer base. Segmentation is a useful and important idea because it helps you clarify the group of customers you are naturally better suited to serve.

By defining your target customers, you can focus limited resources more effectively. Even if you operate within a narrowly defined industrial sector, there will be some customers with whom you have a better fit. It's also important to recognise that there will be some customers whom you don't want to attract.

The approach you take to segmentation depends on whether you sell to consumers or to other businesses. The important point is to have a clear profile of your target segment(s).

Segmentation helps you clarify the group of customers you are naturally better suited to serve

Consumer segmentation

Traditional consumer segmentation approaches utilise attributes such as income, occupation and social status. More recently, you can take advantage of services that classify consumers using locational and lifestyle information.

Business segmentation

Business segmentation starts with the industry or industries into which an organisation sells. First identify the businesses that need your products. Then consider factors such as:

- Geography – Can you supply only in particular locations or more widely?
- Usage – This can be split into size of order and size of customer. For example, it may be uneconomical to supply orders below a certain size. However, to put off buyers from placing orders that are too small, you shouldn't set prices so high that it encourages your customers to shop elsewhere.

The ABC (Pareto) approach

Whether your business sells to consumers or other businesses, you may also have a system that segments size of customer by aggregated orders through the year. This is often referred to as an ABC or Pareto analysis, after the economist who first observed that about 80% of a firm's sales (and profits) derive from 20% of its customers. This basic trading pattern is true of most businesses.

The ABC analysis ranks customers as top (A), medium (B) and bottom (C) performers in terms of sales and profitability. Identifying A and C customers is often clear-cut, but defining the thresholds at which B customers pass up or down is less straightforward. Most people find that they learn from experience and get better at doing this over time. Remember the benefit derives from applying the process so that it works, so don't worry too much about precise demarcations.

Growing with Pareto

Jerry Sandys (a past participant on the Business Growth and Development Programme (BGP) at Cranfield School of Management) grew TDC, the electronics business he founded and ultimately sold in 2005, through careful application of ABC analysis. He identified early on B customers who had the potential to transfer into the A cohort. At the same time, TDC was ruthless about pruning C accounts that would never amount to much.

Your competitors

As a general rule, a business faces two types of competition: direct and indirect. Direct competitors are looking for the same slice of the customer's business as you. Indirect competitors meet the same customer need but by offering different solutions.

It's important to keep abreast of the competition, but most smaller businesses don't have the money to commission market research or for comprehensive market surveys. There are several other ways to keep up to date: the trade press, the internet, competitors' marketing literature, competitors' reports and accounts, and trade fairs. Your sales force and any intermediate suppliers should also be feeding back market intelligence.

Studying the competition is not a substitute for developing a distinct business strategy of your own, but ignoring the competition can be dangerous. A survey undertaken by Cranfield School of Management in association with accountants Kingston Smith showed a clear relationship between high-performing businesses and the monitoring of competition.

KNOW YOUR ABC

As a rule of thumb, for most businesses the A cohort will account for between 60% and 80% of the sales or profit, B will account for between 10% and 20%, and C will account for the rest. Often, the easiest way is to start with your largest customer and work down.

Recognising your worth

So now you know the customers you want to target and the competition you face. But do you know why customers buy from you rather than anyone else? Many smaller firms, including high-growth ones, have no real idea. But if you're aiming to increase your sales, you need to understand how your business wins customers.

The best way to tackle the question is to find out the key factors that make you successful from your customers' viewpoint. These may include: affordable prices, quick response, wide product range or innovative products. As your business grows, and customer and products numbers increase, these key factors should remain most important in the customers' eyes.

Making the most of your existing customers

As discussed in Chapter 2.1, in the research for BGP, 90% of the firms showing consistently profitable growth were doing more of what they already did well – by selling more of the same thing to their existing customers and people just like them. So the growth strategy of least risk is to extract the maximum value from your juiciest customers. We call this 'squeezing the lemon'. When cooking, most people cut a lemon into two, and squeeze one half and throw it away. Sometimes they keep the other half, and sometimes they don't. The result is that most people don't get all the juice from the lemon. Many businesses take the same approach with their customers. There is no plan for developing the sales relationship with larger customers, to encourage smaller customers to become larger ones, and for leveraging existing customers to help find new ones.

Here are some tried and tested approaches to squeezing the lemon.

Paying the right level of attention

Group your customers depending on the stage of their relationship with you. Think of this relationship like a marriage. There are the early days of courting when the customer and supplier get to know each other. If things go well and the relationship develops, a honeymoon period follows. Disillusion sets in if the partners start to take each other too much for granted, and, in the worst cases, divorce results.

It costs far more to acquire a new customer than to retain an existing one

You can give each of your customers the right level of attention if you bear in mind how your relationship stands with each of them on an individual basis. This will also help you identify those customers whom you may have neglected and now risk losing to competitors, as well as those who have defected and could be won back. It costs far more to acquire a new customer than to retain an existing one.

Getting your customers to spread the word

Your best ambassadors are your customers who value you. Speak to them and ask them for testimonials and referrals. Who else do they know that may also benefit from your products and services? Many smaller, growing businesses have customers who are many times larger than themselves. Ask the people who buy from you to recommend you to others in their organisation. And while you're at it, remind them of your complete product range: they might want to buy something else from you.

Being alert to opportunities

Although big company buyers are loath to take risks, they also need to be highly competitive. Often, a rival of your big business customer will find you on the off-chance that your services have given their competitor some advantage. Make the most of these opportunities.

SUCCESSFUL SQUEEZING

Company: Signify
Chief executive: Dave Abraham

Signify helps organisations to secure their computer networks. It provides a secure alternative to pass-words as an on-demand hosted service, based on running IT services on behalf of its customers, and billing them an annual service fee each year.

Signify's chief executive officer Dave Abraham participated in BGP in 2007 and used the squeezing the lemon concept to great effect. He found that four simple steps produced fantastic feedback from customers, as well as great financial results. 'We have built better relationships with some really good customers, better services for customers, significant extra revenue for Signify, and the potential to deliver to those customers additional services that they really want.'

Focus on most important customers

The account manager who was managing all the customers focused on the group that provided the top 80% of revenue (category A). A new recruit was taken on to manage the bottom 10%–20% of revenue.

Customer survey

A short web-based survey gave the company some good pointers to things that it could do better, and produced some unexpectedly good feedback. 'The survey has helped completely change the percep-tion of our employees, especially the new business sales team to realise that we are really good, that customers like us, and that there was evidence to show to new prospects,' Abraham says. 'As a result of the survey, the confidence of the whole company has been lifted massively.'

Customer forum

Ten customers, most of them category A customers, agreed to attend an interactive customer forum. This gave the company a good snapshot of the economy at the time, and their customers' issues and needs, while customers learned about Signify and each other.

Customer meetings, especially with category A customers

Following the forum, the company found that customers used these meetings to tell Signify their priorities. Abraham explains: 'They are asking us for services, being prepared to pay for them, and happy to work with us to identify if there are other customers that would also like the same service. They recognise that, if other customers also want the same thing, they can receive the same service for a lower fee, whilst making it more likely that we will be able to do it for them. They are also more prepared to wait for longer timescales for the service, allowing us to plan better than when trying to respond to new customers that don't yet trust us. We also now understand that whilst our Category A customers are most important to us – in many cases we are also important to them.'

Two for the price of one

Think carefully about the different ways in which you can reach different audiences and tap into new groups of customers. Hotel Chocolat, for example, views each gift order as having two customers: the person who books a delivery of chocolates, and the person who receives them. The buyer is the actual customer, but the recipient is a potential one. Hotel Chocolat makes sure that the recipient knows all about it and its chocolates, creating an opportunity for that person to buy from them on another occasion.

KEEP TALKING

Company: Clough Smith Rail
Chief executive: Tony Simpson

Squeezing the lemon can be as simple as reminding your existing customers of other products or services that you can supply. At Clough Smith Rail, which builds signalling systems, a junior operations manager managed to land a contract worth £2.4 million by doing just that.

A Network Rail executive started talking to the operations manager about other work the public body was planning. The Network Rail executive had not even considered Clough Smith Rail would be interested in this particular type of work. But the junior manager explained how the company could help and got the contract.

Chief executive Tony Simpson has been happy to allow the manager to remain in his operations role rather than promote him to a sales position. 'He just feels great about the fact that he recognised the opportunity,' Simpson says.

How to attract new customers
Customer referrals

Many surveys have consistently shown that the best source of new customers for smaller businesses is recommendations from existing customers and suppliers. This 'word of mouth' marketing often appeals to CEOs who tend to prefer direct interactions with customers rather than impersonal mass promotions. Direct contact means that CEOs often build strong relationships with customers and thus understand customers' needs more fully. And such understanding is at the very heart of successful marketing. For many small businesses, this personal contact between the owner and the customer can represent a unique selling point – in other words, it is the very reason customers buy from you.

Here are some ways to encourage referrals and recommendations:

- Ask existing customers who else might be interested in your products/services
- Introduce a 'refer a friend' scheme with rewards for the referrer
- Ask for citations and recommendations to use on sales literature
- Expose your brand to others by giving existing customers merchandise, such as mugs and pens
- Build a good image of your business by always delivering on your promises to customers and engaging in community events such as charity runs.

PROS AND CONS OF WORD OF MOUTH MARKETING

Pros: Most importantly for growing businesses, word of mouth marketing costs very little.

Cons: Depending on referrals will limit new growth of your business to markets in which you already operate. It also makes planning hard as you can't control what other people say, when they say it or to whom they say it.

Marketing

Promotional activities and advertising

More formal approaches to marketing have their uses, especially when the business has expanded.

- Promotional, or 'below the line', activities, are typically short-term efforts to achieve quick results, such as speeding up sales of old stock or attracting trial purchases
- Advertising, or 'above the line' activities, tend to be used to build long-term customers.

Most growing businesses spend more on sales promotion than on advertising. Promotional opportunities that stimulate interest and awareness among new and existing buyers are very important, for example:

- Ensure all company 'small items' are coordinated with the same image and message, from business cards to Christmas cards
- Take part in exhibitions with specially designed leaflets and brochures
- Experiment with direct mail or email, and telemarketing
- Make your website attractive and suited to your business image.

Advertising, though a powerful way to make your products/ services stand out, is expensive and requires careful control. You can employ a professional agency to help you determine the most suitable advertising mix for your business, particularly if you plan a large campaign. But it isn't always necessary to take professional advice.

The key point is to set clear goals for each campaign, such as building a market share or selling more. Think about the media you want to use depending on the audience you want to target: television, radio, magazines, the internet. For growing businesses, the most cost-effective form of advertising is usually targeted at local and trade-specific channels.

Direct marketing

For smaller business, the most cost-effective marketing is direct marketing. But make sure you are clear about what you want the customer to do as a result of your approach. Whether this is to buy or to make an enquiry, you must have everything ready to respond effectively.

Internet marketing

Small businesses compete equally with big businesses when it comes to the internet

Today, customers, as well as suppliers and potential employees, expect most businesses to have a website. Your drive to attract new customers or recruit the best staff should include a website that is representative of your overall activities. To get the best results, your plans for the internet should be integrated with your overall business strategy. Remember, too, that small businesses compete equally with big businesses when it comes to the internet.

Using a website to drive growth is covered in more detail in Chapter 2.6, but some simple rules for developing a website to promote your business are summarised here:

- *Keep it simple and easy to use* – put your main messages, such as what your business offers, on the homepage. Avoid using any effects for which users need special technology.
- *Make it welcoming* – know all the types of visitor you want to attract and have clear signposts to direct the type of visitor you want the most to the parts of the website you want them to visit.
- *Watch what happens* – it is straightforward to obtain data on your visitors and what they view. This information could help you improve your site and understand your customers better. Make sure there is a way visitors can contact you.
- *Compare your website with others* – monitor the competition and offer something distinctive if you can.

EXPERT OPINION

HOW TO GENERATE SALES LEADS FOR YOUR EXISTING PRODUCTS

How does a business find sales leads? Once found, how do you then talk to them and tell them about your products and services? Generating sales leads can be challenging at the best of times, but now more than ever, it is vital for businesses to ensure that their marketing activity is working as hard as it possibly can in order to win new custom.

As with any marketing exercise, the starting point for success is identifying the correct audience. The variety of demographic information available from business databases allow for very specific targeting. Get this right and the benefits are mind-blowing. The business that does not do this is not only wasting their time; they are wasting their investment.

You want to reach the person responsible for making purchasing decisions within the M25, with more than 50 employees, who operate in the manufacturing sector? No problem; if your data is accurate.

Once you have selected your audience, what is the best way to talk to them? The smart business will use a combination of channels to turn a warm lead into a hot lead. For example, an email campaign followed up by a tele marketing campaign allows businesses to strike whilst the iron is hot.

Because email marketing resides within the digital arena it is possible to see exactly when and who has opened your message. Following up with a phone call whilst your business name is fresh in the recipient's mind gives a significant edge over the competition.

Generating sales leads can be a challenge; Thomson Local has the direct marketing knowledge and experience to help businesses find, talk to and win new custom, helping drive a return on their investment and ensuring that investment works as hard as it possibly can.

To speak to a Thomson Local direct marketing consultant about growing your business, please call 0845 855 9950 and quote AD-02.

- *Look after your existing customers* – ask your customers for their feedback on your website. Online newsletters or discussion pages could help you improve relationships with existing customers.
- *Look out for different expectations* – people have higher expectations of what should happen in cyberspace than in the real world. For

example, they don't want to wait more than a few seconds to purchase an item online even though they will be happy to queue for much longer in a shop.

Getting the most from your salesforce

Your sales team is a crucial communication channel between your company and your customers. That's why it's so important that they are professional and well prepared. Your salesforce should know which products and which groups of customers to target, and keep up to date with competitors' activities.

Try to focus your sales management on three areas: setting and monitoring targets; motivating, training and supporting staff; and recruiting and organising staff.

Your salesforce is the critical connection between you and your customers

Setting and monitoring targets

The simplest sales targets ensure sufficient sales to recover the salesperson's costs. Look into how much time your sales team spends selling and set targets accordingly. In many businesses, this could be as little as a third of salaried time, or even less. You may want to manage the team so that expensive sales staff don't spend time chasing unqualified leads or carrying out routine administration.

Many successful companies use the 'hunters and farmers' model to help their sales staff achieve their targets. In this approach, the sales team is split into 'hunters', who get and nurture new business,

A sales team can be expensive to maintain so make sure it's as efficient as it can be. If a salesperson's salary is £50,000 per year, the real cost to the company after travel, expenses and benefits, is often double that. It's three times the salary if you include sales administration support.

and 'farmers', who manage well-established accounts. The model exploits people's natural characteristics and helps to create effective teams that support each other. Hunters are competitive and often aggressive, enjoy challenges and can handle rejection. Farmers by contrast prefer a steady working environment and deal well with routine administration. Using this model means managers can set and monitor targets partly on the basis of individual performance and partly by team performance, helping to create a sense of shared commitment and responsibility.

Sales forecasting and control

Sales teams are more likely to buy into forecasts worked up on the basis of sound data than those arbitrarily imposed from the top. For example, to achieve last year's sales plus an extra 10%, they need some idea where the extra sales are going to come from. They need to be aware of new opportunities and where to focus their efforts.

Have an early warning system if sales are not going to plan

So ensure that your sales team have access to marketing analysis data. Give them information on known industry or market segment growth rates; estimated market shares for yourself and competitors; and your own initiatives to maintain, grow or disengage from various market segments. Using this information, their task is then to turn your statement of intent into a detailed plan of action. To do this, they should consider sales by month; sales by individual customer account or group of customers; estimates of new business sales again allocated to specific customers; resources needed to achieve this, such as people, budget, sales literature; and any other relevant metrics. And it's worth developing an early warning system if sales are not going to plan.

In the next chapter, we look at how to move into new markets overseas and the things to watch out for along the way.

DEVELOPING YOUR DISTINCTIVENESS

- Is your business still dependent on one product or service for over 80% of profits?
- Do your top five customers still account for more than half of your sales?
- How do you measure customer satisfaction?
- When did you last increase prices and by how much?
- How do your prices compare with your major competitors?
- What is the most cost-effective advertising/promotions medium for your business and why?
- How much do you budget for advertising and for promotional activities?
- When did you last send out a press release and what results did it generate?
- What targets and incentives are set for each salesperson?
- What was your achievement against sales forecasts last year?

! TOP TIPS

! Use segmentation analysis to get to know your customers and your competitors.

! Try to move your category B customers to category A.

! Speak to your customers: tell your existing customers about your full range of products and services, not just the ones they currently buy from you. Ask them if they have any other work that you might do for them, if there are other people in their organisation who might also need your product/service or if they know people in other businesses who might need your product/service.

! Give customers the level of attention each deserves based on their category rating.

! Use a variety of methods to attract new customers: existing customer referrals, advertising, promotions, internet marketing.

! Get the most out of your salesforce by ensuring they are up to date with the right information, well prepared to answer any queries and the personality of the person fits the role (hunters and farmers model).

! Have an early warning system if sales are not going to plan.

GOING GLOBAL:

GROWING INTO FOREIGN MARKETS

THIS CHAPTER WILL DISCUSS:

- Taking your business further afields

- Selecting the best market for your service or product

- The best ways to research your market

- The mechanics of export

- Getting paid

- Exchange rates

- Avoiding legal pitfalls and staying out of the courts

Thanks to technological innovations such as the internet and broadband, to name but two, the world is shrinking. Globalisation is one of the current business buzzwords, and it simply means that domestic markets are increasingly opening up to competition from overseas. So whether you like it or not, you may well find that your rivals are no longer just from the UK. But, of course, the reverse is true, and foreign markets could be just as open to *your* business. This all means that, given the right product or service, there is no reason why you can't take your offer abroad – or export.

> **Globalisation is one of the current business buzzwords**

Exporting can transform a business. If your home turf is saturated or simply not big enough to deliver the revenues you need, the massive markets of mainland Europe, the Americas and the East could be your ticket to further growth. But you don't have to wait for this situation to arise before you dip your toe into the global pond. Indeed, for some companies, exporting isn't an option but a requirement. Most major films and computer games, for example, cost so much to create that they need to sell globally in order to recoup their development costs. And in the technology sector, it's often the case that the only way to cover the research and development expenditure associated with specialist software or equipment is to address an international audience from day one. Export ambition tends to be built into the DNA of high-tech startups.

Taking your business further afield

If your company has the potential to sell into foreign markets, there is a real opportunity to boost your profitability – and very often it will be a lot easier than you might imagine.

Expanding abroad via a third party

Traditionally, manufacturing companies have used 'agents' abroad to make sales, or have appointed foreign distributors. The manufacturer then dispatches the goods ordered, much as it would to a UK company. But there are other ways to export. One route is to license a firm to produce your product abroad. Service businesses, too, can sometimes license or franchise their ideas overseas – and while arguably not strictly exporting, many UK retail businesses have successfully expanded in this way.

Expanding abroad via the internet

Increasingly, companies are exporting using the internet. This is particularly true for specialist businesses, and is very easy to implement for remarkably little investment. Perhaps you have already dabbled with foreign markets without realising it, for example through occasional internet sales. Many UK businesses have literally been taken by surprise when foreign customers find them online. If you have already done it, then consider taking it a stage further. And if you haven't, then now's a good time to consider it – especially if you want continued, sustained growth. With a little effort, it is possible to target customers abroad and develop a strong new revenue stream.

Are you ready to go abroad?

The key to success here is:

1. Deciding whether what you offer will have an appeal beyond the UK
2. Making sure your business is ready to export.

Unless you started out with a global market in mind, it usually pays to build profitability in the UK before looking further afield, because, like cracking any new market, selling overseas is demanding. Sending samples, preparing quotations and familiarising yourself with local regulations eat up time and money that could be used to win customers back home. Also, don't treat exporting as a quick revenue generator. Remember that it's a long-term proposition, and the wins,

Don't be afraid to consider exporting your products or services abroad

although potentially substantial, will be further down the line. So don't rely on exporting to generate short-term cash.

Selecting the best market for your service or product

The first point to bear in mind is that when dealing with overseas customers, however, it pays to be as cautious, if not more so, than you would be when dealing with domestic orders. Make sure you check out creditworthiness. One method is to ask for a list of the prospect's suppliers and ring them up. Most companies will be happy to give their view. Another approach is to request a company status report from the international team in your local Business Link office. (Business Link is the government initiative that offers free help and advice to companies, with sites across the UK. See contacts box.) But remember that this report will contain only such information as your customer has chosen to disclose.

KICKING DOWN THE BARRIERS

Company: Voxar
Founder: Andrew Bissell

In the early 1990s, Andrew Bissell, fresh out of university, created a business in his home town, Edinburgh. The plan was straightforward: to develop software for visualising medical data in three dimensions (3D), and become the world leader in his field. A decade later, he is on the way towards fulfilling those ambitions. Ranked fourteenth among Europe's fastest growing technology businesses, Voxar exports 90% of its products and has a turnover approaching £6m. But this is no textbook study of how to export. At the start, Bissell spent many hours banging on doors that remained resolutely shut. 'We targeted the US multinationals,' he says. 'But they weren't convinced that there was a demand for our product, so we changed tack.'

To kick-start the market, Bissell created a US sales force to sell direct to hospitals. When the hospitals began to request Voxar's technology, the multinationals became interested, opening the way to partnerships with leading suppliers.

Second, in the longer term, it is important to choose your territories strategically. The obvious initial considerations are:

- Whether there is a market for your product, with scope for growth
- Whether the structure of the industry is similar to the UK's
- Assuming that you lack language expertise – whether English is spoken widely in that area.

The best ways to research your market

The basics

As well as researching demand, think about the wider context

A good way to start investigating global markets for your products or services is to focus on your own sector, and how it presents itself on the international stage.

Trade shows and trade journals can provide useful information, and you should also draw on your contacts, talking to people you already know in the industry about global prospects for growth. For example, if there are international trade shows in specific export markets, attend them and try to get a sense of what the market is like there. You can also use the internet to assess where you feel demand for your offer could be highest, and check out overseas rivals, along with those companies that already have an international reach – their websites should tell you which countries they are already exporting to.

The wider issues

Once you have located one or more potential overseas markets that could offer export opportunities, determine whether it is financially worth your while to get involved. As well as researching demand, think about the wider context:

- Is the country politically stable?
- Is the currency volatile?
- Is the economy heading in the right direction?

It's also worth establishing what quotas, duties, taxes and other import and export restrictions apply to your product.

USEFUL CONTACTS

UK Trade and Investment (UKTI): www.uktradeinvest.gov.uk

Business Link: www.businesslinks.co.uk

British Chambers of Commerce: www.britishchambers.org.uk

SITPRO – Simplifying International Trade: www.sitpro.org.uk

British Insurance Brokers Association: www.biba.org.uk

Export Credit Guarantee Department (ECGD): www.ecgd.gov.uk

Where to find advice and help

The UK Trade & Investment website (www.uktradeinvest.gov.uk) is incredibly useful, not least because it holds market reports and the contact details of UK embassies around the world. Most embassies have advisers dedicated to helping British companies establish trade in the country they are based, so you can give them a call.

It's also worth consulting the British Chambers of Commerce Export Zone (www.chamberonline.co.uk). Alternatively, you could commission tailored market information from the embassies through your local Business Link office. Costing on average around £600, the reports provide details on demographics (the make-up of the population, in terms of age, sex, etc.), market size and local contacts to help you identify potential customers and competitors.

You can also make less formal enquiries that will cost you nothing other than a little time and effort. For example, you may have clients who already export, whom you could ask for advice, particularly

FINDING OUT FOR YOURSELF

Although there could well be a lot of official help, and this can prove useful when checking out legislation and trade restrictions, there's nothing like getting under the skin of real businesses for generating the latest and best insight into what's happening on the ground. Try to get 20 minutes with a local purchasing director for a company that currently uses or needs a product or service like yours, and find out what products/services are selling and at what price and how your offer compares on quality. Ask for the names of your competitors and other firms that you can talk to.

multinationals that are already familiar with the market you have in your sights.

It can also prove invaluable to visit the places you are considering exporting to, unless you are content with limited internet sales. This needn't cost the earth – if you have fewer than 250 employees, you may qualify for a grant from the Export Marketing Research Scheme, run by the British Chambers of Commerce. Alternatively, you could take advantage of subsidised travel and accommodation, available to businesses participating in Chamber-led trade missions. Once out there, you have the option of the going through the official channels – such as the embassy, local trade bodies or local authorities – or doing your own thing (see box).

The mechanics of export

It's crucial to find people you will be able to trust and work with

Once you have carried out the necessary research and have identified key export targets, you need to build your strategy for launching your offering overseas. This is clearly one of the most crucial decisions you will make, because even if you have an audience that wants your product or service, if you don't market it to them in the right way, they may not be receptive to it. If you're going to take the time and effort to sell overseas, you should yourself the best possible chance of success.

The virtual option

One option is to start small, by establishing an export-oriented website, so you can assess initial interest, and then consider setting up a physical presence in your target market. However, doing this from the outset, although riskier, will result in a quicker return.

The physical presence option

When establishing a physical presence on the ground, the choices are:

- Appointing an agent to secure business on a commission basis
- Signing up a distributor, who will buy and re-sell your products
- Setting up your own sales force.

Whichever route you take, it's crucial to find people you will be able to trust and work with. So ask your suppliers and investors for recommendations. Also consider partnering with a like-minded business overseas, who might sell your products abroad, while you sell theirs in the UK. In return, you receive a 'royalty' (a fee usually calculated as a percentage of revenue or profit), without the hassle or

THE SMALL PRINT

When deciding on how best to export your products, it's vital to find out in detail the particular requirements of the overseas customers you're targeting, such as trading norms. For instance, in North America it is usual for consumers to be able to return goods to a store for any reason. This risk will almost always lie with the product manufacturer, not the retailer. Meanwhile, in France there are strict laws about the French language content of products on sale there, and unless you keep to the law, your products may not be allowed onto shelves.

This is where joining forces with a local agent or distributor in each territory can be critical, because, as well as understanding local customs and codes of practice, they could also recommend a local lawyer.

risk of having to sell, service and ship your goods to potentially a wide variety of foreign customers. This has the advantage that you will often be paid an advance of royalties, so you have certainty of getting at least something from the deal, with almost none of the hassle and risk.

So there is a lot to consider when selling overseas, and it pays to approach exporting thoroughly to maximise your chances of success. Getting it right will make all the hard work more than worth it.

Getting paid

Expect to wait longer for payment than you would in the UK and build that into the business plan

Late payment is one of the major issues growing businesses face, as they are more susceptible to cashflow problems than larger, more established organisations. This makes effective credit control vital, although it can become more difficult when dealing with overseas customers, because distance, language and unfamiliarity with local laws can make chasing debts a lot tougher. But there are ways to reduce the risk.

Cash in advance

Advantages: Getting customers to pay in advance solves the problem, or it can be alleviated if you can at least secure part payment. Once a trusting business relationship has been established after some time, you can, if required, revert to sending out invoices with set payment terms like 30 days.

Disadvantages: Your customers may not be receptive to this arrangement. Just as you fear not being paid, they may be concerned about laying down money upfront for goods that have yet to arrive.

Letter of credit

A letter of credit is a document issued by the customer's bank guaranteeing payment in accordance with terms and conditions agreed by both parties.

Advantage: A letter of credit will reduce your risk.

Disadvantages: It won't always be appropriate, as letters of credit are complex to administer. For example, for a high volume of small transactions, this payment method isn't really practical. A letter of credit also opens you up to a different kind of risk. The payment agreement is based on strict adherence to pre-arranged terms and conditions, so any deviation from these may mean you won't get paid at all.

Bill of exchange

Advantages: An alternative to a letter of credit is a bill of exchange, where the customer agrees to pay on receipt of the goods and you retain control of any shipped product until payment is made. This is facilitated by a local bank – acting on your behalf – which will execute the bill of exchange by transferring control of the goods when the terms have been met.

Disadvantages: The risk here is that the customer will not accept the shipment, but at least you will retain control.

Factoring

Advantages: Factoring is a way of easing cashflow fears without directly involving the customer, and is growing in popularity. A factoring services company pays a percentage of any money owed to you by a customer as soon as you raise the invoice. So if a company in Switzerland buys £300,000 worth of goods from your business, the factor immediately transfers an agreed proportion of that sum to your account. You don't have to wait weeks or months for the client to pay. The benefits of using the service are often well worth the interest rate and fee that the factor will charge for loaning you the money. The factor also chases the debt on your behalf. In the export market, factoring can be a particularly useful tool as there are several specialist firms focusing on international markets. And while you may find it difficult to chase for payment in a foreign language, your factoring supplier will have the expertise to do that for you.

Disadvantage: In the domestic market, you can expect to pay your factor at an interest rate of between 1.5% and 3% above the base rate set by the Bank of England, plus a management fee based on a percentage of turnover, typically between 0.75% and 2%. Overseas factoring, however, costs about 15% more per transaction because of the complexity. This may seem a little steep, but a factoring arrangement will get cash flowing from your overseas operation while allowing you to sidestep the issue of the payment times. For instance, if you do business with an Italian company, the gap between invoicing and payment can be 90–150 days – and in the meantime you have staff to pay. Factoring removes this particular headache.

You may not always need a factoring arrangement though. In Scandinavia, payment is generally much quicker, so whether or not you use factoring on an ongoing basis may well depend on your experience of the market in question.

Insurance

Advantages: Insurance is another useful option. Export credit specialists will insure you against late or non-payment.
Disadvantages: The cost of cover will vary depending on who your customers are, where they are located and whether the risks are seen (in terms of the payment time) as short, medium or long term.

You can find an insurer through the British Insurance Brokers Association (BIBA). However, for very long-term risks – for instance, when the payment terms stretch out for more than a year – you will probably have to approach the government-sponsored Export Credit Guarantee Department (ECGD) rather than a commercial provider.

Exchange rates

The fickle nature of currencies

Something else to be aware of when exporting is fluctuating rates of exchange – the changing values of different currencies. When you are operating in a foreign market, rather than taking the odd overseas order via a UK website, most customers will want to be invoiced in the local currency.

Protecting yourself against fluctuating exchange rates

Persuading customers to pay you in sterling solves the problem, but if you are up against stiff competition from local rivals, insisting on this could cost you the contract.

Alternatively, you could buy a 'forward foreign currency contract', where you buy or sell a fixed amount of foreign currency at an agreed rate by a certain date to protect you from movements in the money markets. So if you agree a sale worth €100,000 in the belief that it will net you £60,000 in sterling, a forward contract will guarantee a currency conversion at that rate. There will, however, be a fee of a few hundred pounds, but you can factor this into your calculations when you are quoting for the job. This kind of service was pioneered by investment banks, but today the business banking divisions of the high-street players can usually help.

If you're both buying and selling abroad, you can also protect yourself by setting up an overseas bank account and avoid the exchange rate lottery altogether. For instance, you buy from suppliers and sell to clients in euros without converting the cash back to sterling until a time of your choosing.

> **If you can't get paid in sterling, take steps to reduce the impact of currency fluctuations**

Avoiding legal pitfalls and staying out of the courts

In North America, it is normal for consumers to be able to return goods to a store for any reason

- Every company wants to avoid legal disputes with customers or suppliers, especially if this could result in long hours in a foreign court and the big legal bills to match. The key to cutting the risk of this scenario is to ensure that any contract has clear terms and conditions.
- Advice on contractual matters is available from SITPRO, a government-sponsored body set up to provide exporters with information about the documentation and procedures associated with international trading. Good trading and contractual practice is defined by INCOTERMS, a set of rules drawn up by chambers of commerce around the world.
- It's well worth agreeing in advance where any disputes will be resolved and you should aim, where possible, to have any case heard in the UK. However, it's also vital to be conversant with local laws. You could, for example, fall foul of local employment legislation (affecting overseas agents) or product liability rules, and you should also be aware of local taxation issues. For instance, although the USA is undoubtedly a vast and lucrative market with no language barrier, it's also a very litigious place and the penalties for violating trading laws can be harsh. There's also an added complication that if you comply with federal law, you could well trip up on state law.
- Legal issues like this should not put you off entering this huge market or any others, but don't take them lightly and take expert advice.

Finally, remember to take care with the documentation that accompanies shipments. Getting it wrong can mean goods being held up at customs or seized. Once again, the paperwork that gets through the customs in one country won't comply with regulations elsewhere. Happily, shipping companies are adept at this sort of thing and you can also get good advice from your local chamber of commerce.

So far this book has concentrated on growing sales through maximising the potential of your existing offer by encouraging existing customers to buy more, and searching out new markets overseas. The next chapter will look at the growth benefits of moving into new product or services areas – or diversification.

> As the value of currencies moves up and down in relation to each other, sometimes very rapidly, if a local currency falls sharply against sterling between a price being agreed and the invoice being sent and payment made, you could find yourself out of pocket.

! TOP TIPS

! The key to foreign markets is to properly identify the opportunities and take steps to ensure that you are not overly exposed to risk.

! Carefully identify your market and the best way to reach it.

! Assess the risks. Before entering a market assess the political, economic and social factors that could cause problems.

! Take time to find business partners you can trust and who know the local market well.

! Ensure that your business practices are in line with the expectations of customers. Don't assume, for example, that the customer service policies that work in the UK will satisfy customers in France, Germany or the USA.

! Research your foreign customers. What is their trading record and credit rating?

! Take out export credit insurance to guard against not being paid.

! Expect to wait longer for payment than you would in the UK and build that into the business plan.

! If a long wait is not acceptable, consider factoring or payment devices such as letter of credit or bill of exchange.

EXTENDING YOUR BRAND

THIS CHAPTER WILL DISCUSS:

- Deciding whether branching out could boost your bottom line

- Managing the risks of diversification

- Choosing the right management structures

- The power of the brand

- Diversify by acquisition or build from scratch?

Broadening the base of your business by moving into new areas or selling new products or services – in other words diversifying – can provide your business with a major growth spurt if you get it right. There are few more exciting events in business than developing and launching a new product or service, or even snapping up and integrating a new company. You need look no further for the benefits of diversification than one of the world's best-known brands run by arguably the most famous UK entrepreneur – Virgin and Richard Branson. Using your mobile phone while travelling on a train and watching a plane flying overhead, and you are surrounded by Virgin – until recently even the can of cola you were drinking at the time could have been sporting the classic V logo.

The Virgin Group is one of those organisations where diversification has almost become a brand value in itself. Few people expect Branson to rest on his laurels and the result has been an empire of often disparate ventures, united under one name. And while not all of the group's businesses succeed, the sheer volume of its revenues provide an illustration of just how effective a diversification strategy can be in driving growth.

Today, many businesses are emulating Virgin, if on a much smaller scale, branching out into a range of products or services, each targeting a specific market. And while some diversification strategies are carried out under a single company, many CEOs prefer to ring-fence new businesses as separate companies with their own brands, or proceed through joint ventures with others. In short, there are plenty of options to consider, and while the growth prospects of your current business may be limited by factors such as the size of the customer base, by diversifying you can shake off these revenue inhibitors.

Just like exporting, diversification isn't something to be undertaken on a whim, and there may be times when it's better to stick to what you know. Handled badly, diversification can have an adverse impact on your original business, so you need to carefully plan and research your new offering so that it meets customer demand, and then take time to consider the best way to launch it onto the market, whether as part of your original set up or as a separate entity. The same goes for buying a business that you feel is complementary to yours.

Deciding whether branching out could boost your bottom line

Diversifying your offering is a step into the unknown and is likely to be a major challenge. However, there are some good reasons for branching out: these can be 'defensive' or 'offensive', that is taking a pro-active approach to diversification.

> **In difficult market conditions, many CEOs turn to diversification as a way to preserve revenues**

'Defensive' diversification

Providing a boost to your business

Diversification can be a great way to breathe new life into your business and give sales a boost at a time when you are experiencing zero growth, very limited expansion or worst of all a loss of market share as the sector reaches capacity and rivals are undermining your business.

Providing extra revenue during regular low periods

Diversification is also often implemented in response to a business cycle that sees sharp spikes and troughs in profitability and revenues through the year. If you sell ice cream for a living, for example, then a balancing 'cold weather' business will help you escape the tyranny of summer peaks followed by winter troughs. It's a strategy exemplified by travel firm Iglu.com. The company began by supplying ski holidays before moving into areas such as renting villas and tropical holidays to smooth out the seasonal cycle. According to founder Richard Downs, the business was operating at 120% capacity in the winter months and well below that in the summer. The answer was to sell sun holidays as well to the existing customer base.

Pro-active diversification

The Bransons of the world clearly see diversification as part of a pro-active strategy – one in which the management team is constantly looking to new market opportunities and is prepared to leap in whenever a gap becomes apparent. Other companies diversify in direct response to an opportunity that unexpectedly presents itself. For instance, Charlie Osmond, founder of FreshMinds, recalls how his company's expansion into the recruitment market was the result of a single client enquiry. 'We started off supplying graduates for temporary research work,' he says. 'Then one of our clients asked if we could help them find permanent staff.'

The fit between the research and recruitment businesses was almost perfect. The client who wanted a highly educated part-time researcher in March could well want a full-time member of staff, drawn from the same graduate talent pool, in June. Equally, the graduate seeking temporary research work before a world trip could return in search of a career. In both cases FreshMinds was a natural point of contact. 'As soon as we got the request, we knew it would be an easy add-on. We knew that it would be easy to integrate with what we were doing,' says Osmond. 'Now it is hard to imagine one side of the FreshMinds business being so successful without the other.'

The FreshMinds experience illustrates the point that one of the most compelling reasons to diversify is a complementary and strategic 'fit' between one business and the next, and this can take many forms. A common approach is to enter your supply chain, so a supplier of fabricated steel might buy into a steel manufacturer to both boost profits and secure supply.

Other reasons to consider diversifying

Finally, it's worth remembering that by diversifying your business, you can raise revenues while keeping general expenditure more or less fixed, as human resources, payroll and invoicing will require little or no additional investment. Diversification can even be driven by a desire to use up spare factory capacity or space in an office that you are paying for but not using.

There are ways to manage the risks involved

Managing the risks of diversification

Although innovation or investing in new products and new markets is a higher risk strategy than competing more effectively, there are ways to manage the risks involved.

Reactive innovation

The least risky innovation is likely to be the new product or service actively requested by existing customers. When this happens, you often have an opportunity to develop the innovation in close collaboration with one customer, or a select few. This is common practice in many technology-based industries, such as bio-science, information systems and defence procurement. The advantage with this approach is that, if successful, you have a guaranteed sale and, in many cases, help with cashflow. The disadvantage is the danger that the product or service is so customised for a limited group of customers that it can't be sold to a wider target.

Extension of existing product/ service lines

The term innovation doesn't always mean radically new. New products can equally mean simple line extensions to your existing core business. The Austrian company Red Bull has built a significant global beverages business around one product and a handful of variants. Measured by market value, the Coca-Cola Company has been the world's biggest food and drink business for much of its lifetime. Even today, however, more than a century after its foundation, the company derives most of its revenues from its core cola portfolio, of Coca-Cola and a handful of variants such as Diet Coke or Vanilla Coke. In the 1980s, when its management attempted to ditch the old flavour

OLD WINE IN NEW BOTTLES

What appears to an outsider to be radically new or different may just be a clever new combination of existing features and technologies. Many businesses have built strong positions not through innovating a particular technology, but by re-presenting existing technology in a fresh way to the customer. The Japanese industrial strategy of the 1970s and 1980s was largely based on this idea, certainly in the field of consumer electronics, and underpinned the success of companies such as Sony, Matsushita and Hitachi.

and substitute a replacement, loyal customers revolted and forced the company to back down. Since then, Coca-Cola has focused its innovation strategy on a small number of line extensions, carefully researched and tested before they are taken to market. Outside its core cola portfolio, the company prefers to acquire or license new products, which have been successfully developed by other people.

Changing the focus

Companies at the leading edge of technological development are sometimes prone to focus on the features, as opposed to the benefits, to the customer. However, in the commercial world there are no guaranteed prizes for originality.

Risks associated with using the same or a different brand name for new ventures is discussed later.

Choosing the right management structures

Above we stated that diversification didn't necessarily mean change in the basic business infrastructure. However, there are, of course, additional costs associated with staff and management time when

Management teams must be given not only responsibility, but also the power to make things happen

launching a new product or service, so your strategy should take into account the impact it might have on the core business. For example, will your business suffer if certain senior managers donate less time to it in the pursuit of diversifying the company's offering? If not planned for, the dilution of management time can be damaging.

A well thought out management structure can prevent this situation from arising. As an CEO of the business, you shouldn't try to run every business within a group or even take a hands-on interest in every new product launch, while attempting to run everything else

MORE THAN JUST MOVIES

Company: Redbus Films
Chief executive: Simon Franks

Founded by chief executive Simon Franks, Redbus Films began life as a film distributor, moved into film production and has since diversified into billboard advertising and video rentals. At the moment all the divisions are profitable.

According to Franks, the expansion of the group's activities has been anything but ad hoc. As a film distributor, it made sense to move into movie production – not least because one business would become the customer of the other. Similarly, investing in the Video Island online DVD retail business in 2002 gave the organisation an even bigger footprint in Britain's filmed entertainment market. Less obvious was the company's move into billboard advertising under its Xsites OOH divisions. But as Franks explains, there was a commercial fit here as well, particularly in the case of Xsites, which has illuminated advertising screens situated in UK universities. 'As a film distributor we were selling to students. This gave me the idea of advertising on campus,' he recalls. 'The first customer was my own film distribution company.'

Since then, the company has expanded its media business to include roadside advertising under its OOH brand. While the businesses are diverse, Franks says that the company has achieved synergies to keep costs low. 'Everything is run from the same building,' he says. 'The businesses share the same accounting and IT systems.'

While the businesses sit within the Redbus Group structure, each has its individual brands. In this respect, Franks sees no point in trying to emulate easyJet or Virgin, because brand recognition isn't a factor for him. 'People don't watch a film and think "Redbus",' he says. On the other hand, he can justifiably claim to have a corporate profile where it counts – within the film industry. 'We have a lot of relationships,' says Franks. 'We're in constant contact with a lot of the film companies in Soho.'

EXPERT OPINION

DEVELOPING PROJECT MANAGEMENT COMPETENCE

Peter O'Neill of ESI International advises on the best way for growing companies to approach improving how they run key projects

As companies grow, it's often the case that competence in identifying, defining, selecting, planning and executing projects becomes more critical to success. Projects are likely to expand in size, number, complexity and type – and previous relatively informal approaches are no longer likely to be sufficient. To complicate the problem, staff often need to acquire these skills at the same time as senior managers are working on the challenging question of which approach to project management methodology the company should adopt or develop.

The managing director of an expanding niche manufacturing company raised this issue while attending a project management event last year. One of his concerns was that generic project management training for his staff might not suit the specific project situations that the company faced. Conversely, he also felt that it would be best if staff knew the basics so that they could contribute to the process of developing an appropriate company methodology.

The solution that we agreed was to organise an in-house workshop, which used current and potential company contracts as examples to teach skills and techniques appropriate for the type and size of the projects. As an added bonus, two outputs of the workshop were a 'wish list' in-

dicating the areas where staff felt that a company methodology could help them and an indication of the concerns that they had – for example, that a company approach might be too restrictive or involve too much 'paperwork'.

The resulting decision was to concentrate on developing consistent use of the estimating and planning tools covered in the workshop, and to hold back on any further methodology components while focusing on these areas.

The general lesson is important. Expanding companies often rightly identify the need for a more consistent approach to managing projects, but can try to adopt (or be inappropriately sold) a level of methodology far beyond their current capabilities. My advice is to start with the basics and ensure that these can be applied successfully and consistently to the specific projects the company is involved with.

Peter O'Neill, MBA, PMP is a senior instructor with ESI International, the world leader in project management and business analysis learning. He is also an Associate Fellow at Warwick University Business School.

For more information, visit www.esi-intl.co.uk

as well. Instead, create a situation where you oversee everything that is happening within a group, while setting up teams to run different projects from day to day.

This idea of delegation doesn't often come naturally to CEOs, as it's viewed as a loss of control. But it must be embraced for the business to take significant steps forward. For it to work, management teams must be given not only responsibility, but also the power to make things happen. You have to empower them to make decisions – and reward them for successful ones.

Indeed, one way of diversifying successfully is to encourage existing staff or talented outsiders to take charge of their own projects. This has been the approach taken by serial entrepreneur and one of the original starts of BBC TV's *Dragon's Den* Simon Wodroffe. Having made a killing from the Yo! Sushi restaurant chain, he set about launching other business under the Yo! banner. His strategy was to provide his chosen managers with support rather than hands-on management time. 'We don't launch a business unless someone is driving,' says Wodroffe. 'I tell people: 'This is your business, you run it. I am a service to you.'"

The power of the brand
The case for using the same brand

Which brand name to use is a key risk management decision to make when considering diversification

As the ubiquity of Virgin or easyJet demonstrates, if you have a brand that has a resonance with either a mass or niche audience, you can apply it to range of often very disparate businesses. The key to success here is to understand the strengths of the brand in terms of what it represents to the consumer. Once you have done that, you can look at businesses where it will make sense to use that trade name. Get it right and you can save yourself time and money on marketing names that are new to the market.

The most obvious way to exploit the power of your brand is to expand into closely related business areas. Iglu was already in the

> Don't fall victim to brand overstretch. For instance, Virgin is seen as a so-called challenger brand that moves into markets and shakes them up. Sometimes it works – as with the company's airline and mobile phone business – but other ventures have been less successful. Certainly, Virgin Cola didn't give Coca-Cola or Pepsi many sleepless nights.

travel business through its skiing operation, so – aside from the associated name – it wasn't an enormous leap to expand into other areas of the holiday market.

The case against using the same brand

As illustrated in the box above, it doesn't always pay to launch your new product or service under the same name or brand as your existing offer. In fact, this is one the key risk management decisions to make when considering diversification. Do you launch your new project under the wing of your existing company (or companies) as a means to sell more goods to existing customers, or do you create an entirely new brand and/or a new company?

There is a strong argument for ring-fencing new ventures – or separating them from the core business. If set up as a different company, a loss-making new venture is likely to be less of a drain on an otherwise profitable core business or unlikely to inflict the same level of reputational damage on a sister or parent company.

Managing the financial risks

In many cases, however, you will want the new product or service to make a direct contribution to the growth of your existing business, and it may also be important to tie it in with the current brand. And although no one launches a new product expecting it to fail or underperform, you have to face that possibility, so how do you set about limiting the potential financial or reputational damage that can be caused by a project failure?

> Don't forget that the decisions on how to structure the new business could have tax implications and you should plan accordingly.

If you opt to launch within a single company structure, you should ensure that budgets are in place and that the business plan includes targets and milestones to help assess whether the new product line is delivering on its promise. But as you are, to some extent, diving into the unknown, be flexible and pragmatic about these targets, and review them once you know more about how the launch is proceeding. On the other hand, you might opt to use the same brand but under a different company structure. For instance, you might take a stake in a business that carries your company's name, while allowing the managers or another business party to invest in and even drive the project.

Diversify by acquisition or build from scratch?

Look for complementary businesses opportunities

It's that eureka moment. The instant when you see the way clearly ahead. New product lines perhaps, or complementary businesses that will not only fit with your existing services, but also enhance your offering to new and existing customers. But after that moment of inspiration, it's time to face the practical planning issues and one of the key questions you may have to ask yourself is whether to build the concept from scratch and take it to the market or diversify by acquisition. For instance, if the plan involves a new product line, do you launch it yourself – with all the research and development and market research that is involved – or buy up something that is already in existence. Of course, your strategy will depend on circumstance and your own inclinations, but it is worth considering the pros and cons of launch and acquisition strategies.

The case for diversifying by acquisition can be compelling. If you have the cash – or if you can raise it – you can launch into a market at

GOING TO EXTREMES

Company: Extreme Group
Chief executive: Al Gosling

Al Gosling, chief executive and founder of the Extreme Group, is obviously not one of those individuals who adhere to the adage 'sticking to the knitting'. While the companies operating within the Extreme Group are all, in one way or another, linked by the theme of extreme sports, they collectively cover an ever-widening range of activities, including media (internet and television), retailing and drinks marketing.

Gosling has used a number of strategies to expand his commercial empire, including joint ventures and acquisitions, but he has a particular enthusiasm for developing new ventures and product lines in-house on relatively modest budgets. He spends somewhere in the region of £500,000 or less developing projects, but stresses two key factors that have proved vital to this success. 'A hands-on approach is essential and you have to do your research,' he says.

Gosling also makes acquisitions when appropriate, such as buying a chain of surf shops for £16m. The attraction, says Gosling was the retail infrastructure rather than the brand. 'We wouldn't pay a premium for someone else's brand,' he says. Indeed, the shops are due to be gutted and reframed in the near future.

a speed and on a scale that would prove difficult if you were moving from a standing start. But there's a caveat here. To make an acquisition strategy work, you have to buy the company. So always be clear on what you require and stay clear of acquisitions that won't help you deliver on your goals.

For some, nothing will compare to the satisfaction that can be gleaned from a launch, whether it be a standalone enterprise or as part of an expansion plan. But you do have to accept that it will be a challenge. Spend £500,000 on an existing business and you know – more or less – what you're buying and where it stands in the market. What's more, it will be generating revenue from day one after the acquisition. Start from first principles and you will have to put up development money that will sustain the project.

The next chapter covers in detail one of the most important adjuncts to growing your business sales today – maximising your online presence and other e-marketing strategies.

! TOP TIPS

! Don't diversify simply because you're bored with what you're doing.

! Never overstretch your brand into unsuitable business areas.

! Don't diversify prematurely. Try to wait until your existing businesses are performing as planned.

! Avoid spreading yourself too thinly across new and existing product lines.

! Be wary of associating your existing, successful brand, with an untried or risky product.

! Look for complementary businesses opportunities.

! Ensure that there is enough management time available to launch a new business while maintaining the old one.

! When setting up new management teams, ensure they are empowered to drive the business forward and properly rewarded.

! Budget properly and consider the most appropriate ownership structure.

! Always consider the tax implications.

THE NET EFFECT:
GROWING YOUR
SALES ONLINE

THIS CHAPTER WILL DISCUSS:

- E-commerce: the basics
- Reaching an internet audience
- Email marketing
- Analysing success
- The social networking media: Web 2.0

These days, consumers and businesspeople spend more time browsing the internet than watching television, whereas companies are increasingly sourcing suppliers online using search engines. Consequently, it almost seems reckless not to have a well-developed online presence – which means both a regularly updated and engaging website and the ability to sell products online. Yet according to research by the Federation of Small Business, only a fifth of small-to medium-sized businesses are currently trading online. This means that not only could you be missing a trick if you aren't trading online, but also that you can still get there before the majority.

Setting up or upgrading your existing website to a transactional website – one that can handle online sales, or e-commerce – will cost money and management time, but prices have fallen as many companies now offer this service. You may also have to do some restructuring of your business to be able to supply goods sold online, essentially coping with the additional orders and also training staff to process orders online. The question, however, is not whether you can afford to embrace e-commerce, but rather whether you can afford not to. And the chances are that your competitors are thinking the same thing right now, or have already taken steps towards trading online, if they aren't doing it already.

Selling online will increase your geographical reach at very low cost. Regardless of where you are based, you could be trading with new customers anywhere in the UK – or indeed the world – without necessarily having to spend money on new offices, warehouses or sales agents. So if you haven't thought about selling online, there's no better time than now to put together a web strategy.

The question is not whether you can afford to embrace e-commerce, but rather whether you can afford not to

E-commerce: the basics

E-commerce is more suited to businesses that offer goods rather than services, and will be more relevant to certain products over others. So you first need to assess whether the product or service you offer lends itself to being sold online. For instance, if you're selling

INTEGRATING CUSTOMER SERVICE

Today's customers channel hop. Sometimes they research online and buy over the phone or in person. On other occasions they will check out products in a retail store or warehouse, but make the purchase via a website.

The same channel promiscuity is evident even after a transaction has taken place. If a customer wants to check on the status of an order, he or she may phone, email, or join an interactive chat session. But whatever the channel, service has to be good.

Getting customer service right across multiple sales channels is certainly a challenge, and as a recent survey revealed, even the big players sometimes struggle. When customer experience consultancy Foviance tracked the customer service standards across 25 major name retailers, a very mixed picture emerged. Although a number of companies – notably John Lewis, Argos and Amazon – scored very highly, other household names fared less well. Asda failed to respond to email and phone queries. Foviance described HMV's call handling as 'poor' and the now deceased Woolworth demanded that customers register before allowing them to make email product enquiries. The survey illustrates the difficulty of creating a seamless experience and there's a lesson there for all businesses.

Often the problem stems from companies thinking of the online and offline sides of their operations as two different businesses and this can manifest itself in a number of different ways. It may be that online and offline sales are recorded on different platforms, making it difficult for staff to provide joined up customer relations.

The answer is to ensure that all sales and stock information is available on one database. This can be done by collecting data from point-of-sales and web shopping carts, and putting it on a single customer relationship management system.

However, getting the technology right is only part of the story. As far as customers are concerned, whether they buy online or offline they are dealing with the same company. Internally, it may be a different picture. For instance, in the retail market, store managers have their own sales targets to hit and they won't necessarily welcome customers who, say, come in to look at goods and perhaps try them out, but buy from the website a week or two later, with the consequent sale attributed to the online side of the business.

But in the multi-channel world, it is no longer possible to attribute sales to one channel or another; you have to look at the totality of the business in terms of total revenues and profits. Staff should be taught to think in the same way.

luxury villas on the Spanish coast or made-to-order components for the European space programme, there probably won't be much scope for direct transaction. Any sale in these types of market sector will require considerable negotiation over price and specifications – something that the internet isn't particularly suited to. However, you still need to ensure that your website provides as much information as possible about your products and (ideally) plenty of opportunity to open a dialogue – such as making sure your website attracts potential customers and encourages them to make online enquiries when they pay a visit. If, on the other hand, you sell the type of product that can be bought online – anything from CDs to car insurance to renting a holiday villa – you should think about adapting your website so that it can handle transactions.

If you have any doubts, take a look at what your competitors are doing. If they're selling on the web, it's not only an indication that it can be done, but also a warning that you might be missing out on market share.

Technology requirements for e-commerce

There is a tendency to think that e-commerce is synonymous with credit card processing, but that isn't necessarily the case. If you trade on the basis that customers place an order and subsequently receive an invoice, all you do is provide clients with a secure username and password, giving them access to a section of the website where orders can be keyed in. But if you require payment at the point of sale, you will need to have a credit and debit card facility as well as stringent security measures in place to ensure that you maintain the confidence of customers and comply with data protection laws.

Technology-wise, to trade online the basic requirements are:

- A merchant account with a bank, which holds your payments
- A electronic gateway linking your website to the bank's systems
- The necessary software to capture and process credit card data.

MOVING THE GOALPOSTS

Company: Pharmacy2u
Founders: Daniel Lee and Julian Harrison

You have had an idea that could revolutionise an industry. The only trouble is, it's illegal. That's exactly what Daniel Lee and Julian Harrison faced when setting up Pharmacy2U, the UK's first internet and mail-order pharmacy. And incredibly, they have overturned the legislation forbidding their business from trading.

Back in 1999, sending medicines through the mail was strictly prohibited, but Lee, whose family business was retail pharmacy, and Harrison, a management consultant at Andersen, were sure there was a market there.

'I'd been looking into e-pharmacy around the world,' says Harrison. 'We felt we could make a reasonable case to the Royal Pharmaceutical Society of Great Britain (RPSGB) that it could be done in a very professional way. So we built strong business processes to show we could use data powerfully to create an auditable system without the need to see patients face to face.'

The business was launched without the approval of the RPSGB, but once it was up and running the regulator agreed to amend its code to allow Pharmacy2U to trade. It's now the UK's largest dedicated internet and mail-order pharmacy, safely dispensing private and National Health Service (NHS) prescriptions and selling 3,000 over-the-counter products online. The founders have taken on around £4m in venture capital and private investment to develop the mail-order platform, while introducing new processes, such as the electronic requesting of repeat prescriptions. In 2001, Pharmacy2U was chosen by the government to lead a two-year NHS pilot project to develop an electronic prescription system to monitor what's being prescribed and dispensed, replacing the paper-based version.

Pharmacy2U has been profitable since 2003, growth has been 30% year-on-year, and this year's revenue will be £11.5m. Once the electronic prescription system is finally rolled out, there will be no stopping them.

Maintaining online security is a technical challenge, so even if you have a merchant account with a credit card company, it's probably easier to outsource transaction processing to a specialist online transaction provider, such as WorldPay and Secure Trading.

You will also need the shopping cart software that allows customers to stack their goods in a virtual basket and pay for them in one transaction. Today, this technology is available off the shelf and any good web design company will build such a system into your website.

Finally, you should have a connection between your internet transactional system and your back office accounts. This will cut down considerably on the amount of staff hours needed to transfer data across.

Creating a truly professional web presence

You don't have to be technologically gifted or a design genius to create your own website. There is downloadable software available with templates you can use to create a serviceable website. However, you may need something more than serviceable if you want your website to:

Good website design is a matter of combining form with function

- Reflect your company and your brand
- Be simple to use, effective and engaging for the visitor
- Stand out against your competitors.

To create a truly professional web presence – which is what you should be aiming for – you may need to employ a professional web designer. Also, building an e-commerce section, although relatively straightforward for an experienced web designer, could be tricky and time consuming. That said, if you are up for a challenge, with clear ideas of what you want and confident of your design and technical abilities, you can save your business money by doing it yourself.

You don't have to conform to a standardised design, but before briefing the company that will be creating your website, think carefully about your audience and what the site will be used for. This is partly a matter of combining form with function. If you sell nuts and bolts or electronic components, visuals probably don't matter too much, but you will need to provide easy navigation to perhaps thousands of products. If you're in the fashion business, then you need to think about the kind of online environment that will either drive direct sales or encourage customers to visit your shops. That may well mean a major

WEBSITE BASICS

Most websites conform to a three-column design: a menu on the left side, core content in the middle and special offers or announcements on the right side. In a transactional website, all of these columns will have links that allow the user to go directly to the appropriate part of the website, while a search engine provides an alternative means of navigation.

emphasis on graphics. Communicate your requirements clearly to the design agency. Avoid ostentatious designs with lots of animation, as this can prove annoying and distracting, take time to load up, and deter visitors, who today are more time-poor than ever. Getting to the point quickly and saying what you do on the homepage can also help your website get noticed by search engines.

Reaching an internet audience

Specialists do very well on the internet

It has been almost 15 years since online retail pioneer Amazon set up shop. Since then ambitious electronic traders have moved into every available niche. This means there is now a well-developed and growing online customer base for a huge number of products – customers who are adept at searching out the best bargain or right product for themselves. There are huge numbers of companies vying for their business, so how can you make your online voice heard?

Specialising

Specialists do very well on the internet. If you can offer something that isn't easy to buy on the high street or locally, then customers have a reason to come knocking on your virtual door. If a local record shop is simply competing with Virgin and HMV, then the lion's share of the business will go to the big players. If, however, it's offering something that's difficult to find – a good selection of world music, or albums imported from the USA – there will be a market. The same could be said for suppliers of specialist electrical parts or other such technical items or rare books.

It's often the case that a certain product will sell well enough nationally – or even internationally – to support a business, but wouldn't have a big enough market in most towns or cities to warrant a bricks-and-mortar shop. The great advantage of the internet is that it allows you to access that niche national – or international – market.

TURNING VISITS INTO SALES

Company: GetGeared
Founders: Mark McCance and George Braun

GetGeared has proved that it's the overall web offering, not just a fancy website that brings in sales. With just a £1,000 investment in an off-the-shelf e-commerce website, the company has seen dramatic growth in its first two years.

Mark McCance and George Braun, both executives more accustomed to the big business budgets of PC World, Wanadoo and Pearsons, launched GetGeared (www.getgeared.co.uk) in 2004. An internet-based business selling clothing and accessories for motorcyclists, it looked to profit from the increasing number of people opting to commute our congested roads on two wheels. Stocking top brands such as Highway 1, Vanucci and ProBiker and with exclusive UK distribution rights for the UK market, Get-Geared's progress has been rapid. It currently attracts 90,000 monthly visits with 800 orders per month, putting it on course to generate sales of £1m this year.

Braun puts the growth down to providing a pain-free experience for customers and the ability to offer a far wider range of products than could be sold from one physical site. Major emphasis has been put on customer service, ensuring positive word-of-mouth recommendations, while it has invested in features such as live stock availability indicators and fraud screening technology to secure customer payments.

Braun says the company's online success has made traditional retailers with far bigger budgets sit up and take notice. 'If you offer better choice, suppliers react both positively and negatively. We had a few ring up and try to persuade us not to stock certain brands, including threatening to cut off our supply routes. We didn't change our plans, though.'

Discounting

From insurance to CDs, discounted goods still account for a huge amount of trade on the internet. In the early days, it was a simple proposition. Companies such as Amazon could take advantage of the lower overhead costs associated with centralised warehousing to offer goods more cheaply than they would normally be available. Latterly, we have seen the rise of price comparison sites that allow customers to track down the keenest prices.

If you're only trading on the internet, then discounting to pump up sales can be a winning strategy, but it's a bit more complex if you sell through other channels too. If you're not careful, you could undercut yourself and potentially undermine your pricing strategy. To do it successfully, you can use the internet to market special offers or end-of-line goods, but your business plan needs careful thought.

Leveraging your existing brand

The starting point for many companies is to use the internet as an additional channel for existing customers. In the retail market, this often means accepting that consumers increasingly use the channels that suit them at any particular time. If John Smith decides to buy an ipod when he's working close to the high street, he may well pop into the local electronics store. If the mood takes him at seven in the evening, he will use the same store's website. Increasingly, he will also mix up the channels. Retailers such as John Lewis and B&Q allow customers to buy online and pick up in-store. But the multi-channel approach is not confined to the consumer market. Many business customers will buy online one day and pick up the phone to place an order the next time, depending on what is convenient. This emphasises the importance of your website reflecting your existing brand.

Your website should reflect your brand visually, with respect to corporate colours, logos, etc., and deliver the same key messages to avoid confusing the online shopper, and to make it clear that the site is an extension of your business. This also goes for everything from the domain name to policies on delivery and customer service, as any interaction a customer has with your website – whether it's positive or negative – will ultimately reflect on your company and its brand.

Ensuring quality service

Online trading has the potential to become a major revenue stream, so it's important to invest in the resources necessary to keep it running smoothly and effectively. This means making sure that it is regularly updated with new products and prices, and that staff are on hand to answer queries and complaints and fulfil orders. In the retail sector – where trading volumes tend to be large – many companies have struggled to match the level of service that has become the norm in offline shops. Mail-order companies traditionally have fared better, simply because e-commerce is just another version of distance selling. But whatever your company's background, providing a good service is essential.

" **Whatever your company's background, providing a good service is essential** "

That doesn't necessarily mean spending a huge amount on technology. Yes, the big names in retail invest millions in their websites, but you can build a basic transactional website for as little as £500. How much you spend will be dictated by customer expectation, the brand values of your own company and what your competitors are doing, but outside the consumer space, it's often enough to present the products professionally and provide an appropriate means of payment.

Marketing your website

To help attract the most business to your transactional website you will need to market it effectively. The first priority should be to make sure that when customers use a search engine, such as Google, MSN or Yahoo, to search for a product you offer, your website should be

SEARCH ENGINE OPTIMISATION

The process of raising your profile in the online search rankings is called search engine optimisation. Today, this is all about the content of your website and the links you have to other relevant websites, more than anything else. Google pioneered the technique of ranking websites and internet pages according to the number of links leading to them, so you should aim to set up reciprocal links with websites that are complementary to yours.

the first – or at least high up – on the list of search results. This is vital because search engines are the main source of new visitors to websites.

The written content of your website is also important, and, where possible, should include words and phrases – known as keywords – that customers would use when searching for your product on the internet. For instance, if you sell cameras, you have to think of the various words that a customer might key into a search engine to find the cheapest prices on, say, a new Canon. Include these words on your webpages, and it will help you climb the rankings. The more information that you provide on a given product – the full specification of that brand new Canon – the more likely you are to pull in the casual searcher. Remember that it's in Google's and other search engines' interests to produce the most relevant results for their users, and so they use techniques to scan websites for key content.

You can get professional help to optimise your website, but be wary of companies that promise the earth and guarantee the top spot forever, as this is rarely achievable. It's now more difficult than ever to fool search engines, and those websites caught using underhand methods can get blacklisted. Look for a realistic approach and ask for testimonials before writing a cheque.

Paying for online advertising is a surefire way of making it to the first page of search results. For example, you can use pay-per-click advertising, such as Google Adwords and Yahoo! Search Marketing.

AFFILIATE MARKETING

Essentially, setting up an affiliate marketing programme means recruiting other website owners to carry links to your website. If you sell CDs, for example, you might recruit affiliates from content-driven, non-transactional websites, such as those provide music reviews. The idea is that a music fan reading a review of a new album on your affiliate website can then link to yours to make the purchase. In return for carrying the link, affiliates get a commission, usually on every purchase.

The same model can also be applied to price comparison sites. These websites also direct traffic to online retailers and take a commission. The key here is to think carefully and creatively about possible affiliates, as they could prove to be a valuable way of generating online business.

In this bidding system, you decide how much to pay, so you have full control of your costs. Obviously, the more you pay, the higher you will appear in the listings. However, if you're bidding against major league rivals, then be careful of spending too much money that won't be justified by increased sales.

Online advertising is also a possibility, but unless you are a major brand, the response rates are likely to be low, unless you focus on buying space on niche websites that your target audience visits in high concentrations. You should also make sure that your website is promoted outside the internet – or offline – by drawing attention to it on any marketing materials you produce, from business cards and stationery to flyers, magazine advertising, etc.

EXPERT OPINION

STARTING YOUR SEARCH

Lucy Cokes, director of Guava Digital Marketing Agency offers more information on the importance of search engine marketing.

Search engine marketing essentially focuses on two distinctive means of promotion. The first, Search Engine Optimisation (SEO), is concerned with the natural rankings that the search engines give to your website (such as listings on the left-hand side of a Google page) based on its content, quality links to the site and how the site is structured, among other things, and determines where your site is listed when potential customers are searching for a certain keyphrase.

The second important search engine marketing tool is Pay-Per-Click advertising (PPC), which involves paying to promote your website through advertising against targeted keyphrases, as mentioned previously. For example, if you own a car dealership in the North West, one of your keyphrases may be 'second hand cars Liverpool'. If you pay to advertise with one of the search engines, you can write a short advert that will appear when a search is made that fits with your specified keyphrase. It is important that your advert captures the attention of the person searching and that it is succinct.

Depending on the scale of your business and the demands on your time, you may be able to run PPC advertising campaigns in-house, but like any other part of your business you will only get results if you are prepared to invest in it. If you are planning to undertake the work yourself, do your research, investigate your market, learn about how search engines work, think about your customers and look into what your competitors are doing.

If you are planning a new website, get a reputable SEO agency on board from day one. That way they can work alongside the web developers throughout the project, and ensure that the website is constructed with good search engine visibility in mind. If you already have a website that is under-performing, look into appointing an agency with proven results, but be prepared to be flexible, as they may suggest radical changes to the site.

Search engine marketing is unique in its ability to produce measured results and provide excellent return on investment. The key is to look into appointing an agency or qualified individual as soon as possible, ensuring that you research their previous work and credentials. Once you embark on a solid search engine marketing campaign you will quickly see the power of search and its ability to generate business for your company.

For more information, visit www.guava.co.uk

Email marketing

Email marketing can be an effective way of reaching your target audience and by including links to your website it can generate instant interaction with customers, thus growing your sales. It's also far cheaper than traditional direct mail. Once you have bought the necessary software to send bulk emails, and prepared the email and your database, you can dispatch the necessary emails for practically nothing. This means, unfortunately, that there is a tendency to overdo it, to the annoyance of potential customers. As a result, the response rates can be low, but even if just a handful of people out of several thousand click through to your website and make a purchase, it's possible to get some kind of return on your investment.

The low cost of sending emails in bulk has fuelled a tendency to use the medium as a blunt instrument

However, the silent majority – those who hit the delete key without opening the message – represent lost business and a wasted opportunity. More damagingly, an increasing number of consumers will report marketing messages as spam, with the result that further communications are blocked by ever-vigilant internet service providers (ISPs). Indeed, if an ISP decides you're a spammer, then it could block all emails to and from your company. An ill-targeted email campaign can do as much harm as good so to reap the full rewards from your email marketing, you need to think more strategically.

Keeping it relevant

The first step is to understand that email isn't that effective as a customer acquisition tool. If you buy a list and begin to mail out to people who have never before engaged with you or your company, you may be breaching the Data Protection Act. And if you're emailing consumers you are creating a negative impression. What's more, as mentioned earlier, the response rates are likely to be low.

Email marketing is far more effective once a relationship has been established with a customer, as it can be a great way to reinforce customer service, highlight offers and reignite interest. And if you can maximise the chance of a customer opening your message rather than simply deleting it, you will have established a major engagement tool. The key is to make the content of the email as relevant as possible to the customers you are targeting.

Where you start should reflect the priorities of the business. For instance, online gaming company Virgin Games targeted its early emails at two consumer groups – those who spent a lot of time and money, and those who dropped out. In the case of the latter, the aim was to find out why they left and offer incentives to get them back and playing. Equally, you can use a previous purchase as the basis for promoting the next. If someone buys crime novels from an online bookstore, it's a fair bet that they will want to read more. It makes sense, then, to send information on new releases within that genre. Of course, some purchases are one-offs. When your customer buys a state-of-the-art camera, the chances are they won't by another for a few years, so offering similar products won't do much good. But what you can do is offer accessories or cut-price prints from digital files. Also, if you have a broad product range, you could send information out about other state-of-the-art gadgets, as the customer is likely to be interested in these.

Segmenting your audience

Depending on the size of your customer base and the breadth of your offering, you should tailor a wider range of email messages to a number of tightly focused customer groups, by dividing up your database accordingly. Doing this is probably easier than you think. Unless you're a retail outlet selling lots of low-value goods, when a transaction is made, you probably have the names, addresses and email addresses of your customers at least. Then there are purchase records, which give you a reasonable idea of what each customer has bought and is, therefore, interested in. From this you can begin to build profiles, and divide your target audience into sub-groups – perhaps in terms of types of products they buy, the regularity with which they make purchases (high value customers versus low value) or whether they have begun an online transaction then abandoned it. Then you can create mail messages that are relevant to the different sub-groups.

Segmenting can be done in-house by your marketing team or you could recruit a specialist in this field. Alternatively, you could outsource this work to an agency.

Digging deeper

The real benefit of email marketing over traditional direct mail is that there are more accurate ways to measure its effectiveness, so you can plan further campaigns accordingly. Today's technology allows you to track the delivery of the message – did it arrive and was it opened? Web analytics software enables you to monitor a customer's behaviour when they click from the email through to your website.

All this information can be brought together onto a single platform that will help you to more accurately segment your customers, building on the initial work you will have done based on initial contact details and purchases. For example, you can track which customers have been viewing which products on your website. You can then automate email campaigns based on that information.

Analysing success

One of the phrases that you hear over and over again from internet professionals is that the web is a totally accountable medium. And it's certainly true that with the right software, everything you need to know about your customers can be laid out in front of you. For instance, if you are selling online and you have taken the trouble to buy advertising space at other websites, paying good money to secure a high position in both paid and natural search engines, then you will be able to see in fine detail exactly how successful your strategy has been. You will know where the customers clicked through from, what they did

THE ART OF SUCCESSFUL EMAIL MARKETING

- *Start small*: Use the information you have to create a limited number of customer segments and target tailored mail messages accordingly.
- *Build on your information*: As customers respond to your emails, use the information to create new and more precise segments.
- *Test and test again*: The segmentation of your consumer base is always going to involve assumptions. Those assumptions should be tested on an ongoing basis.
- *Build profiles from a broad base of information*: In addition to the information that customers volunteer about themselves you can extend their profiles using behavioural data (what they buy, where they visit, etc.) and demographic information extrapolated from postcodes. For a forward-looking view of the customers, predictive modelling tools provide an indication of cross and up-sell opportunities.
- *Experiment with subject headers*: This is a tricky area. The header that encourages the biggest response in terms of open rates may not generate a high rate of conversions. Conversely, a very specific header may prompt a relatively small percentage of recipients to open the message, but those who do may be more inclined to click through to a landing page and make purchases.
- *Work with ISPs*: They often take a stricter line than legislators on what does and does not constitute spam. It pays to give assurances that your mail campaigns conform to best practice. Consider joining the Good Mail initiative. Mail carrying the Good Mail stamp will not be blocked by ISPs.
- *Take note of those who don't respond to mail messages*: If customers don't respond to mailshots, consider targeting offers to reactivate their interests. However, if there is still no response, drop them from the list. Smaller lists can be better lists.

when they arrived at your website and just how many converted from browsers to customers.

The good news is that software that will deliver this information to your desktop needn't cost a fortune. Indeed, one of the most powerful tools (Google Analytics) is available at no cost, and if you want something a little more sophisticated, there are agencies across a range of price points that will collect and analyse data on your behalf.

Using analytics

The key is to make sure that you use this invaluable information to hone your sales strategy and move the business forward. This sounds obvious, but currently many companies are failing to get the most from the online tools at their disposal. One major obstacle seems to be the sheer amount of information available from analytics tools, which can make it difficult to focus on the data that matters. But there are ways to cut through the noise and find the information you want.

The first step is to tailor analytic reports to the goals of your business and to recognise the metrics that are important, that is where your customers are coming from – search engines, online banner adverts, websites with links to yours, etc. These data might tell you that search engines are delivering four times as many customers as banners and that people linking through from affiliated websites represent just a fraction of your traffic. This doesn't necessarily mean that you cut down on banner advertisements and focus on search, because it may be, for instance, that those who click through from a banner are more likely to make purchases. Once you know this, you can work out what the return on investment from each of your channels actually is.

The second step is to segment the view of where customers are coming from: by individual site, banner location or search engine, by region or even by country. If you combine these data with an analysis of what customers are doing, you can customise your website to specific groups within your overall audience. For instance, if you have an international audience, you may find that the landing page – the place on your website where customers first 'land' once they have been directed – is better for your UK visitors than it is for your American customers. Once you know that, you can tailor the landing page to each group, or go one stage further and create a separate website – known as a microsite – for them within your main website.

Thirdly, analytics software is also a useful means of identifying problems. If the figures tell you that the average person is spending two minutes on your website, that's comforting to know. If on the other hand, 80% of arrivals log off within seconds, then you have identified an important issue and can set about resolving it.

Shaping your offering

Analysis of customers can also help shape your company's offering to the public. By taking a close look at where people are going on your website and what they choose to buy, you can establish exactly what your customers' preferences are. Once you know this, it's possible to focus your online marketing on the most popular products and buy stock armed with a clear idea of where the demand is.

Analytics tools don't stand in isolation. The information you have gathered on customer preference can be transferred to other tools, and once you have gathered names and email addresses, and created customer segments, as described earlier, you can use it to better inform your email marketing – or other techniques, such as direct mail – by more accurately targeting groups of customers through offering products or services that are tailored to their previous choices.

The social networking media: Web 2.0

A staggering 194 million people worldwide are actively using social networking websites such as MySpace, Bebo and Facebook, with the estimated user base in the UK alone coming at 4.48 million, according to research carried out by advertising agency Universal McCann. And while the audience remains heavily weighted towards teenagers and twenty-somethings, the age range of users is slowly but surely broadening.

At the same time, the principles of social networking are also being applied to a business context. Sites such as Linkedin, France's Viadeo and Xing provide businesspeople with a means to make contact with

The internet now has a massive, broad and growing audience

peers, find service providers, locate business partners and recruit. And they are proving very popular. The biggest player, Linkedin, now has 11 million members worldwide and has passed the 1 million mark in the UK.

Using the social internet to market and sell

Online social or business networkers exchange information and interact with each other rather than being passive receivers of content. This means the operators gather a huge amount of information about their users: age, gender, location and interests – it's all on the social network databases. The upshot is that these sites are becoming increasingly effective advertising platforms. If you want to target your advertisements at a very tightly defined group of people – and get more bangs for your bucks in the process – social networks will help you do that.

However, the potential of social networking sites goes beyond advertising. Increasing numbers of businesses are building their own communities on social sites, giving the audience an opportunity to engage directly with them. At first glance, this is mainly the preserve of the big brands, but businesses of any size can communicate with customers, using Web 2.0 tools, such as blogs (interactive web journals) and forums. You can either do this through a social network or by incorporating social elements into your own website.

The advantage of interactive communications of this kind is that it invites comment. Talk about your company or products on a blog and you will get customers posting responses telling you what they think. That might not always be comfortable reading, but at the very least you will get to know your market. Equally, a customer forum will encourage those who use your products to get together and swap advice and tips. By building loyalty in this way you will grow sales. In addition, by allowing your customers to create content you will also become more visible on the all-important search engines.

Using the internet to the full

You may think that embracing the logic of the social internet is a bridge too far for your business or that your product or service might not be appropriate to sell online. But remember that the media and technology landscape is changing, and that there has been a significant shift online. Consequently, the internet now has a massive, broad and growing audience, and you ignore it at your peril.

As explained above, by moving into the realm of social networking, you will find lots of ways to get involved online beyond selling your products, ranging from advertising and marketing to building active communities of customers, which can generate loyalty and help keep your business directly in touch with the people who are buying its products or services – this is essentially what harnessing online social networking can achieve in a practical sense. What's more, you can measure the effectiveness of your activity far more comprehensively that you can beyond the online world.

The first chapter of Part Three will introduce the second approach to growing your own business – buying and growing existing businesses.

AN ONGOING COMMITMENT

If you do decide to embrace Web 2.0 as part of your market strategy, remember that you have to stick at it. Even something as simple as a blog has to be updated constantly if it is to be of interest. Nothing looks worse than entries that are months out of date. Remember also, that it is in the nature of social networks that there will be negative as well as positive comments, and you have to be prepared for both.

! TOP TIPS

- ! Decide whom you want to reach online – all of your audience or just a part of it?
- ! Tell your existing customers – and use search engines to attract new ones.
- ! Never forget customer service. One bad experience and customers won't return.
- ! Invest in search engine optimisation and keyword marketing.
- ! Use email marketing as an effective way of reaching your target audience
- ! If sales or customer response is disappointing be prepared to rework the website.
- ! Gather data on customers and use that information to target relevant messages.
- ! Use analytic reports to find out where your customers are coming from – search engines, online banner adverts or websites.
- ! Use analysis of customers to help shape your company's offering to the public.
- ! Ensure that the look and feel of your mail messages match your existing brand values.
- ! Social networking sites can be effective advertising platforms.
- ! Social networking allows you to build communities online, allowing your customers to tell you what they think & to create content about your brand.

PART THREE

ACQUISITIONS

ACQUISITIONS:
THE FASTEST
WAY TO GROW

THIS CHAPTER WILL DISCUSS:

- Reasons to acquire another business

- Advantages of acquisitions as a growth strategy

- Funding acquisitions

- Alternatives to full-blown acquisitions

The word acquisition means 'purchase' and in business relates to one business buying all or part of another. Acquisitions became a glamorous activity in Thatcher's 1980s Britain, as many large companies bought others, filling newspapers with headlines reeking of money and success. But acquisitions can be, and often are, every bit as useful for small- and medium-sized businesses too. Acquisition provides a means for businesses of all sizes to grow more quickly than would be possible organically, which is why acquisitions are sometimes described as a shortcut to growth.

However, remember that buying a business isn't a race, and absolute care needs to be taken before embarking on the acquisition process. Get it right and the rewards can be big, but many acquisitions don't go smoothly, and a bad acquisition can severely wound the buyer.

Reasons to acquire another business

Here we discuss why and when might acquisitions make sense. Common reasons for wanting to buy a business are:

- Increase market share
- Enter new market
- Acquire key supplier
- Acquire new technology
- Acquire key people
- Acquire a key customer
- Belief you can significantly grow the value of the business being bought
- Buy and build strategy
- Cheaper than organic growth.

> **Acquisitions are sometimes described as a shortcut to growth**

The first five are all things which you might normally achieve in the usual course of business. The reason to buy another business to reach these is that it would enable you to achieve one of these objectives much faster or more profitably than you could by hiring people, launching products and so on within your existing business.

The business you acquire will be already up and running with revenues and profits whereas it might take you a year or longer to get to the same stage organically.

Equally, it could also be a way of reducing risk, as new launches or expansion into new markets inevitably involve risk, especially if there is already someone doing what you want to do now. First, your new launch might not work, or at least it might not work as well as you need it to. It may be there is enough demand in a market for one nicely profitable business but not two; to launch into that market you would need to hope that the other business decides to leave you to it. This assumes the market can't grow fast enough into being sufficiently large to support both of you, otherwise you would simply both lose money. Buying their business gives you profitable access to that market without the risk of your launch failing. Second, it might be cheaper to buy an existing business than to launch one. If you want to grow in a particular market, new product launches or significant marketing investment might be more expensive than simply buying a business already there.

Occasionally, there are specific people or teams or technologies which you might want to grow your business, and the only way to secure them is to buy the company which employs or owns rights to them. This might apply to creative industries that own intellectual property, for example, or to manufacturing industries that want sole ownership of certain significant new technologies currently owned by another business. In these instances acquisition is usually the only way to achieve a particular objective. For instance, in January 2006, marketing business REaD Group bought direct mail company My Right to Privacy (MRP) to develop an existing service online. REaD Group chief executive Mark Roy knew he needed to invest in online technology and skilled individuals to make the service work.

'We were looking to put our solution online,' he explains, 'but we didn't have the skills in-house and thought the only way we could acquire them was to buy them in. MRP had some great technology, so we approached them to buy their business.' The theory worked in practice and, using MRP's skills, REaD Group now has a strong online offering to complement its offline services.

Buy and build strategies

Buy and build strategies are where a business sets out to buy several businesses and grow them. Clapham House (see Chapter 1.3) is an excellent example of a business with such a strategy; it bought a number of restaurant brands that it proceeded to expand by rolling out the restaurants into lots of new locations. This strategy is common with retail and leisure, but can also apply to media and other businesses.

If a seller is keen enough to sell, it might be worth buying a business just because you know it's worth more than you are paying for it, and that you will be able to make it worth far more. From time to time opportunities to buy a business for less than it's really worth do arise, usually because the seller wants to sell quickly. Equally, you may feel that you can make a business worth considerably more than it is today. The private equity industry is built around this premise – it buys large businesses that it believes it can turn into more profitable businesses. Sometimes a buyer believes a business might have a hidden asset, which could be sold off for worthwhile money, while leaving the intact core business still worth more than it was before.

STRATEGIC VERSUS OPPORTUNISTIC ACQUISITIONS

Acquisitions can be described as either strategic or opportunistic. Strategic acquisitions are those where a company has a particular strategy to expand in a certain way, and buys businesses to help achieve that growth. In practice, many acquisitions are opportunistic – companies which have an opportunity to buy a supplier, customer or competitor do so even when they had had no prior strategy to grow by acquisition.

In a downturn such opportunities will usually be far more plentiful than normal as many businesses face a tougher time. Some owners will be keen to sell out quickly rather than putting in hard work into running a business through a risky time. Others might run into or anticipate financial hardship, and choose to or even be forced to sell, perhaps by an administrator. Barclays Bank's acquisition of part of the Lehman Brothers investment bank in late 2008 is a good example of an opportunistic acquisition.

Advantages of acquisitions as a growth strategy

Cost synergies

When you buy a business, you have an opportunity to benefit from 'synergistic' cost savings. The enlarged business should have the revenues and gross profits from both businesses while spending less on functions such as administration and back office processing than the two businesses used to – so your net profit should be higher both in pounds and as a percentage of revenue.

The same principle applies when companies expand geographically. If you have two office equipment outlets in the West Midlands, buying up similar stores elsewhere in the country will boost sales while opening the possibility of centralising key administrative functions. In recent years, we have seen a rash of this kind of deal, with the creation of nursing home chains and multiple dental practices – even the funeral business has got in on the act. And although the revenue for each component business doesn't necessarily rise, the costs fall.

Vital to achieving these business synergies is carefully planning the integration of the two companies, so that staff remain motivated and the necessary departments are combined with the minimum of fuss. Managing integration can be a complex process, and it's worth spending plenty of time and effort getting it right as it holds the key to a successful acquisition.

Revenue synergies

A dream ticket for an acquisition would be achieving synergies on two levels – not only from operating together under one more cost-efficient company structure, but also from the combined businesses being able to sell more than was previously possible individually. Typically, this is achieved when the products of the two companies are different but complementary. For instance, when a computer hardware and

LET THE PEOPLE GROW

Company: The Hot Group
Chief executive: Tony Reeves

In the post-2000 environment of low unemployment and skills shortages, recruitment was a flourishing business, but it wasn't always easy for smaller players to make a decent profit. 'You have to get to a turnover of at least £2m before increases in revenue begin to make a real difference to the bottom line,' says Tony Reeves, chief executive of The Hot Group, a recruitment firm that put technology at the centre of a business that involves both traditional branches and web operations.

While the company's ultimate priority is to expand organically, the past few years have seen it make a number of acquisitions to increase its footprint in the recruitment marketplace. Since its formation, it has acquired recruitment websites, such as GisaJob, as well as people-based agencies, such as ASA Recruitment. All of these have given the Hot Group scale in the market place and, as Reeves points out, there is considerable scope to grow revenues while instituting savings. 'We consolidate the back office and put in our technology,' he says.

But not all acquisitions are the same. Often, acquiring a website means retaining the brand, but not the people or the technology. On the other hand, when you buy a traditional agency, you are buying people and skills and you have to keep them on board. And whether growth is achieved by acquisition or organically, Reeves stresses that having the right people is crucial. 'The reality of growing a business is allowing the people to grow,' he says.

software supplier buys a systems integrator, the result is a company that can not only sell the kit, but also the installation and systems management expertise. This creates the opportunity for the sales force from each business to sell the other's services and products to their existing clients.

Such a revenue-based strategy has been used a number of times by IT company Avanquest, a business that has made around six acquisitions of owner-managed information companies. 'I want to know if I can take that business and create more value by selling its products and services to our customers, and taking what we already have and selling to its customers,' says managing director Chris Thomson.

Funding acquisitions
How much do acquisitions cost?

Acquisitions sound expensive. Perhaps it's the word itself, or because we usually hear the word being used in association with major headline-making deals. But the reality is that acquisitions needn't be expensive. There have been numerous famous acquisitions for £1, such as when Ken Bates bought Chelsea Football Club, but that too is misleading – the businesses you can buy for £1 will almost always come with numerous liabilities as well as assets. However, you can buy a worthwhile business from as little as a few hundred thousand pounds, and the vast majority of acquisitions each year will be for businesses changing hands for less than £5 million.

If you go after the number one player in the market, you need to be prepared to pay top dollar. But if your budget is limited and you have confidence in your ability to turn an under-performing company into a cash cow, companies that are struggling provide opportunities for bargain hunters.

Raising capital for acquiring another business

One big advantage of acquiring a business is that it will generate revenue from day one. But there is also a corresponding big disadvantage: you will have to pay for it – or at least a significant proportion of the total cost – up front.

Raising capital is always a challenge, but ironically it can be easier to strike a deal with investors or banks for acquisitions than for organic growth. This is because the investors can see precisely what your business would get for its money, reducing their perceived risk considerably. In the past 20 years banks have been willing to lend against cashflow, too, where they can see the ability of your enlarged business to repay the loan you would need to make an acquisition. It's too early to tell whether the current banking climate will still see

> **It can be easier to strike a deal with investors or banks for acquisitions than for organic growth**

lending like that, but it's certainly still well worth discussing with your bank manager.

Venture capitalists and business angels are often willing to provide funds for expansion through acquisition, though all the normal criteria of what they will invest in and on what terms would apply – see Chapter 4.5.

Alternatives to full-blown acquisitions

Depending on your objectives, there are some cheaper alternatives to full-blown mergers and acquisitions. If it's skills you're after, poaching individual members of staff or teams is undoubtedly more cost-effective than bidding for the entire group. A certain amount of care is required here, at least in assuring yourself that the people you are after aren't subject to contracts that will prevent them from working for rival companies such as yours for a stated period of time.

You could also consider buying certain assets rather than the whole business. Retailers often sell off small groups of stores to other retailers, for example, and media businesses often sell individual properties, such as magazines, websites or book lists. If your plan is to move into other regions or countries, but you lack the infrastructure (or the money to build it), you should consider options such as joint ventures or franchise deals.

If your takeover plans were aimed at securing favourable terms from trading partners, taking a minority stake might secure the same result. For instance, let's say you are considering buying a supplier to both secure a source of vital components and keep costs under control. You might be able to secure the same outcome by buying a sufficiently large stake to give you a real say in the operational decision making of that company.

Although an attractive option, you should expect and allow for some negative surprises in any deal, and the next chapter discusses the reasons why acquisitions are very vulnerable to failure.

IS MAKING ACQUISITIONS RIGHT FOR YOUR BUSINESS?

If you're looking to secure a mix of higher revenues and stable fixed costs in a short time, nothing can beat an acquisition. And while there are plenty of other good reasons to hit the acquisition trail as listed above, it's important that you know exactly what you want to achieve from each transaction.

- Are you sure that it makes more sense to acquire rather than launch into the market?
- Does your business have the financial and management wherewithal to not only complete the deal, but also manage both the old and new parts of your business properly afterwards?

Avoid getting caught up in the excitement of buying a company. You will have laid the foundations for a successful acquisition when you have:

- Set clear goals that you want to achieve through the acquisition
- Identified the right target
- Made sure you have the necessary finance in place
- Paid close attention to the cultural differences and how you can align them.

! TOP TIPS

! Acquisitions and mergers provide businesses an alternative way to grow other than organically.

! Acquisitions can be strategic or opportunistic.

! Acquisitions can deliver very rapid growth as the business you acquire will be already up and running with revenues and profits.

! When you buy a business, you can benefit from 'synergistic' cost and revenue savings.

! It can be easier to raise capital for an acquisition through investors or banks than for organic growth as they can see the end product more clearly.

! Cheaper options include well-thought out strategies to attract skilled people from other companies and buying only certain assets of a company. Before setting out to acquire another business, make sure you do your homework – will it be cheaper than a new launch, do you have enough money, will the two businesses complement each other, etc?

WHY ACQUISITIONS CAN GO WRONG

THIS CHAPTER WILL DISCUSS:

- The right deal, but the wrong timing

- Needing a 'fresh challenge'

- Overpaying

- Misunderstanding the target

- The benefits that don't materialise

- The failed integration

As discussed in the previous chapter, for businesses with ambitious expansion plans, acquisitions can be a fast track to growth, and could carry less risk and cost than gradually building your business. The caveat is that this is only the case if you approach acquisitions carefully and strategically, with clear goals and parameters. This is because statistics tell us that the majority of acquisitions do not deliver the expected benefits. The exact proportion varies depending on the survey, but if the business consultancies that produce them are to be believed, the failure rate is sizeable, and could be anything between 60% and 80%.

A large percentage of mergers and takeovers fail to deliver the expected benefits

Although not all unsuccessful takeovers inflict serious damage on the acquiring company, it's important to understand why deals go wrong so that you won't be deterred from pressing ahead with a good takeover opportunity just because of the statistics. Also, even though a deal which fails to produce all the expected benefits may be considered a statistical failure, it may nevertheless be an acquisition which still made sense; failure to achieve all the desired benefits doesn't mean that the enlarged company fails altogether (though there are certainly examples of that happening).

The right deal, but the wrong timing

A common mistake is not to take a step back to consider whether the timing is right. Let's assume for a moment that your business is successful and you have an opportunity to acquire a company that could genuinely enhance your sales and profits. The main question to ask yourself is whether your management team has the necessary time available, beyond running your business, to dedicate to making the acquisition a success. For instance, if your strong performance levels involve everyone in your team working long hours, then you need to honestly assess whether your team will have the time or energy to cope with the extra workload that a merger or takeover will undoubtedly generate, including identifying opportunities, negotiating the deal, carrying out due diligence checks and working with lawyers and accountants. So before going for an acquisition, no matter how tempting, make sure you have the internal resources in place to handle it.

The key here is to be realistic and only press ahead with acquisition plans when the timing is right with regard to your existing business, both strategically and financially, and it makes sense within the current commercial climate. Too often those involved, from the CEO down to the management team and investors, let their ambitions get the better of them. Mergers and takeovers are often seen as a sign of corporate virility. When one business takes control of another, it's a sign that the acquirer has the financial wherewithal, dynamism and strategic ambition to become a better company. It makes everyone feel good – from the shareholders, the advisers and, above all, the management team that pulled it off. But that good feeling won't last long if the deal doesn't live up to expectations. The saying 'buy in haste, repent at leisure' has never been more applicable than with acquisitions, and it's an error numerous entrepreneurs have lived to regret; land-grab for its own sake is a dangerous game.

The disaster that was the merger of media giant Time Warner with the then all-conquering internet brand AOL could be said to be an example of muscle flexing over brain power. What appeared initially to be an inspiring and ambitious piece of empire building, with the pre-eminent new media company of the day merging with a content-rich titan of old media, was shown, as the deal quickly turned sour,

SHOULD AN AILING BUSINESS BE CONSIDERING ACQUISITION?

Before taking over another business your company should be ready to tackle the often complex challenge of integrating the acquired business into your working practices and culture. If you're struggling to hit sales targets or keep costs under control, the opportunity to acquire a competitor might appear to offer a route out of your present difficulties (and in some cases it might be exactly the right course of action). However, if your business is unstable, the wisest short-term strategy is usually to address the problems it is currently facing, rather than taking on a challenging project that may or may not deliver the goods.

to be simply the hubris of first generation internet companies that thought they could do no wrong. Following the collapse of the dot com bubble, the value of the new company's online assets dropped and the resultant goodwill write-off forced the merged group to report a massive $9bn loss. AOL founder Steve Case was subsequently ousted as chief executive and, by 2007, plans to sell the online division were made public.

Needing a 'fresh challenge'

Beware buying out of boredom, too. If you have spent a number of years building a company, you might think of making an acquisition because you need a fresh challenge. So when a buying opportunity presents itself, it's all too easy to throw caution to the wind in the desire for an exciting new business project. Once again, it pays not to let your heart rule your head.

This was one of the few mistakes made by mail-order shirt company Charles Tyrwhitt on its journey from back-room mail-order operation to a £60m turnover multi-channel retail brand. Founder Nick Wheeler admits that his decision to buy children's clothing retailer Patrizia Wiggins was fuelled by the need for a fresh challenge, coupled with belief that the acquisition would enable his company to leapfrog into a new market. In fact, retail proved to be a different market to mail order and Wheeler found it impossible to turn the struggling company round. The result was that Charles Tyrwhitt lost more in one year attempting to integrate Patrizia Wiggins than it made in the previous three. Buying a business solely to shake yourself from a torpor is not advisable.

> **Buying a business solely to shake yourself from a torpor is not advisable**

Overpaying

Another often repeated mistake is to overpay to complete a deal. When acquiring a company, you should set a maximum price you're willing to pay, and be prepared to walk away if the seller insists on a higher price. Avoid getting caught up in a bidding war that results in you making a

> **Many companies pay too much for the business they are buying**

deal that is hard to justify in terms of the returns. The most striking example of this error was the Royal Bank of Scotland's (RBS) recent acquisition of ABN Amro bank, which ultimately proved disastrous for RBS. The same principle can apply to smaller companies. It's important that you know what the business you want to acquire is worth to you. It doesn't matter what it's worth to anyone else; if you can buy the business for less than it's worth to you, go for it. Otherwise, move on. There is always another deal, no matter how much you might convince yourself that any one deal is 'The only one' for you.

The acquisitions market will of course be influenced by the wider economic climate; boom years result in a sellers' market, with plenty of finance around to fund deals, while a credit crunch results in a dramatic downturn in deal volumes as sellers sit on their hands and fewer buyers have access to finance. Deals can often fail to get off the ground because a buyer or seller (or both) lacks a keen awareness of the prevailing market and they fail to structure the deal accordingly. There's always a way to get the structure right, despite market conditions. For instance, in a depressed market, if you are buying a company with growth potential from a reluctant seller, you can structure the deal to give the outgoing owner a share of the upside as the company grows over time. As the company grows, the seller's remaining stake also increases in value. And when the time comes to sell those shares, the one-time owner not only gets a second opportunity to cash in, but also the shares are worth much more.

> **Many purchasers fail to grasp the disruptive impact a distressed and under-performing business can have on their company**

Misunderstanding the target

Failing to achieve a comprehensive understanding of the target company and the market it operates in is a common pitfall. An insufficient assessment of the compatibility of the company you're looking to purchase in terms of its management style, financial structure and business practices can be disastrous. Getting it wrong at this stage of a deal betrays that the purchaser has not been clear enough about what they were looking for. A proper due diligence process can provide the headline figures on sales, costs and profits, but to be absolutely sure that an acquisition will deliver the results you want requires a much more detailed investigation. Here are some of the key factors acquirers fail to consider fully.

- *Knowing where the sales come from* – is the company exposed to a few big clients who could cancel contracts at a moment's notice? If so, that would make the transaction extremely high risk. And why do customers buy from this particular company? Is it because of good marketing, the perceived quality of the products or close relationships between its staff and the customers they serve?

- *Why the business is successful* – a clear impression of whether a company's approach to the market will fit with yours is crucial. For example, if you are both selling a similar product but your company focuses on customer service and build quality, whereas your potential acquisition piles high and sells cheap, you need to carefully consider whether the two businesses are compatible. That kind of situation can present an opportunity, allowing you to address two different sets of customer. Also, acquisitions can go awry if a post-acquisition strategy to avoid one part of the merged business cannibalising the other isn't established at this stage.

- Why the business isn't successful – if the business isn't successful (i.e. the acquisition is a fire sale) an understanding of what went wrong and attending market conditions is even more crucial; entrepreneurs often let their ego do the talking and assume they can fix the problems of a company picked up for a knockdown price. A detailed understanding of exactly what went wrong and how deep problems run in distressed assets is invaluable and will tell the purchaser if they have the capability to turn the company around. If the market the company operates in has moved on, what looks like a bargain could become a very expensive mistake. Has the business had key assets and capabilities stripped away? Has it retained crucial IP? Will key staff be retained? Many purchasers fail to grasp the disruptive impact a distressed and under-performing business can have on their company. If it's a full-blown turnaround,

THE IMPORTANCE OF DUE DILIGENCE

Company: Dreams
Founder: Mike Clare

Following its launch in 1985, bed retailer Dreams largely pursued a strategy of organic growth – expanding into fresh territories under its own steam by opening new stores. However, in 2006 the company seized an opportunity to break into the Scottish market through the purchase of Off to Bed, a retailer with eight shops. It was Dreams' first acquisition, and it illustrated the importance of strategic planning.

Off to Bed was a struggling business available at a knock-down, six-figure price and there was little time for due diligence. As a result, Dreams founder Mike Clare found that he had bought a company that was no longer advertising its existence and where a cost-cutting approach included switching off in-store heating, an economy measure that was unlikely to be popular in Scotland. But there was an upside – the workforce was eager for change. The staff were generally happy about the takeover, not least because Dreams standard rate for salespeople and managers was more than they were being paid previously. Dreams brought in a new energy, too, with Clare setting targets for the big promotion period of January, even though one or two stores weren't entirely suitable.

But tough decisions had to be made, and in 2007 Dreams was forced to plan for store closures in Scotland and cut back in pre-existing expansion plans. This left Clare wondering whether taking advantage of a fire sale was the right decision. 'We got a warehouse and some staff, but I don't think we'd rush into another acquisition,' he says. 'It took up a lot of management time, plus expenditure on advertising, shop-fitting, recruitment. But it's more than that with the disruption and change and other hidden costs.'

Predictably the people element was as big a challenge. Dreams, like any company, has a culture and style of its own. 'There was some passive resistance,' recalls Clare. 'We were naïve to think it would be easy.' Off to Bed hadn't done many promotions and its employees didn't want the store to open late and on Sundays, even though they weren't being asked to work more hours. 'There was also the issue that we're an English company coming here,' says Clare. 'We learned a lot and might have done things differently with hindsight.'

What's more, Scottish consumers didn't know the Dreams brand, even though the company had sponsored the ITV drama *Heartbeat* and increased its ad spend from 8.5% to 14% for six months following deal completion. Clare was forced to conclude that buying the chain might not, after all, have provided a short cut into the Scottish market.

it will require distinct skills, which may mean costly professional help and even a new management team.

- *Why they are selling* – why has the seller put their company on the blocks? Spend time getting an understanding of the seller's motivations. Are they retiring or seeking a new challenge? Alternatively, although the historical numbers may be strong, just how rosy is the future looking? Check the closet for skeletons, as you don't want any jumping out once the deal is done. Your legal and financial advisers should be red hot on this, but it's worth repeating that you need to know whether there are any legal actions waiting in the wings, outstanding disputes with Her Majesty's Revenue and Customs (HMRC) or contractual issues with staff or customers that could throw you off course.

The benefits that don't materialise

Post-acquisition, if the organisation isn't stronger than the original component parts in terms of costs and sales, the deal is a failure. Realising the benefits of an acquisition can be challenging.

Cost synergies should be the easiest to achieve, but larger organisations often find that the expense of merging accounting, enterprise resource planning and customer relationship management systems can, in the short and medium term, outweigh any financial gains.

The first 100 days are vital, and sometimes you have to be tough

Revenue synergies also are difficult to realise, perhaps because they rely on external factors that are easy to overlook during the assessment process. The 1980s and 1990s saw a raft of financial and property services sector mergers, with building societies and banks buying estate agency chains. The logic was simple. A customer would visit a local estate agency in search of a home and once a property was found, the agent could direct his or her client to a mortgage adviser who would sort out the finance. Once hooked, the customer would also have access to related products, such as home insurance and life cover. However, this model didn't always produce the expected boom in profits. For one thing, customers didn't always like putting their financial services eggs in one basket and preferred to shop around. And the hard-sell image of an estate agency didn't fit comfortably with the customer's idea of the kind of service a bank or building society should be offering.

So it's vital to understand how your customers will react to the new set up of both companies before predicting revenue synergies or there's a danger that the acquisition won't come off. It may be a question of playing a hunch, but it's worthwhile carrying out customer research and talking to your own salespeople about their view of the market.

The failed integration

The biggest challenge facing any management team is the integration of two or more businesses and many do stumble. Once the contract has been signed, you face months of work that will draw on both personal and managerial skills, and there are countless pitfalls waiting to happen.

You need to bear in mind that you will be dealing with new people, many of whom will be long-standing employees of the acquired company. Both staff and management are bound to have certain misgivings about their future, new working practices and fitting in with the culture. It's dangerous to assume that these issues will sort themselves out; people may eventually become accustomed to a new set up – or simply leave – but damage may have been done in the meantime. Common mistakes include the management team not appreciating how much work it will need to put in to gain credibility and trust from the people in the acquired company and not honouring commitments made during the merger. The smart acquirer resolves issues as quickly as possible to maintain the momentum and vibrancy of the merged business. Consultants agree that the first 100 days are vital, and sometimes you have to be tough. Ducking the issues or procrastinating jeopardises merger projects.

Some companies are very tough indeed. When Hanson Trust bought Imperial Group, the latter had around 90 managers in the top two grades at Imperial Tobacco. Within a short period of time, only the sales director and finance director remained. This approach can work, but it's a high risk one. Generally, it suggests that the acquirer's management wants to assimilate the new subsidiary into an established way of working rather than recognising the merits and culture in the acquired firm. This can poison the integration process.

Whether your approach to the integration process is to placate staff, slap down those who prove obstructive or clear out the management from the acquired business and replace them with your own people, making a takeover work requires strong and decisive leadership. The whole process can be streamlined after the merger and any conflict kept to a minimum by forward planning. Where the transition process

PEOPLE MATTERS

If buying in expertise is your goal, remember that the uncertainty of an acquisition often provides the catalyst for key staff to up sticks and leave. This won't be too much of a problem if your intention is to buy a brand rather than the people behind it. For instance, in this era of internet trading, you might buy the URL of a well used e-commerce site in order to exploit its loyal customer base, while using your existing order processing and fulfilment operation to deliver the goods. But if the acquisition is a people business, you have to keep the key players on board.

One way to do this is through autonomy. You buy the company, but leave the existing management in place and offer incentives for performance. The advantage here is that you have people in position who know the business (and its customers) well so there is minimal disruption. It's a strategy that tends to be successful if you're buying a complementary business rather than taking a competitor out of the market.

However, in many cases you will need to make changes and you need to be clear from the start what that means for both you and the staff of the target company. The first 100 days of any merger are vital in terms of integration, but you need to think about a plan well in advance.

Customers can be an equally tricky proposition. While an acquisition should deliver more of them, they certainly can't be taken for granted. Sometimes, when a business merges with another, its customers will vote with their feet and go elsewhere. In some cases, bigger customers will have contracts containing change of ownership clauses, which gives them the right to cancel orders in the event of the supplier changing hands. However, even if that's not the case, you will need to convince the loyal customers of the business you acquire that the new company can supply as good a service as the old. If personal relationships between customers and sales staff are important, do your best to hold on to key staff.

is lengthy and crucial decisions protracted, a pessimistic reaction in the acquired firm can become permanent.

To avoid these pitfalls, take steps to meet and greet your target's employees in advance to help reassure them, while working out how many staff you will need to keep and who you will have to lose. Openness and honesty will really aid a quick integration and getting to know your new employees will also help you assess the level of cultural fit, which will give you an additional feel for how smooth the integration process is likely to be.

By this time, you would have a good idea whether making acquisitions is the way forward for your growth business, and in many cases it will be so. The next chapter will cover the key issues involved in searching and approaching the right targets for making a successful acquisition.

PEOPLE POWER

Company: Loch Fyne Restaurants
Financial director: Helen Melvin

Helen Melvin, financial director of Loch Fyne Restaurants, the seafood restaurant chain, was shocked at the amount of time it took to integrate Le Petit Blanc, a business it took over in 2003. 'We thought it would be a lot simpler than it's turned out to be,' she says. This is explained in part by the opportunistic nature of the deal. Le Petit Blanc was in administration when Loch Fyne moved to buy the assets for four of its restaurants for £1m.

'We also underestimated the cultural differences of the businesses,' recalls Melvin. Unfortunately, some of the remaining members of the management team proved more resistant to change than had been anticipated. 'We walked on egg shells for a long time, so that we didn't seem like we were coming in dictating to people,' says Melvin. She admits a firmer stance might have been better. 'In hindsight, the question is,' she adds, 'is your own management team strong enough to win them round or are you going to waste too much time doing this?'

It's an easy trap to fall into and Loch Fyne is far from alone in that respect. In order to get a workforce on board after an acquisition, it often pays to listen and attempt to placate, and where possible, to get to know the inner workings of a company. However, it becomes unhelpful without a degree of assertiveness and the generation of a strategic plan to cure any ills and achieve alignment with your own processes and objectives. Ultimately, this acquisition was made to work and the Le Petit Blanc brand is now profitable.

! TOP TIPS

DON'T

! Be tempted to buy another company because you're bored or think it would look good on your entrepreneurial CV, unless you can justify the acquisition in terms of real returns and tangible goals; focus instead in building your business organically.

! Assume that a bargain is good value – it can be tempting to buy a struggling business at a knock-down price, but be sure you have the time and skills to successfully integrate it into your existing company.

! Buy the first business that comes along – you may have identified growth by acquisition as your key strategy, but don't rush the process. Assess as many takeover targets as possible and choose the best fit.

! Get caught in a bidding war – set a ceiling for what you are prepared to pay and stick to it.

! Get bogged down – if integrating the acquisition target with your own company is likely to be a protracted and expensive process, consider walking away.

DO

! Look at cost and revenue synergies – but make sure you have check out how customers might react to the new set-up before making any predictions.

! Check out the reasons for the company being sold – does the CEO simply want to retire or is there a potential problem that the historical numbers don't reveal?

! Explore the customer story – why are customers buying from your acquisition target? Is it the price? Quality? Customer service? Does the target's business model complement or enhance yours?

! Ascertain whether the management of the acquisition target is behind the deal – if key staff leave when you need them, what impact would that have?

! Look for skeletons in the closet – are there any pending legal actions or tax disputes that could make life difficult when you take control

SOURCING AND APPROACHING TARGETS

THIS CHAPTER WILL DISCUSS:

- What type of company to look for

- Making the approach

- The role of advisers

There is no single way to find the ideal business(es) for you to buy to help your company grow. Ask a dozen CEOs about the circumstances that led up to them making an acquisition and you are likely to hear a dozen different stories. In some cases, the deal may have been an opportunistic response to an out-of-the-blue phone call offering a business for sale. In others, the acquirer could have spent months researching the market and looking for suitable acquisition prospects, beginning with a long list and narrowing it down to just one or two candidates. Then there are recommendations by advisers, introductions through friends of friends or business partners and contacts made through networking events.

Where you should start depends on what you are trying to achieve. If you are planning to take a competitor out of the market, you will probably have a good idea of the target companies, even if you won't necessarily know whether the owners are open to a deal. But if you are looking to acquire a company that will give you a foothold elsewhere in the UK or overseas, more research will be required. So where exactly do you begin?

What type of company to look for

Staying with what you already do strategy

In acquisitions, the lowest risk strategy is usually to stick to what you know, such as buying a competitor to boost your market share and cut costs. This can be a good plan, and the search process starts by making a list of key rivals. Then you need to define your acquisition strategy. Are you looking to buy businesses at bargain basement prices? If so, you can narrow the list down to those rivals that are known to be struggling, but are nonetheless picking up enough trade to make them interesting. Alternatively, you might be looking to buy a

> **Gathering as much information as you can on potential targets is absolutely essential**

bigger and more profitable rival through a reverse takeover. Again that narrows the field.

Diversification acquisition strategy

If your plan is to diversify your offering, your search should be directed at complementary business that present opportunities to cross and upsell a wider range of products and services. For instance, an online car insurance company might join forces with a business offering general insurance, with a view to selling more of everything to the combined customer base. In theory this is a smart move, as it will create a new business that is more than the sum of its component parts. By selling complementary products, the combined company – or companies within a group – have an opportunity to sell more to existing clients. Rather than simply adding one company's revenue stream to another – which would in itself mean higher profits – you can genuinely enhance the sales opportunities.

The key to a successful diversification acquisition strategy, however, doesn't lie within the companies involved, but with the response of the market to the move. A supplier of office hardware – PCs, photocopiers, etc. – might reasonably assume that if it purchased a stationery supplier, its existing clients would buy both product groups. In practice, the customers might be very happy with their existing stationery suppliers, with the result that the expected upturn in revenue doesn't occur. So spend some time finding out what your customers want. For instance, if a significant number have been asking your salespeople for an additional service that you don't currently offer, that could point the way to one or more strategic acquisitions. Let's say you're an IT company selling accounts packages. You find that a number of your clients are asking for advice about other solutions, such as ERP (enterprise resource planning) or CRM (customer relationship management) systems. They're long-standing customers and they trust your expertise, so potentially there is real opportunity, provided of course, you can find the right strategic acquisition prospect.

Identifying potential targets

There are two main routes to take when pinning down acquisition targets: do the research yourself or get professional help.

Researching yourself

If you are researching the market yourself, the internet is probably the first port of call. It's an immensely powerful medium, but don't forget the press too. Businesses are advertised for sale in local newspapers and trade magazines, so it's worth a trawl through the relevant publications.

Then there are trade shows and other sector-based events. These are good hunting grounds that offer the opportunity to meet potential targets face-to-face and get a sense of their abilities and unique selling points. What's more, establishing a relationship with a business you could acquire might make a future deal easier, and it could also put you at the front of the queue when the owner decides to move on. Predictably, owners nearing retirement age are more likely to consider this.

Don't forget your own contacts either. Suppliers or distributors are useful sources of insider information about acquisition prospects and some of the best tips come from word of mouth. Indeed, the companies that make up your supply chain may themselves present acquisition opportunities. Buying into your supply chain – such as a manufacturer taking control of a distributor – is a tried-and-tested acquisition strategy and if you have good relations with your trading partners, you may well be the company they call first when an CEO decides to sell.

Getting professional help

Moving on to professional help, your business adviser or an accountancy firm may help you track down the companies to target for acquisition. An accountant in a corporate finance practice will have a wealth of contacts, including business owners who wish to discreetly sell up. What's more, any corporate finance adviser worth their salt

---

USEFUL WEBSITES FOR SEEKING INFORMATION ON ACQUISITIONS

- Acquisitions International – www.acquisitionsinternational.com
- British Embassy – www.ukembassyhomepage.com
- UK Trade & Investment – www.uktradeinvest.gov.uk
- Companies House – www.companieshouse.gov.uk
- Dun & Bradstreet – www.dnb.co.uk
- FD Centre – www.thefdcentre.co.uk

---

can match buyers with sellers in vertical market segments and advise on whether the takeover or merger would provide a good fit.

Specialist mergers and acquisitions (M&A) brokers also have a sense of what is rumbling beneath the surface and can often identify potential targets that aren't yet on the market. Getting to know them may bear fruit and lead to giving them a mandate to buy. Acquisitions International, owned by BCMS Tradeplan, is a respected player that identifies and approaches on your behalf those companies not formally for sale, both in the UK and abroad. For foreign acquisitions, you can also request international directories from the British Embassy, UK Trade & Investment and the British Library.

Apparently healthy profit and revenue figures can hide some nasty shocks, so approach all takeover opportunities with care

Obtaining detailed information

The secret behind choosing the right company to acquire is all in the detail. So gathering as much information as you can on potential targets is absolutely essential. Some of this can be sourced from the company's website or via news media. Then there are official sources, notably Companies House, while credit reference agencies, such as Dun & Bradstreet, furnish additional details and also provide reassurance that your target is in good shape. For a small fee, a number of companies, such as the FD Centre, will keep tabs on a list of potential targets over a prolonged time period. Such advance spending can prove to be a smart investment.

QUESTIONS TO ASK YOURSELF

Once you have identified a business and made the initial approach, it's time to start asking some fundamental questions about your own motives, the intentions of the seller and your ability to make the acquisition work.

Start by looking at yourself. Why are you interested in this business and is it really right for you? Do you have the resources to make the acquisition and integrate it with your existing company or group?

Does the seller have a current business plan? Indeed, do they have any business plan? The business plan – or its absence – may tell you a lot about the business, its history, the owner's view of its future and their interest in selling.

Will you be able to work with the seller? If you should purchase the business, the chances are you are going to be dependent on the seller for information, contacts and resources. Based on what you know now, what do you think your relationship with the seller is going to be like? Can you expect that to be a positive experience? If you see signs of a 'difficult' person in the initial purchase investigation stages, it may become more stressful for both parties as things progress.

Do the numbers add up? Regardless of the response to the business plan question, access to the 'real numbers' behind the business is crucial. This may be more challenging than you would expect. Business owners are often reluctant to share operating and financial data, often for tax and competitive reasons, even when they are in a 'selling mode'. Ask if the financials that you will review are 'recast financial statements' and, if so, what adjustments have been made to these statements? Be as specific as you can when you gain information about the source of these statements. You may not receive any meaningful financials until after signing a confidentiality agreement and proving you have the financial ability to make the purchase.

Are you going to be able to add value to the business or is your goal simply to keep 'the machine' running? Once you have purchased the business, what are your objectives? Are you planning on owning the business for the next 20 years, or growing it over the next five years and then looking for the opportunity to sell? This will have an impact on the intangible assessment of what the business may be worth to you and help assess the potential challenges ahead. Beginning your business plan will help to clarify your objectives and the business potential ahead.

Some industries compile yearbooks, some offering a forensic breakdown of sales. Again, check the trade press for information, as businesses are often willing to provide financial information details to sector-specific publications. Remember, though, that any research you do – either at arm's length or over a business lunch with a trading partner or rival – won't give you anything close to a complete picture. Companies with a turnover of more than £5.6m must file audited accounts at Companies House and companies listed on capital markets must be totally transparent in terms of their trading records. However, you will be largely looking at historical data, and there won't be an opportunity to dig deeper into the current standing and future prospects of the business until negotiations and the 'due diligence' checking process begins. Apparently healthy profit and revenue figures can hide some nasty shocks, so approach all takeover opportunities with care.

Making the approach

How you approach your target is critical

Buying another business could be the most important transaction you ever undertake. It could kick-start your company to the next level, transform its growth chances and ultimately make you a good amount of money when the time comes to make an exit. Equally, it's likely to be life-changing for the seller, who will need to be convinced that the price is right, that market conditions are conducive to achieving the best deal and that his or her business will be in safe hands. This makes how you approach your target critical.

The circumstances surrounding the initial contact can vary enormously. In some cases, buyers make an offer out of the blue – either cold to a company that has been identified as a potential prospect or to a long-standing trading partner. In other cases, the target will be up for sale and marketing itself through advisers or the press. And of course, if the seller is actively looking for a deal, they may ring you direct. Regardless of the circumstances, though, there are some golden rules:

- Handle the initial contact sensitively. Even if an CEO wants to sell, they won't necessarily warm to arrogant buyers. Often it's best to suggest meeting to discuss potential areas of common interest; you don't need to straight away say 'I want to buy your business'. Your intention about buying is probably best communicated later on, after at least one meeting.
- Explain clearly your reasons for wanting to buy. Understandably, a business CEO may be suspicious of any approach, and unless you can impart your strategy effectively, they could be forgiven for thinking that you are on a fact-finding mission aimed at gleaning business intelligence. So tact and openness is everything.
- If you prefer to put an initial approach in writing to show you mean business and formalise the process, make sure that the letter doesn't end up in the wrong hands. If another member of staff sees it – the CEO's PA, for example – it could cause panic at the company, a situation that could scupper negotiations before they begin.
- If you are making an unsolicited offer, send a letter to the business CEO's home address, then follow up with a phone call.
- If the deal matters to you, be prepared to be persistent.

WHERE SHOULD YOU MEET A POTENTIAL BUYER?

Generally speaking, informal meetings are a good thing, especially if they are held on neutral ground. Let's say you plan to make an offer to a trading partner in your supply chain – a supplier perhaps. Doing it at your offices might make you feel comfortable, but it won't necessarily put the supplier at ease. It would be better to organise a lunch or a meeting for coffees to take soundings. Such informal discussions help to establish a strong rapport and understanding, something that's important for both parties – you could be working with the outgoing CEO for some time and these occasions also provide you an opportunity to sound out their motivation and get a feel for the factors that could make or break a deal. If they hope to retire in the near future, money might be the main factor. If they are younger and ambitious for the company in question, they may respond well to an offer that allows them to cash in, but remain as managing director of an autonomous unit within a group.

THE RELUCTANT SELLER

Company: Xchangeteam
Founder: Emma Brierley

The founder and chief executive of £6m turnover recruitment company Xchangeteam, Emma Brierley, has made two acquisitions since launching the business in 1999, purchasing recruitment counterparts the Davis Group and BDG Group. Brierley heard about the latter through a mutual contact, although the business was not up for sale. Brierley called its founder, Valerie Gascoyne, and suggested they meet.

'We had several meetings over about a year before she was ready to sell,' recalls Brierley. 'Over that time we got to know each other very well and understood one another's business. You have to look at everything and open communication is the key to making the relationship work. It's very emotional for an entrepreneur to sell their business, particularly if they weren't originally looking to do it.

'Valerie had been running her own business for more than 20 years, so it was a big decision for her to come and work for someone else. However, the deal meant that she would be freed up from a lot of the responsibilities she didn't really enjoy and enabled her to spend more time with clients.'

After selling her business Gascoyne joined the Xchangeteam as its chief executive. Her two-year earn-out is ending, but she will stay on as a director. 'It certainly wasn't just the money, as it wasn't enough to retire on,' says Gascoyne. 'I thought it was attractive to be a part of something bigger. We got on as people and that was the first step – I was fortunate in finding the right company.

'The culture fit was a major element, too; there was a lot of synergy. And I'm probably better off financially than if I'd stayed with the business, but I sometimes miss the freedom. However, I don't plan to start another business – I hope to help Emma grow this one.'

Mark Roy, chief executive of REaD Group recalls the first call he made to acquisition prospect MRP. 'Initially, they said that they really weren't interested, but they went away and discussed the idea,' he says. 'Later they decided they would have a meeting and we got moving from there.'

The role of advisers

The right professional advisers can help you enormously with the acquisition process, especially if you have not been through it before. There are three types of adviser you might use:

- A *corporate finance firm* can help scout for acquisition targets, negotiate the deal and even arrange finance
- A *lawyer* is essential for turning the bare bones of a deal into a sensible contract – expect to be taken aback by the amount of documentation that a deal needs
- And you might want to ask your *auditors* to go and do financial due diligence on the target before you complete a deal – essentially they would do a small audit of the target for you.

One major advantage of using advisers is that they should be less emotionally involved in the deal than you. On the other hand, your adviser(s) stand to earn good fees if the deal goes through and therefore there is a danger that some advisers might encourage you to proceed with a deal which is not right for you. Most will be above that, but it's always worth knowing their perspective.

If an CEO plans an exit, they will typically work with advisers for a period of months or even years before a sale. The advisers will help their client prepare the business for sale in terms of its structure, management team and systems, and they will also advise on an exit strategy. In other words, they know their clients on the seller side very well indeed. The advisers will also sound out the market. Indeed, the advisers have a key role in identifying potential buyers and will often make the first call or arrange an introduction. So they will be the ones to talk to you about the business on offer and why it's being sold. You will tell them about the plans you have to expand through acquisition. In an ideal world, that should make the first meeting with the seller a lot less awkward.

Working with an adviser is by no means essential and while some CEOs like to involve accountants and consultants early, others like to handle the initial introductions themselves. Again, the approach you take will depend on both circumstance and your preferences.

Remember that one thing is certain, even if you get a positive response to your overtures, a long process consisting of review and analysis of costs lies ahead before you sit down at the negotiating table. That's what we will be looking at in the next chapter.

! TOP TIPS

IDENTIFYING A PROSPECT

! Draw up a list – if you're planning to buy up competitors, make a list of rival firms. Similarly, if you're planning to expand geographically by buying businesses in other regions, decide on a location, research the market and list the likely candidates.

! Decide on strategy – are you looking for bargain basement prices or do you plan to buy out a bigger and more profitable competitor? A strategy of this sort will help you narrow the list of candidates.

! Use advisers, brokers or business transfer agents – these professionals can help you locate acquisition prospects. Newspapers and trade magazines can also provide a useful source of information.

! Use your own contacts – business partners or friends can be a source of information on companies that are coming on to the market.

! Research the prospects carefully – you can get a certain amount of information from the internet and Companies House, but you should also use credit ratings agencies to build a picture of the financial health of your target.

MAKING THE APPROACH

! Be tactful – if you're cold calling someone to explore the possibility of making an offer for their company, they are bound to be wary and very possibly hostile. Handle the situation with care.

! Be transparent – openness about why you want to buy the business is crucial. Equally, you should be clear about the owner's reasons for selling.

! Make sure any written approach goes direct to the owner – it may be advisable to write to him or her at a home address, rather than running the risk of other members of staff prematurely seeing your offer.

! Be persistent – if your offer is rebuffed, don't be afraid to modify it and try again.

! Talk informally – by meeting a potential seller over coffee or a meal, you have the opportunity to sound each other out ahead of any formal offer.

! Use advisers – they can not only help you identify prospects, but also make introductions.

GETTING YOUR MONEY'S WORTH: NEGOTIATING THE RIGHT PRICE

THIS CHAPTER WILL DISCUSS:

- How much is the potential acquisition worth to you?

- Common methods of valuing a business

- What can effect the price

- Risk analysis

- Structuring an acquisition

Clive Sanford, Magus Partners

Acquisitions are different from the normal routine of business and almost always involve the exciting prospect of an immediate and substantial improvement in your own business. Yet, precisely because they are outside the norm, and often a new experience for CEOs and their management teams, making an acquisition is fraught with a different type of business risk. Most experts identify over-paying as the biggest single cause of acquisition failure, as all too often buyers go into discussions and negotiations with a target without a detailed plan concerning valuation.

Determining how much to pay for a business you want to buy is a mixture of detailed business review and analysis, an assessment of your required rate of return, deal tactics and market awareness. So this is often a hugely involved process, even for a relatively small transaction, and usually very time-consuming. There is as much art as science involved.

How much is the potential acquisition worth to you?

Establishing how much the business is worth to you involves the calculation of how much more the combined business might be worth once you have achieved the benefits of the acquisition, compared with how much it's worth now. Although not all the difference might be attributable to the business you are buying, this will give you an absolute maximum figure that you might be willing to pay for the business you are considering buying.

Use a healthy dose of realism and even cynicism when making your assumptions

This calculation rather pre supposes that you know what your business is worth now and what it might look like after the proposed acquisition. For now, ignore what your business might be worth were you to sell it, and focus on its profits. So the next step is to work out how much more profit you might make after the acquisition. Of course, there might be non-financial reasons why the business is attractive to you, and you should consider those also, as a separate issue.

Calculating the synergistic benefits

Draw up a comprehensive list of all the effects of the deal, noting when the benefit might take effect and what it might cost, if anything, to achieve that benefit. Typical costs would be redundancy payments for any staff no longer needed, the cost to get out of any property or other arrangements which you would no longer need. Some cost savings might be almost immediate, whereas others might take years to come through. Once you have made this list, you should draw up a detailed analysis of how the combined business will look, highlighting the benefits from the acquisition. The easiest way to do this is on a simple spreadsheet (see example below), with your profit and loss information in one column, and the potential acquisition target in the next, and a sub-total column adding the two together, representing what would happen if you owned both businesses and ran them separately, precisely as they are today.

In the next column you can then start to make adjustments for synergies – whether increased revenue, reduced cost of goods, or reduced overhead costs. And the final column will then be the expected final result, showing what you expect the combined business to make in profit once the synergies have fed through. You should probably do this analysis for at least three years after the acquisition, allowing time for the synergies to come through.

Use a healthy dose of realism and even cynicism when making your assumptions. Merger and acquisition (M&A) history is littered

MISCELLANEOUS BUT IMPORTANT ITEMS

When reviewing your target's earnings, it's important to adjust for exceptional and non-recurring items – both positive and negative – as well as considering how sustainable they are. Perhaps the current owner takes a larger salary than the manager you will employ to run the acquired business after a deal (a positive adjustment) or perhaps the target has recently benefited from a one-off contract which temporarily inflated its profits (a negative one).

with projected cost savings that never materialised. And be aware of the risk of 'negative' synergies – for example, a customer of both your current business and your target might decide it still requires two different sources of supply after the deal is done, in which case your enlarged business may actually lose some turnover.

Other non-financial tangible/ intangible benefits

Next make a list of the potential non-profit benefits you think acquiring this business might yield. It may be that your target offers a threat from having launched a newly patented product that competes with your current business, or has just the right product to fill a gap in your product line, or even has a highly regarded production director who would be a perfect replacement for one of your key people who is about to retire. These attributes also have a value – admittedly more from a defensive perspective than in terms of growth – and need analysis in the same way as synergistic benefits.

Generating a positive perception in the marketplace through effecting an acquisition is another potential driver of value. 'It will be well received by our customers' or 'We'll go up to n^{th} in the league table' are both well-worn phrases, heard many times over the years. Inevitably, such thoughts are largely intangible in nature and, therefore, somewhat difficult to place a monetary value on. From a hard-nosed financial perspective, therefore, you should probably consider them as the 'icing on the cake', rather than the principal reason for pursuing a deal in the first place. Nevertheless, there are cases where these benefits have identifiable value – for example, the acquisition may allow you to be of a size to win a valued place on tender lists not currently available to you. Unless there are very clear tangible results expected from this, it's usually best not to place any monetary value on these benefits, but rather to bring them into your decision as to whether or not to proceed with the deal in due course.

We find new ways to get your company noticed

In today's market place
Calashock Marketing can
really help your business
move to the next level.
Don't be left behind, let us
help you get noticed!
We offer full-service
marketing & design support.
Call us on 020 8440 9535
and see how we can make
your marketing
go further for less.

calashock
marketing

Benefit from a flexible FD

Employment and Health & Safety Legislation
Why Do I Need to Bother?

Human Resource & Employment Law

Employment law is an extremely complex area. A wealth of existing legislation is being continually added to by new legislation.

Equal Opportunities Legislation has grown significantly in recent years, including legislation outlawing discrimination on the grounds of religion, race, sexual orientation, disability and age discrimination. This will impact on many areas of employment including recruitment, provision of benefits and retirement. Businesses can potentially face unlimited damages awards in discrimination cases and employment disputes are time consuming and costly.

The Employment Act 2002 made it a legal requirement for all organisations, regardless of size, to follow minimum discipline, dismissal and grievance procedures in certain circumstances. These changes mean that where dismissal is the outcome of a disciplinary procedure, an employer's failure to comply with the minimum procedures will lead to the dismissal being automatically unfair, leading in turn to hefty financial penalties.

Health & Safety

The Health & Safety at Work Act 1974 requires employers to provide a safe place and safe systems of work for both their employees and anyone else who comes into contact with their business e.g. the public, contractors etc. In addition to the Health & Safety at Work Act, the Health & Safety Management Regulations require that all work activities and locations are assessed for risk and that the risks identified are either removed entirely, or reduced by the introduction of control measures.

Owners ultimately hold the responsibility for Health & Safety in a business. They may delegate the authority to carry out Health & Safety duties but they cannot delegate the responsibility. The law places responsibilities on owners to prove "due diligence". The consequences for serious breaches of Health & Safety legislation can be punitive and with the introduction of the new legislation on Corporate Manslaughter, compliance is vital.

There is a major need for businesses to review their Human Resources/Employment Law procedures, the wording of their Contracts of Employment, the preparation of their disciplinary/grievance procedures and their understanding of forthcoming employment legislation to ensure they are complying with requirements and that procedures are being implemented in a fair and consistent manner.

With well over 1 million days being lost to accidents in the workplace and some high profile cases emerging, where small companies have been ordered to pay substantial amounts for failure to observe and put into practice the correct Health and Safety Procedures, again the time is right to review Health & Safety systems and procedures.

The Xact Group is offering a no obligation compliance assessment of a businesses procedures and systems in these key areas.

Contact us on:

0845 665 3006

The Xact Group Ltd
email: enquiries@xactgroup.co.uk
www.xactgroup.co.uk

X A C T

The Sun never sets on a...

...Business that keeps Trading

Don't let tight marketing budgets restrict your business growth.

When under pressure to deliver within tight marketing budgets, it's more important than ever that you efficiently develop new business leads and generate sales.

Direct marketing offers both measurability and accountability, making it the ideal choice for growing businesses that need to show a return on investment.

> " As a start-up business, I invested £395 in Thomson Local Business Search PRO. I was very pleased with the response rate (more than 2%) and I have had about £20,000 worth of business from the mailing so far. "
>
> I.P. Messenger, Camea Ltd

> " We have been using Thomson Local data and Strata Mail for some time now, our direct marketing is now a much more cost effective solution for us and the end results have shown a fantastic return on investment. "
>
> Conosco Computer Support

Call **0845 855 9950** quoting AD-02

Talk to a direct marketing consultant at Thomson Local and find out how we can help you generate new business.

THOMSONLocal™

Deciding your limits

You shouldn't pay as much as it will be worth to you, though, to allow room for something to go less well than you expect

By this stage you should have a clear sense of what the combined business looks like, and you can consider how much you would be willing to pay to move your current business from where it is now to where it could get to with this deal. As a principle, you should seek to pay a price that reflects only the stand-alone value of the business you want to buy. But sometimes people pay more than the estimated stand-alone value, and if your target is worth considerably more to you than its standalone value, you should consider paying more. You should try not to pay as much as it will be worth to you, though, to allow room for something to go less well than you expect.

The above analysis will give you what the absolute maximum that your business should pay for the business it might buy. That is not the same as what you should pay – it may very well be that you might pay considerably less than that, as we shall now see.

The underlying value of any business is a multiple of the earnings it can sensibly expect to generate in future

Common methods of valuing a business

There are several established ways to value a business: net asset value, discounted cashflow, multiple of turnover and multiple of profit.

Net asset value

The simplest valuation method is net asset value – what the value of the business's assets are after taking off all its liabilities. This makes sense in that the underlying net assets are at the core of what you are buying in financial terms. You need to make a qualitative assessment of the assets – audited accounts are supposed to value assets at the lower of cost and 'net realisable value' (NRV) but what does that mean:

WHEN TO CALCULATE THE NET ASSET VALUE

Net asset value will underpin any valuation – it's rare to pay less than the underlying value – and may well be a key driver to valuing an unprofitable acquisition target, but, if the deal concerns a profitable business, then other methods are usually more appropriate.

- What is the real value of fixed assets?
- Could you sell them for the balance sheet value?
- Will a bank lend against them at these figures?

In practice, it's not quite what you might hope – NRV purports to represent a 'going concern value', rather than a 'forced sale' value, with the consequence that fixed assets (other than freehold property) are usually stated at a higher value in the target's accounts than you could readily sell them for (or borrow to buy them).

Then there are the other assets to contend with – what is the age profile of debtors and will you really be able to collect them all? Are all stock items in the current catalogue and how long has the stuff been 'Available for sale'? A cautionary example of this is a £3m deal where it transpired that while the ongoing production was sold within about three months of manufacture there was an underlying £1.5m of stock that had hardly moved over the previous five to six years. Even so, the owner claimed it was 'still good and will sell eventually'. This was his honest opinion – but it won't surprise you that the acquirers took a rather more jaundiced view.

Discounted cashflow analysis

Theoretically the most accurate way to value any project, including acquisitions, is a discounted cashflow (DCF) analysis. A DCF analysis calculates the 'present value' of a series of future cashflows, with the present value (PV) being the maximum price an acquirer should

COVERING ALL BASES

It is best to do the DCF analysis twice, with and without the benefits of synergy, therefore establishing a range of values reflecting both the stand-alone value (i.e. excluding synergy) of the target and its value to you.

Table 3.4.1 provides an illustration, assuming the target business generates cash in Year 1 of £1m, increasing by 5% each year for the first 3 years and then remaining flat, with synergy benefits in Year 1 of £400,000. Discount rates of 15%–20% are considered appropriate.

Table 3.4.1 Example of a discounted cash flow					
	Year 1	Year 2	Year 3	Year 4+	Total
	All values in £ × 1000				
No synergy					
Cashflow	1,000	1,050	1,103	1,103	
Discounted (15%)	870	794	725	7,350	9,738
Discounted (20%)	833	729	638	5,513	7,713
Synergy					
Cashflow	1,400	1,470	1,544	1,544	
Discounted (15%)	1,217	1,112	1,015	10,290	13,634
Discounted (20%)	1,167	1,021	893	7,718	10,798

What this table indicates is that a range of £9.7–£13.6m is appropriate to pay for this particular target using a discount rate of 15%, dropping to £7.7–£10.8m if the required rate of return increases to 20% – the significant variation confirms the sensitivity of the calculation to the chosen discount rate. The discounted Year 4 figures reflect the (stable) cashflows for Year 4 onwards into perpetuity. The ranges are quite broad given the importance to the overall cashflow of the projected synergies.

The above is a simplistic illustration but it shows that the DCF technique, although very powerful, can be extremely complex give the number of variables it incorporates. As such, it is most often used in sizeable transactions where large sums are involved and accuracy is required. It tends not to be used as often in smaller business deals, but its principles are well worth remembering.

be prepared to pay. The notion of present value revolves around the notion that for most people have that having £1 in your hands today is worth a little bit more than the promise of £1 in a year's time – the value of the promise being less due to inflation than the risk that something might happen to prevent you getting all the £1 in a year's time. DCF is a bit like applying an interest rate in reverse – taking it off money you expect to receive in the future, rather than adding it to money you put in a bank today.

When carrrying out a DCF, the 'interest rate' is called a discount rate (DR). This should reflect your cost of capital. There are plenty of books defining cost of capital, but in simple terms it needs to reflect what the money you use for the acquisition actually costs you (whether in loan interest or in dilution if you raise share capital to fund the deal) and the opportunity cost – what else you could do with that money. The rate should also take into account the risk of the business you want to buy – some businesses are riskier than others, and to take that into account the discount rate should be higher for such businesses.

To work out the present value of an acquisition you need to estimate how much money you expect the business will pay out in future. You should take into account not just profitability but also changes in the working capital needs, necessary capital expenditure, tax payments, loan repayments, etc.

Multiple of profits

Valuing companies based on a 'multiple of profits' is a quick and simple route to an approximation of DCF – profits are (sometimes) an approximation to cashflow and using a multiplier is an alternative to a complex calculation to derive a discount rate. Although it's more user-friendly, this method is not uncomplicated in itself and needs care in its application.

Probably the most recognisable multiple is the P/E (price/earnings) ratio, which appears daily in the media against the names of Stock Exchange listed companies. This figure is the result of dividing their market capitalisation (a known figure for listed companies – their number of shares multiplied by the price per share) by their most recent post-tax profits. 'P/Es' are often quoted in negotiating meetings for private companies and they are a useful aide to valuation. Even so, they vary so much – according to the size and quality of the company concerned, its sector, whether it has recently reported results (so the market appreciation is up to date) and, of course, its prospects – so it also has to be 'handled with care'.

As an indicator, private company P/Es are often considered to be 25%–40% lower than their quoted peers – simply to reflect the lack of marketability of a private company's shares (rather than any qualitative aspects). Have a look at the *Financial Times* or use one of the online services and you will see the variety of P/Es for different sectors and company sizes.

EBITDA

Many people use slight variations when valuing private businesses, including multiples of 'sustainable' EBITDA (earnings before interest, tax, depreciation and amortisation), EBITA and EBT. As a general rule, EBITDA is favoured for three reasons:

- Excluding interest allows the financing structure of the target business to be addressed separately. So, the net cash or debt (excluding the normal working capital requirement) within the target is dealt with as a separate part of the valuation process. For example, assuming a multiple of 5, a target with EBITDA of £500,000 will be valued at £2.5m plus its net cash, so if it has £250,000 in cash its value would be £2.75m whereas if it has an overdraft of £300,000 it would only be worth £2.2m.
- Depreciation and amortisation are non-cash items that relate to past capital expenditure (Capex) and acquirers can easily adjust the valuation for any capital spending they plan in the future.
- There are a myriad of different tax rates, particularly across geographical jurisdictions, so excluding tax is deemed to remove potential anomalies.

Sustainable earnings

We have again mentioned the term 'sustainable' when referring to the target's earnings. This is crucial; the underlying value of any business is a multiple of the earnings it can sensibly expect to generate in future. Yet in any one year many one-off or unsustainable factors can affect earnings. For example, has a business had a particularly good or bad year? Is there something happening in the industry that will improve or hinder the company's prospects? What earnings can you realistically expect from the target in the future? In addition to gaining a good understanding of these issues, as well as recognising excessive reliance on particular customers or suppliers, a way of lessening the impact on valuation of recent figures is to use a weighted average of earnings over the past few years. An example is shown in Table 3.4.2.

Table 3.4.2 Example of weighted earnings multiple			
	Earnings	**Weight**	**Weighted**
2007	500	3	1,500
2006	425	2	850
2005	400	1	400
		6	2,750
Weighted average earnings			458

What this table demonstrates is that the 'base' level of earnings for valuation purposes is reduced by nearly 9% (500 down to 458) when adjusting for the latest year having seen significant growth. It may be, of course, that this recent level is, in practice, sustainable – as the potential buyer you will need to make assumptions about this and many other factors, and these can have a significant effect on the price you are willing to pay.

The 'multiple'-choice question

Once you are comfortable that you have a good handle on your target's sustainable earnings, inevitably the $64,000 question is 'what multiple to use'? Perhaps equally inevitably, there is no simple answer. Multiples often reflect the size of the target (the bigger the

WHICH METHOD?

- A possible method of deciding on a multiple which offers a direct comparison to other yield-generating investments, say, share dividends or bank deposits, is to consider return on investment (ROI). A 5 times multiple, for example, implies the need for a 20% return (pre-tax).
- Computing the payback period of the acquisition is another way of looking at multiples. Before considering the effect of tax, a three-year payback period would require a 3 times multiple – tax will lengthen the period, of course. If you choose to focus on payback, do remember to consider the cashflow, and not just earnings, implications.
- One scenario where you might pay a higher multiple than usual is where there is a genuine 'strategic need' to acquire the target business. It may be that, for example, your target has technology that you need or perhaps there would be serious consequences to your business if another party acquired the target.

deal, the higher the multiple), expected growth prospects and quality of earnings (how risky or reliable they are). A business expected to shrink or not grow is worth less than one that is expected to grow fast, and the multiple should reflect that. And the riskier the business, the lower the multiple which is usually used.

The multiple you use should also take into account your own required rate of return taking into account the perceived risk. A pretty reliable rule of thumb is that private company multiples tend to be in the range 3–8. This is a pretty wide range, and working out where any one company belongs within the range depends on its sector and circumstances – which is why there are professional mergers and acquisition advisers to guide you through the maze!

Just remember, the higher the multiple, the lower the return and longer you have to wait for payback.

Goodwill

Two businesses with precisely the same earnings and risk profile but with different levels of net assets should, intuitively, justify different valuations. The explanation is that one of them must have 'excess' assets (namely assets surplus to those required within the business) – perhaps fixed assets or stocks – and as a possible acquirer you need to evaluate what the difference is made up of and adjust the valuation accordingly. If it is simply retained earnings in the form of cash, then it's hard to argue against the vendor keeping that in addition to the underlying target valuation. The difference between the valuation you pay and the net assets you acquire is known as goodwill, which is particularly relevant to the purchase of a business, rather than a company's shares – see more on this below.

What can effect the price?
Competition

It is often said that there are three values for any business:

- What the Seller wants for it
- What the Buyer values it at
- What the Buyer has to pay for it.

What the seller wants to get is generally irrelevant to potential buyers. You should be prepared to pay up to what the target is worth to you. Often, the asking price will be on the optimistic side. It's only on the rare occasion you might value the target at more than the vendor wants – perhaps due to the opportunity for synergy.

At the end of the day, all the technical valuation work in the world is irrelevant if someone else is prepared to offer a more attractive deal to the vendor than you. The underlying circumstances of the sale will potentially have a significant effect on the eventual deal and certainly have an impact on how much you should offer to pay. It's worthwhile considering what the circumstances might be.

- *'Auction' sale* – this is where a vendor conducts a structured process – usually involving professional advisers – to invite potential bidders to put forward offers based on a reasonably detailed

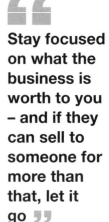

Stay focused on what the business is worth to you – and if they can sell to someone for more than that, let it go

package of information. There may be several rounds of bidding and, usually after the first round, the opportunity to meet with the seller and management team, typically in the forum of them making a presentation and a subsequent question and answer session. This process is designed to force potential buyers to offer the highest possible price to stay in the process as they are unaware of who the competitors are and what other bids they may have made. The process is typically used for larger transactions – it is expensive – but, if you are involved in an auction, then be prepared to offer/pay at the upper end of your valuation.

- *Informal sale* – this is most common for private companies. Many of the stages and processes are similar to those in an auction, but the process is less rigid and there should be more opportunity for contact with the vendor. Information specific to each interested party (for computing synergies) should be made available and a sale will typically not be concluded without each interested party having a further opportunity to increase their bid. So you could take a more aggressive view on a lower offer, leaving something in reserve from your valuation.

- *Unsolicited approach to the business owner* or a vendor responding to an advertisement by you seeking acquisition opportunities, for example, are obvious ways in which you can narrow the field of competition and, therefore, enhance the opportunity to pay less for your target. If there is genuine interest in a sale, it is difficult for the vendor to put discussions with you 'on hold' while seeking to generate competitive interest, so these situations will tend to reduce how much you have to pay.

- *Forced sale* – it may be that the vendor has to sell, such as where the target business is having financial difficulties or even is already in administration. In such cases, *timing* often becomes an important factor and your ability to move quickly might offer a significant reduction in what you need to pay. For example, if a business is losing £10,000 a week, then an offer of, say, £5,000 below its (realisable) NAV would seem attractive if the deal can be completed in a week. Indeed, if no one else could complete a deal for, say, two weeks, then £15,000 below NAV will still be attractive to the vendor. You need to be aware of any advantage you have in such situations – it can be extremely valuable.

- *Prices paid for comparative deals* – these are also relevant, though they don't affect how much the business will be intrinsically worth to you. There are several databases with details of lots of private company sales, and the terms of a transaction involving a similar business to your target will provide a good indicator of what you might have to pay. One problem is that these databases are expensive and usually available through a professional M&A adviser. Perhaps more importantly, deal terms are often not entirely clear and it can be difficult to find a precise match. Nevertheless, these types of data are valuable when considering who the potential competitive buyers are likely to be and what a 'market-tested' valuation of your target is likely to be in practice

- *Established sector-specific valuation metrics* – in several sectors, turnover-related multiples are used and these have tended to become the 'standard' valuation methodology, regardless of return- or asset-based techniques. A couple of examples are the manned guarding sector, where a typical valuation of goodwill was based on 40p–50p in the £ of contracted turnover and the photocopier sales and service marketplace, where typical valuations are based on one to two times contracted service revenue. They are both sectors where a buyer is expected to absorb the target business into its own and, therefore, reflect synergistic benefits. From your point of view, it's crucial to stay focused on what the business is worth to you – and if they can sell to someone for more than that, let it go. Don't be tempted into paying more!

The vendor's agenda

The vendor is the single most important party in (virtually) every sale process because, whether an individual or another company, it will make the key decision to accept a buyer's offer and complete a transaction... or not. Any buyer who can develop an 'edge' over other would-be purchasers will have found another way of potentially reducing the need to pay the top price.

The headline price isn't always the determining factor in a vendor choosing whom to sell to. The key is to identify a vendor's true priorities and address them in your offer. Factors which often play a significant part in the decision include: whether or not the vendor wants an ongoing role; how key staff will be treated; and whether you represent 'a good home' for the business in the vendor's eyes.

What, if any, role does the vendor want in the business post-deal? If retirement is being contemplated, then there is less likely to be any 'personal' side to the decision but if, for example, an CEO is seeking to remain with the target in some capacity, then his or her assessment of, and empathy with, you will likely play a significant part in their decision. There have been plenty of deals where a vendor simply doesn't get on with a potential purchaser and, as a result, another bidder wins almost by default. In practice, this may lead to a vendor telling a buyer that he or she is 'preferred' and giving them the opportunity to match any higher offer which comes in.

The vendor's relationship with their employees and how they identify with the business are other factors to consider. The business may be family owned and long established and well regarded in its sector. Perhaps the team has been together for a long time. In such cases, it's possible that the vendor simply won't have any interest in a buyer who plans to shut down the business and change its name, absorb it into their own operations and make the long-standing workforce redundant. Indeed, this is probably one of the most common influences on whom a vendor selects to sell to.

"

The bigger the target is relative to your current business, the greater the risk "

Risk analysis

Once you have done the number-crunching and are serious about putting in an offer to pursue a potentially life-changing acquisition, it's time to pause – what can go wrong and how might the risks be mitigated? It's difficult to quantify the degree of risk in making an acquisition, but it's generally higher than buyers perceive. There are some obvious reasons for this:

- However many analyses of the target you have done, you won't know everything
- However nice the selling management team members have seemed, you can't know them properly until you have worked with them for a while
- However well you think you understand the marketplace, something may be around the corner you couldn't possibly have foreseen
- However dispassionately you feel you have analysed the business, what is the risk that you have missed something because of your desire for the deal?

  Try to assess the principle areas of risk:

- Is the business dependent on a particular customer or supplier?
- People issues are often underrated – what is the dependence of the target on an individual, or more likely a small group?
- How will they feel about the deal and how will they want to behave afterwards, especially if they receive significant sums from the sale or are close to retirement?
- How significant is the deal to your current business? The bigger the target is relative to your current business, the greater the risk.

Structuring an acquisition

Having identified the risks involved, they must be factored into your valuation. One way of doing this is to increase the rate of return you require from the deal, which you can do by reducing the multiple of sales or profit that you offer; this can clearly have a material effect on the valuation. Otherwise you can *sensitise* the projected earnings – effectively assume that 'something goes wrong' – and see how it affects the valuation. The downside of these adjustments, of course, is that the vendor will be unimpressed with your negativity, you are reducing the price you are prepared to pay and therefore reducing the likelihood of winning the deal, on the basis of 'what ifs' – when nothing has actually gone wrong.

Earn-out structuring

A recognised way of overcoming (at least some of) these risks is to make some proportion of the amount you pay dependent on future performance of the business. If the business does indeed do as well as the seller wants you to believe it will, then you can pay the higher sum; if it doesn't, then you pay less and the deal still makes sense. Examples range from the highly complex – such as a deal where the eventual consideration was linked to profits over the 10 years' post-completion with annual payments and various earnings thresholds – to a simple 'you'll receive an additional £x after 3 years if customer Y has continued to spend at least £250,000 a year with us in the meantime'.

The use of earn-out structures like this is a complex topic all on its own. The performance-related proportion of the overall consideration can be a highly emotive subject and you need to find a structure which provides 'reasonable' risk mitigation without making your offer totally unattractive to the vendor. It is much harder to achieve deals like this when you plan to absorb the target business into your own, and it is most appropriate when the seller is remaining in charge of the target business after the deal and/or is comfortable that you will not be able to (negatively) influence the performance benchmarks being met. Offering bank guarantees for any guaranteed element of future payments can make it much easier to persuade a seller to accept this sort of structure.

Offering shares/sharing equity

Offering shares in your current business as part of the payment for the acquisition, or leaving the vendor with a proportion of the equity in the target, are two other ways of reducing risk. These both reduce the cash you need to do the deal initially and certainly tests the seller's belief in the post-deal environment, although it is less commonly used in the private company marketplace where CEOs are less keen to dilute their own equity position. This approach is also more limited in application when vendors are seeking an immediate exit, for example in a retirement situation.

Tax on acquisitions can be complex, and can affect sellers and buyers very differently. Tax advice is essential in any acquisition.

Clearly, accurately assessing the 'negotiating margin' is one of the key skills in trying to make a successful acquisition, and the next chapter looks at this point in more detail.

! TOP TIPS

! Conduct and document a detailed review of any business you are considering buying. Make sure you understand the drivers of its earnings, market position, customer/supplier/employee relationships and how it would fit with your operations. Consider the synergies which the acquisition might have for your business.

! Review the target's assets and liabilities, in order to determine what they're really worth – rather than simply accept balance sheet value.

! Consider negative synergies – contingent liabilities that might crop up when a deal is done or the acquired business is integrated.

! Decide what rate of return you're seeking from the deal and how you want to measure it. This must take into account the quality of target's earnings and the cost of capital.

! Adjust your valuation according to the nature of the sale process, the number and nature of competitive bidders and how strong your relationship is with the vendor.

! Adjust your valuation for risk – sensitise the projections or increase the required return and also consider the opportunity for using deferred consideration or a purchase of assets rather than shares.

! Take advice from professionals with experience of acquisitions of this size, and also, ideally, who understand the business sector. Financially, a lot can be riding on the outcome, so there should be significant value added from involving a specialist merger and acquisitions adviser in the valuation – and other – stages of the process.

DOING THE DEAL

THIS CHAPTER WILL DISCUSS:

- Preparation and tradables
- Starting the negotiation
- The formal meeting
- Talking numbers
- Structuring the deal
- Managing due diligence
- Closing the deal

By now you would have done your research, identified your acquisition target and made the approach. If the response is positive, it's time to sit around a table to negotiate the best deal. This is arguably the most exciting part of the acquisition process, as this is when reality bites and you are on the verge of buying up a company and its employees and taking your business to the next level. And if you have not been here before, it is probably the most significant step you will have ever made.

Some deals go through remarkably quickly, but in others the negotiations and due diligence fact-checking processes stretch over months of intense work. And even if there is broad agreement on price before formal talks begin, although it can help, it's no guarantee of a successful conclusion. A great many deals come unstuck over details – some seemingly minor – at the negotiation stage, while others stumble when due diligence reveals some hitherto unsuspected problem. This is all part of the acquisition process, and if a deal fails on these grounds it does so for good reason, so you should view it less as a failure and more as successfully determining that this was not the right company for you to buy at this time – and move on. Whatever the eventual outcome, you still need to give the deal-making your best shot by rolling up your sleeves and getting the negotiation ball rolling.

So how can you maximise your chances of success?

ACROSS THE TABLE

At this point, remember to bear mind the person or people you are buying the company from. They will be handing over their baby to you, and either recasting their working life as an executive within a larger group or planning a move to pastures new. An appreciation of what they are going through will help here, as although there is little room for sentiment in business, an empathetic approach will help the deal-making process run more smoothly. Try to win over the seller and develop a good and amenable relationship. After all, there is a lot at stake for both of you, as each will be attempting to secure the best possible deal, while at the same time agreeing a formula that will stick until the contracts are signed.

The question now is how can you maximise your chances of success?

Preparation and tradables

Once your target has expressed some interest in selling, request them to send you as much information about their business as you think you need. This should include detailed sales and profit analyses for the past few years, forecasts for the current and next year, details of any staff involved, any property or other significant commitments, and possibly details of research and development or new product development. There is always an element of give and take here – your target will not want to give you too much information too early, because in case you withdraw, they don't want you to know all their secrets. So this process tends to go through several stages. And many targets won't have all the information you need straight away as it will take them time to pull it together.

You should develop a list of all the information you think you need before you ask for it; then as you and your team review the early information you are sent, you are likely to have a series of additional information requests which come out of the information you review. At some stage you need to decide whether you want to buy the business or not, and if you do, move on to the negotiation stage.

Starting the negotiation

> **Money won't be the only thing on the table**

There's no right or wrong way to start negotiations. Some experienced CEOs recommend an informal start – over coffee, a meal or a round of golf. This is a chance to talk about issues such as price, the future of the to-be-acquired or -merged company and the aspirations of buyer and seller in a relaxed and neutral environment. You could argue that this is part of the approach rather than the negotiation proper, but at the very least it will give you a good idea of what the seller is looking for and whether it's worth progressing further.

Objective of negotiation

The purpose of a negotiation is to reach an agreement. By this point you should have a strong idea of how much you are prepared to pay, and the seller will also have a figure in mind. If you are lucky, there won't be too much of a gap between the two. If there is – but both parties are still keen to do a deal – the task is to find a mutually acceptable formula. The thing to remember is that money – while hugely important – won't be the only thing on the table. Agreeing on a figure is vitally important, but there are other things to consider, not least the co-called 'tradables'.

The tradables

Tradables are the bargaining chips that often enable two parties to work towards a deal, even if they don't initially agree on a headline amount. From the seller's point of view, the tradables could include the time that he or she will be required to stay on at the business once it has changed hands, an agreement about an ongoing role within the company or a deal to preserve the autonomy of the operation within a larger group. For instance, if you are making an acquisition, a pledge on keeping key managers in their posts or offering the vendor an attractive consultancy may prove to be effective sweeteners. The tradables will be different in every deal, but the key for all parties is to remember that they have more to deal with than might be initially apparent.

So besides thinking about what the tradables might be, use any preliminary informal meeting with the seller to glean an idea of what he or she considers important. In terms of your own approach to negotiations, it's useful to think about what you 'must' get out of the deal, what it would be nice to have and the elements that are totally negotiable and potentially useful as bargaining chips.

The formal meeting

Informal meetings help with the groundwork but sooner or later you will be sitting in a meeting room, possibly flanked by lawyers and accountants, attempting to fine tune the details of a deal – possible the most important part of the acquisition process as stated above. Although integration of both companies once the deal has been struck is key to a successful acquisition, formally negotiating terms decides how much you will be spending and if no agreement can be reached then the process stops there.

The importance of this stage can make it a daunting prospect, but you shouldn't to be overawed by the situation. Key to this is detailed preparation beforehand, so that you feel as confident as possible about your offer. Remember that, even if you are the owner of a relatively small organisation dealing with a bigger one, as the would-be buyer, you are likely to be coming into the negotiations from a position of strength, if only because it is your cash on the table. So take time out to take a deep breath and collect your thoughts before you are joined by the other party.

Ewan McLeod, an entrepreneur who has been in a number of negotiations, even advises against sitting down in the foyer ahead of a meeting. 'What happens is that you settle into those big comfortable seats and when the other team arrives to take you upstairs, you're struggling to get to your feet. It instantly puts you on the back foot,' he says.

Location can be important, too. If possible, you should arrange to hold the meeting on either your home turf or neutral ground. That way you will feel more comfortable and in control of the situation.

Finally, you need to honestly consider whether you are the best person to lead the formal negotiations. To many of you, negotiation will be the meat and potatoes of the entrepreneurial life and you will want to play a hands-on role. However, if you feel you lack the confidence or experience to handle a multi-million pound deal, your advisers will be able to do it for you. Whether these are lawyers or accountants specialising in corporate finance, they will have taken the lead role

INFORMAL TALKS

Company: Last.fm
Former executive chairman: Stefan Glaezner

When the founders of web 2.0 music site Last.fm were asked by global music giant CBS to consider the sale of their business, the first priority was to build trust between the parties. The Last.fm team had been considering either a trade sale or private equity investment to raise cash to develop the business further and, on the face of it, the CBS offer was manna from heaven.

'When they approached us, they told us they wanted Last.fm as a kind of outsourced new media think tank,' says Stefan Glaezner, serial entrepreneur and at that time executive chairman of Last.fm. 'We knew the power that CBS had and we wanted to ensure that once the sale had gone through, Last.fm's founders would be allowed to continue to run the business in the way they wanted to.'

Perhaps surprisingly, the $280m price tag was agreed relatively quickly, but the Last.fm team was determined to establish whether the deal would really provide the company with the autonomy within the group that had been promised. The crucial factor was a series of both formal and informal meetings, during which time the details of the deal were sketched out and trust established. The agreement went through with the management team in place.

in a great many acquisitions and handing over the reins to a skilled negotiator may improve your chances of securing a successful deal.

Talking numbers

Although, as pointed out earlier, there is more to discuss than the price you will pay for the company, talking numbers is the crux of the matter. A lot is at stake here, but thrashing out a deal can be both exciting and enjoyable, if approached in the right spirit alongside advisers you have complete confidence in; and you will certainly benefit from the experience.

One of the biggest questions is when to show your hand

Ultimately it resembles a game of poker. One of the biggest questions is when to show your hand – or put an offer on the table. Do you move first and risk either going in too high and having an over-generous offer instantly accepted or tabling a low figure that threatens to break the deal at the outset?

- Some believe it's the negotiator who pitches in first with a figure that most closely matches his or her aspiration who secures the deal. The logic is that by knowing what you want and being forcefully clear about it, you direct all subsequent discussion towards that figure
- Others feel more comfortable letting the other party fire first, and once an offer is on the table you explore and critique it, armed with the fact that your opposite number has already shown their hand.

The truth is that either technique can be effective, depending on the personalities involved. The key thing is that whenever you table a figure (or make a counter-proposal), it is important to state clearly what you want, while you should avoid striking an agreement that you may come to regret For example, consider you are anxious to do a deal and your opposite number tables a proposition that seems close enough to what you want to make an agreement possible. It's late, everyone is getting tired, so you agree in principle. That night, however, you begin to argue with yourself. The proposal was close, but not close enough. Perhaps you should have pushed a bit harder to get exactly what you wanted. And by that stage, you have a king-size dilemma. Do you bite the bullet and press ahead with the deal on the basis of that broad agreement or do you go in the next day and re-open that particular aspect of the talks?

Many deals fall apart because deep down either one or other of the parties is unhappy with what they have agreed or they have a change of mind. So make it crystal clear what you want and don't agree to anything in the heat of the moment, unless you are sure it's right, even if it seems close to your demands.

It's important to come up with a formula that all parties can get behind

Structuring the deal

Once you have agreed on a figure, it's time to discuss the nature of how the payment will structured, because it's not always necessary to pay the full amount of the agreed sum up front. Certainly if you are buying another fast-growth business, where part of its value to you is its future potential rather than current sales, there should be an 'earn-out' element to the deal. For instance, you might agree to pay 60% of the agreed value of the target company on completion, with the rest payable once certain financial targets have been met within a certain period of time. The advantages of this approach to the buyer are that not only do you pay less up front, but you are also protected from underperformance by the simple fact that you won't part with the full value unless the payment of that sum is justified by sales. What's more, if the original owner is staying on for a period time, he or she has a clear incentive to deliver results.

However, earn-outs are less popular with sellers as there is no guarantee that they will ultimately receive what they consider to be full value. So it's important to ensure that the seller can live with the initial payment and that it is in line with their plans for the immediate future. If not, they may simply walk away. Before agreeing to the earn-out, the seller will need to be assured that any targets are achievable and both parties must agree on a formula to measure performance. And

PEOPLE ISSUES

When the assets of a business are sold – as opposed to the share capital – employees are covered by the TUPE (Transfer of Employment (Protection of Employment) regulations. Essentially, TUPE ensures that the new owner of the business takes on the obligations to staff who had been in place under the previous regime. Put simply, under TUPE the employee's terms and conditions cannot be changed. This can be something of a handicap if you want to completely re-engineer the way a recently acquired company works and the regulations also bring to light issues that should be addressed in the due diligence process.

For instance, the TUPE regulations state that once a sale is in train staff should be consulted. In practice, this hardly ever happens and in theory aggrieved employees can take legal action against the employer. So you should check whether the seller has managed the risk effectively. Or to be more, precise has action been taken to minimise the chances of a case being brought by staff who are unhappy with the sale. Keeping staff onside after the transaction will also minimise this risk.

When share capital is sold, employee rights are also protected because although ownership of the company has changed, the corporate entity is the same. That's not to say that jobs are protected – simply that employees enjoy the same statutory entitlements.

this can present quite a challenge. Unless the soon to be acquired firm is to be ring-fenced within a larger group, integration with another company will certainly affect performance in ways over which the seller has no control.

The seller may also express concern about the timetable. If sales or profits take a dive in the first six months or year after completion, before heading skywards, the former owners could lose their chances of a full payment, despite longer-term success. The upshot is that although earn-outs are good news for buyers, it's important to come up with a formula that all parties can get behind.

Managing due diligence

Once a broad agreement has been reached on price and tradables, it's time to begin the due diligence process as you and your advisers establish whether the company that you have agreed to buy (as described to you by the owner), matches the business in reality. This should involve a comprehensive process of assessment that typically lasts about three to four weeks, although there is no set timetable.

When you consider the sheer amount of information to be checked over, it's no surprise how long due diligence can take – and where do you get all this information from? Well, if a business has been preparing itself for sale, its advisers (along with the finance director) will have put together a due diligence pack. This should contain all or most of the relevant information. Anything that isn't there you can ask for, although it would be reasonable for the seller to insist on a non-disclosure agreement while all this is going on. And, of course, information is also available from Companies House and credit reference agencies.

During the due diligence period, you will be given access to the books of the target company. However, the process is about much more than the historical and current trading figures. For instance, you will need to look at employment and staffing issues. Who are the key staff? Are their contracts properly drawn up? Is there any ongoing litigation under employment or equal opportunities laws?

Then there is intellectual property to consider. Does the company actually own what it says it does? For instance, if its business is reliant on a database of customers or targets, is that record owned by the company or simply rented from a third party that could easily sell the details to rivals? Alternatively, if the company has developed a technology or software platform that is vital to its success, does it own the rights exclusively or do others – perhaps former employees who developed it – have a call on it? Again, is there any litigation in the pipeline?

You also need to look closely at the operational health of the company. The books may appear healthy, but are the customers happy? Are there any major supply contracts that are about to come to an end and, therefore, liable to be lost or renegotiated? And, yet again, as this point cannot be emphasised too much, is there any risk of litigation?

The due diligence process should also embrace the company's relations with bodies such as HMRC. Is there any dispute over payments that is likely to come to the boil minutes after the ink has dried on the acquisition contract?

On the customer side, you or your advisers should look at major contracts. If you can, talk to the seller to establish whether or not there are any outstanding issues.

So what happens if the due diligence process reveals gaps in documentation, which in turn raise questions about, say, the ownership of intellectual property? Equally what do you do if it emerges that a major client is about to terminate a contract? Due diligence often uncovers skeletons that are either deal breakers or cause for some serious re-negotiation. In some cases, you can ask the seller to indemnify you against future problems. For instance, if there is no proof that the company owns a particular piece of software, you could agree a clause in the contract that would ensure you are compensated for any legal claim. However, if it emerges that the seller is been deliberately evasive over certain issues, the deal may not survive the due diligence process.

How long should all this take? There is no single answer to that question, but you should assume several weeks as a minimum unless there are exceptional circumstances. As a potential buyer you should have a timetable in mind and try to stick to it – after all, protracted wrangling can kill a deal. Equally, though, you shouldn't try to rush the process. For one thing, that might look a bit desperate and cast you in a position of weakness. And unless you take the time that you need to get the deal you want and do the due diligence properly, you could end up making a bad mistake.

However, once a deal has been struck, you should certainly agree a schedule for the subsequent completion process.

Closing the deal

Once terms have been agreed, the purchaser normally gets their lawyer to draw up a contract, which will typically be the subject of a

---

ESSENTIAL CHECKS

Company: Loch Fyne Restaurants
Managing director: Mark Derry

When restaurant chain Le Petit Blanc fell into administration, it was still enjoying high visitor levels. It was this that convinced Loch Fyne Restaurants co-founder and managing director Mark Derry that it could be turned around after an acquisition, but the due diligence was all important.

Derry focused on finding out where and why money was flying out of the business. 'We got to see the sales books and profit and loss account, which showed the labour costs were far too high,' he recalls. 'They had marketing managers for each of their four sites, there were too many chefs and the food was costing a lot to produce.'

Successful due diligence in these circumstance is dependent, to a large extent, on the goodwill of the seller, and Derry found that Le Petit Blanc's management was very open to letting his team take a forensic look at the books and the wider business. However, even if you trust the vendors, the message is always to dig as deep as you can. If you are buying assets, make sure they exist.

Derry went ahead with the acquisition and decided to integrate everything but the actual Le Petit Blanc restaurants into Loch Fyne. 'You have to fully integrate, otherwise the costs are too high and you can't keep an eye on problems,' he explains. 'We don't like surprises and get sales reports sent to our mobiles at 9am every morning. You need an open book to manage cashflow.'

Le Petit Blanc is now back in profit and has bolstered the group's overall turnover to £30m.

huge number of amendments once the lawyers of both sides get to work. Typically, the lawyer will also draw up a disclosure letter, which will require the owner of the target company to reveal any additional information that could affect the value of the purchase.

In the last hours before the deal is closed, or in some cases the last few days, the parties involved will meet to go through these documents. These can be intense meetings, involving not only the executives and legal teams of the buyers and sellers, but any banks or investors with a direct interest in the deal. It's a formal process and with larger deals there could be up to 50 documents to sign. Even at this late stage, problems can arise that will either delay or prevent the transaction from going through. Thorough due diligence, however, should reduce the risk of late shocks.

The final meeting will usually kick off with a list of issues that need to be resolved and warranties or indemnities to cover the buyer's risks are often high on the agenda. Even at this late stage, issues such as the valuation of net assets – say old stock held in a company's warehouse – can be a sticking point. There can even be last-minute attempts to re-negotiate terms and no one really knows whether the deal will go through until the final signatures are drying on the paper. The only consolation is that as the legal teams do their work – often in break out huddles dispersed around the room – the chances of success increase as the meeting goes on.

If things go according to plan, when you emerge into the fresh air, you will be the proud owner of a company that will significantly enhance your ability to grow.

Once the deal is done, no doubt you will feel like celebrating. Buying a business can be a stressful affair so certainly take the time to enjoy a glass of champagne and congratulate your team for all their hard work. However, signing the deal is not the end but rather, to paraphrase a great man, the end of the beginning. The next chapter discusses the next major step in the process – how to merge the two businesses smoothly and effectively.

! TOP TIPS

SMOOTHER NEGOTIATIONS

! Do your preparation – Research the other party carefully, ahead of the meeting. Why is he or she prepared to sell? What motivates your opposite number? How can you use this information to move the negotiations forward?

! Decide what you want out of the deal – The seller will have a number in mind. But what are you looking for in terms of price and structure?

! Think about tradables – What bargaining chips do you have at your disposal to sweeten the deal? For instance, would it help if you offered to guarantee the jobs of key staff for certain period or allowed the seller to retain some shares and stay on in an executive role?

! Feel confident – Take some time to focus ahead of the meeting. Don't allow yourself to be fazed by an imposing meeting room or the other party's array of high-powered advisers. If you don't feel confident, let your advisers lead the negotiations.

! Be prepared to walk away – If the terms demanded by the seller are unacceptable, and it's clear they won't negotiate, don't be afraid to walk away.

CHECK WHAT YOU ARE GETTING FOR YOUR MONEY

! Carry out thorough due diligence – If you rush the process, you might find that you have bought more (or less) than you have bargained for.

! Examine every aspect of the company that has an impact on value – In addition to the financials, ask for the documentation that will provide you with information on employment issues, intellectual property ownership, customer relations and outstanding litigation.

! Have a timetable in mind – Don't rush due diligence, but set a provisional time limit for the process, and if it looks as if talks are getting bogged down, reassess your commitment to the deal.

! Structure the deal appropriately – You needn't pay all the money up front. An earn-out arrangement is common.

AFTER THE DEAL:

WORKING TOWARDS SUCCESSFUL INTEGRATION

THIS CHAPTER WILL DISCUSS:

- Planning the integration
- Communicating with people
- Assigning responsibility
- The timetable for action

A key factor in the success of your acquisition is how well you integrate the new company into your existing operation. This will be a challenging period for you personally and will test your entrepreneurial talents to the full. However, it's also going to be an exciting time and if you get it right you will be ready to grow your business in a way that many other CEOs don't.

Business folklore suggests that there is a crucial period of 100 days in which you need to set the foundations of the integration: the early stages are the make or break period for the merging of the two businesses. Also, what you achieve with your newly acquired staff and customers in the first few weeks and months will remain fixed in their minds going forwards. Although the exact timescale for integration will depend on the company you have acquired, you need to get started quickly, and ideally you will have got the ball moving before you have actually bought the new business.

Get to know as much as possible about your new company before you buy it. Although you will have gone through a proper due diligence process, you also need an implicit understanding of how the company 'feels'. Understand its culture and the mindset of those who work for it (see Chapter 3.2 and 3.5).

Planning the integration

Integration planning should have started before the deal was signed and hopefully you have appointed key people to help you bring the businesses together. In order for your integration to work well you must ensure that your management team understands its roles as well as the overall goal of integration. Some questions you need to consider are:

- How are new clients going to be managed?
- When will new services be offered to them?
- Who is going to be managed by whom?
- What are the lines of communication to be?

Ideally you will have got the ball moving before you have actually bought the new business

> ## WALK THE TALK
>
> A common reason for acquisitions failing to deliver on their promise is that CEOs haven't come up with an effective integration plan. And sometimes even if there is a plan, acquiring companies don't necessarily stick to it. Don't fall into either one of these camps. Instead, envisage how in an ideal world the merged company will look, create a plan to make that a reality, and then stick to it – and change it if circumstances indicate something else may be better.

You know your business well so think through what your acquisition FAQs are and work with your management team to get some answers.

A time for clear leadership

In an acquisition the main thing to get right is how you handle people

Map out your existing business and the newly acquired business in detail and discuss with your team where the dots must be joined. Before you bought the business you should have had a clear idea of why you thought it was going to add value, so start your planning with that goal in mind. Things such as reporting lines and responsibilities have to be agreed in advance and need to be clearly communicated. Ensure that your existing team understand the extent of their involvement and don't try to consider the integration as a 'land grab exercise' on an individual basis. Be firm and fair, make decisions and then stick to them. If you have never done an acquisition before then you are probably beginning to realise that this is going to be a test of your leadership abilities – you are right, it is.

Communicating with people

CEOs often worry about areas such as IT or accounts when buying another company. And, while it is true that they are important, it is also the case that technical matters can be fixed when broken by what are usually fairly straightforward means. However, the things that can't be repaired as easily are relationships; in an acquisition the main thing to get right is how you handle people.

You will most likely have a big part to play in both the acquisition and the integration. As the owner of the acquiring business you will be seen as a figurehead whom people will look to for guidance and support. Be prepared to spend plenty of face-time, particularly at the start of the process, and meet as many new people as you can – clients, staff and also suppliers. People often don't react well to change and can become anxious if they feel their livelihoods are at risk in any way. A big part of your role in this process should be to make sure that you personally communicate a clear message to all of the key people involved. Typically people want to know the same thing: 'What does this mean for me?' and for staff there's always the additional question of 'Is my job safe?' Be ready to answer these questions fully and honestly and explain to all concerned what the benefits are designed to be. Make sure that your message is consistent and that everyone in your team is on the same page when discussing the future of the business. This applies to newly acquired staff just as much as it does to customers and suppliers.

Prepare in advance written formal communications and press releases in your name and send these to relevant parties such as clients, suppliers, staff and members of the press. The buzzword for you is communication and lots of it. You might well feel like a parrot constantly repeating yourself so be certain in advance that your message is strong and clear and you are really confident in it. Also be prepared, mentally and emotionally, to spend a lot of time phone bashing.

Assigning responsibility

Buying another company is a time-consuming process and you already have another business to run. It is important that you keep driving your business forwards while you work on the integration. But remember you can't do everything and will have to defer responsibilities to others to make sure you meet all of your targets.

Keep driving your business forwards while you work on the integration

If you do have a large team of managers or senior people to draw on this is easier. However, many CEOs don't and you might have to consider bringing in some additional help. There are a number of options that you might consider here:

- Bringing in an interim manager to take a role in the integration, preferably someone with experience in acquisitions who can take a clearly defined role for a set period
- Allocating the role to an existing staff member; some of them might relish the opportunity to be involved in such an important process
- Looking to the management from the incoming company to play a part – they know their own business well and it is a good opportunity for you to get genuine 'buy-in' from your new employees.

The route you take will depend on your resources and circumstances, so planning is vital and, of course, try to enjoy the journey. Giving the employees of the company you have bought a big say in how they should be integrated into your business is a brave strategy, but it is a great way to get them to buy into your culture and embrace it, while feeling valued. If managed well, this can cut down on the number of leavers and provide motivation to get the business moving quickly. They will also pass their enthusiasm for the new set-up on to their customers.

A DIFFERENT APPROACH

Entrepreneur: David Evans

David Evans is an experienced entrepreneur who has been making acquisitions since the 1980s. He takes a somewhat unusual approach, but one that works for him. He believes that the incoming staff are the best ones to create an implementation strategy, although this must be done in the framework of his business. He always makes a presentation to the whole company after he buys a business. Then he tries to get the new staff to buy in to his philosophy, and unveils nine main parameters he calls the Grass Roots Management System, which cover the whole business. Once that is done, he assembles a team of people to draw up their own plan on how they are going to fit into his business and begin the integration.

'We then monitor the plan with key performance indicators, which are the same across the group. However, the plan is only as good as the people working on it,' warns Evans.

The timetable for action

Arguably your first 100 days begin about a month before you make the deal. By now you should have a clear plan of action and have highlighted goals and ambitions that need to be met. Your team should be briefed and 'the message' communicated to everyone involved in the integration. However, you will soon have to start working alongside your new employees who most likely will not know you and may not have even been told that the business was up for sale.

> **The first 100 days are crucial**

The next chapter, the first in the last part of this book, will take a close look at the impact of growing your business on your human resources and what to watch out for while hiring people.

THE FIRST 100 DAYS

Days 1–10

- Keep the information flowing: Immediately after the acquisition has gone through, there are likely to be a lot of nervous people around and your first priority should be to let people know what is going on. Panic and rumours can spread like wildfire so stop this at the source and get some genuine information out there. Often redundancies go hand in hand with acquisitions, frequently on both sides, and the best way to allay any fears is to open the channels of communication immediately. That means meeting everyone personally to communicate your plans for the new-look business.
- Show confidence and spread reassurance: In essence you need to lead by example, so be prepared to answer questions at this meeting. Inevitably, people will want to know if their jobs are safe and whether their role will change. The chances are they will also be anxious to know how departments will be restructured and whom they will report to. The key is to assure everyone that the merger is in their interests, while being careful not to make over-optimistic statements that could backfire on you at a later date. At the same time, you should make clear that there are changes ahead.

To summarise: The first couple of weeks are primarily about communication and making sure everyone is getting on with their work. It might feel like you have two different companies although hopefully people are now becoming accustomed to the change.

Days 11–30

Don't hold back on your plans for too long, so start making changes that will help you to maximise value from the combined business. Exactly how you go about it will depend on your personal style.

- The case for early change: Some would argue that you should go in with a plan and implement change as quickly as possible, whereas others would take a more cautious and conciliatory approach. If you opt for the former, it means stamping on a few toes and unsettling a lot of people. It could also involve redundancies and a period of uncertainty for everyone involved. However, this can lead to cost savings faster and if handled well might also lead to a speedier integration. Tough decisions will have to be made, but as the proponents of rapid change would argue, by doing it early, you can do it cleanly.
- The case against early change: However, there's another argument that says wait a while to give you time to assess the strengths and weaknesses of the combined workforce and the business itself. Once you know that, you can implement changes based on greater understanding. There seem to be a lot of advantages in this second approach – after all why did you buy the business if the first thing you are looking to do is to dismantle it? And after two weeks are you really sure about what you have bought? Perhaps the big deciding factor is the feedback from the clients on what the change has meant to them. It's hugely important to ensure that what the customer sees is a change in ownership, not a decline in standards of service.

To summarise: You need to ensure everyone gets their job done effectively so customers don't have any reason for complaint (they will be watching to see… and competitors will be keen to poach on any sign of weakness). If this isn't being done successfully then you will need to start implementing changes faster.

Days 30–60
- Implementing/modifying the plan for change: By this stage, feedback from your implementation team, new staff and clients will be flowing in. This should be informing your strategy of how you are going to change the company and merge it with yours. A detailed plan of how you will manage the integration should have been prepared before you bought the company, but don't be afraid to modify this in response to what's happening on the ground. For instance, when Networks First bought ANS in June 2007, the new managers expected to be able to run a dual accounting system. However, when this proved to be impractical, the two systems were merged early on.

- IT and finance: Unless you are talking about the merger of a vast corporate with an unwieldy array of disparate computer systems and networks assembled over tens of years and multiple mergers, rationalising accounting and other IT packages shouldn't be a major problem. However, don't neglect the important task of implementing financial controls as soon as you can. You will need to clarify for new and existing staff who can spend what, which bank accounts should be used, and make sure all outstanding payments due to the acquired company are collected so the money keeps flowing.

- Handling culture change in the workplace: As mentioned above, dealing with the people can be a major challenge and requires a softer skill set. For instance, if the company you buy has a regimented nine-to-five way of working and you take a more flexible and results-focused approach, then this is a clash, which you must address. Over time staff grow accustomed to their working patterns, and build their lives around them. Indeed, some may even have taken the job in the first place because of a particular shift pattern. So be sympathetic and don't be too quick to lay down the law. Instead, you need to talk to staff and if there is a need for change, explain why. It may be that flexible working patterns are essential to survival. For instance, if competitors are offering 24/7 customer support, then it's important to make clear that failure to match that offer hands the rival a competitive edge. It may not be easy to persuade people that working late is necessary, but explaining the reasons will go a long way to helping you win the arguments.

- Re-establishing the hierarchy: To a great extent, the people issues will depend on the nature of the post-acquisition plan. If the fate of the acquired business is to become an autonomous unit within a larger group, its staff may see very little difference, especially if the remaining management team remain very much in charge. Things are a little trickier if you're planning to put your own managers in place, either to replace or enhance the original team. In these situations, there can be some confusion over who is in charge. For instance, let's say that the managing director stays on in a consultancy role for an agreed period, but they are clearly taking instruction from a group managing director, who is also on site. The question that staff will be asking themselves is who they should be approaching in the case of a problem arising. It's human nature for staff to gravitate towards their old boss, which can be frustrating for the new person in charge. Alleviate this problem, and other similar ones that may arise by clearly communicating the new management structure, while ensuring that the two individuals are not apparently playing the same role. For instance, the old managing director could spend more time working from home or at client sites, leaving the new man free to get to know staff and the way the company works.

Arguably the biggest potential challenge comes when two businesses merge physically, sharing offices and reassigning jobs within a new structure. Although people will see new opportunities and forge new friendships, you need to be prepared to cope with the disappointment and occasional hostility of those who feel they have lost responsibility or been given a less interesting job under the new regime. Keep such issues to a minimum by clearly communicating any plans to change or adapt roles, while encouraging feedback from staff and dealing with any individual queries or complaints quickly and effectively, explaining that the new regime has been brought in to benefit the business as a whole.

To summarise: The key is to be sympathetic to the feelings of your staff – both old and new, and clearly explain your position, while sticking to your decisions and assigning tasks on the basis of what is good for the company.

Days 60–100

- Planned changes underway: If you haven't yet combined your account and IT systems, now is the time to do it. You also need to take the plunge on reporting lines. This can be very positive, particularly if you have tools and methods that can benefit the acquired business.
- Networking opportunities for old and new staff: This is also a good time to ensure that there's plenty of interaction between old and new employees. Joint projects should be launched, and your new clients should be experiencing the benefits of dealing with a larger company. Damian Broughton, founder of Danbro, which provides accountancy services to contractors, has bought accounts from a number of different companies. He says: 'We contact all customers over the phone as quickly as possible after we make an acquisition, but leave it for two to three months before we start to offer additional services, as we don't want them to feel bombarded.'

To summarise: Hopefully, the majority of staff at the acquired company will stay on. It's inevitable that some will leave, but you shouldn't pander to the minority and must now boldly implement your changes. Culturally, there might still be some way to go if your company was very different to the one you bought. However, as long as you have most of the key players onside and embracing your vision and values, then the foundations of overall cultural change should be set.

THE 30/60/90-DAY PLAN

Company: Gyro International
Chief operating officer: Richard Glasson

The chief operating officer of global marketing agency Gyro International, Richard Glasson, has a 30/60/90-day plan for when his company integrates an acquisition. There is always someone who is responsible for the plan, although that is never the person who brokered the deal. The first 30 days, in his view, should be about communicating with staff and showing that they aren't an interfering employer. He literally aims to do as little as possible for the first month. After 30 days they begin to introduce some of the tools and systems to the new company, although these are always presented as a benefit not an order. After 60 days, increased interaction is encouraged through joint projects, and the specifics of the business are addressed. However, Glasson will only acquire businesses that are both successful and culturally similar to his own.

'My view is that you can't integrate a business that isn't already right for your company,' he says. 'I think the integration should be an extremely straightforward process.'

! TOP TIPS

! Plan ahead – the first 100 days are crucial but they begin before the deal is signed. Start planning as soon as possible.

! Set your message – be able to communicate why this is a good deal and what it means for the future. Ensure that everyone is on message.

! Meet everyone in the first week – be prepared to answer questions about what the change in ownership will mean for the various roles and job security.

! Ensure that you speak to staff yourself – there's nothing more unsettling to staff than hearing from a third party that the company they work for has changed hands. You are the figurehead so get involved directly.

! Be honest but positive – the deal should be a good thing and suggests promise of a better future. However, don't over-egg it or raise expectations to levels that can't be sustained.

! Assign roles – you need a team behind you and in front of you. Make sure everyone understands their role. People who aren't involved in the business shouldn't get distracted from what they are doing.

! Get help if necessary – if you don't have enough expertise to hand, consider bringing in some outside help.

! Be prepared to stand your ground – get your plan sorted and then make the changes required. There will be a few grumbles but don't let this distract you from your main task of getting value from your deal.

! Impose a timetable for change – consultants agree that the first two to four months are crucial in terms of successful integration. You will need to identify the changes that need to be made during this period and establish a timetable.

! Be prepared to change the plan if circumstances dictate.

PART FOUR

EQUIPPED FOR GROWTH

HIRING RIGHT:
STAFF, MANAGERS AND DIRECTORS

THIS CHAPTER WILL DISCUSS:

- Maintaining the drive and company values

- Reviewing your management set-up

- Delegating effectively

- Hiring senior managers

- Hiring directors

- Executive coaching

- Stepping aside: hiring a chief exeutive officer

- Staying on top

It comes as a surprise to most growing company CEOs that management phases are very similar across the majority of growing businesses:

- The start-up phase is full of energy, passion and a strong connection to customers
- As the business grows it takes on junior staff to help 'do'
- As numbers grow beyond 10 staff, a modicum of management structure is needed, so typically one or two people are promoted from within and the business continues to add more do-ers
- Next the business may hire a manager from the outside, in a specific function (marketing or finance, say) and then not a very senior manager...

The growth continues until one day the balance between customer complaints, internal staff battles, a dip in internal morale and a realisation that they still have more to do than they can get done suggests that the business has more problems than the CEOs know how to solve. Most of the highly successful companies run by now-celebrity CEOs have gone through stages very much like this. The trick is to come through structured to enable growth to continue. Those

FAMILIAR UNHEALTHY TRENDS IN GROWING BUSINESSES

- The founders do less of the direct customer interaction
- Managers who excel at one level are frequently not right for the same role in a larger-scale operation
- Early team members resent, sometimes subconsciously, the inevitable lessening of the time they get to spend with the founders
- Later hires join an established operation that is already at least somewhat successful and less needy, spend relatively little time with the founders, and feel much less passion and loyalty as a result
- Founders aren't usually trained managers and hence may not set up great management systems
- Founders have a growing amount riding on the way the business runs, given its current significance to their personal net worth, and therefore find it harder than ever to delegate responsibility which they fear might harm their baby.

that do can go on to become substantial businesses and turn their founders into very wealthy people. Those that don't typically decline; some die, others might sell but not for substantial valuations. A few choose to stay small and stay at a level their CEOs can handle.

Almost all CEOs know that they face some of the problems outlined above, but presume that the problems are unique to their business, and feel both a little ashamed, and determined to fix them – usually by trying to work even harder. It can be incredibly powerful to realise that not only are these sorts of issues not a function of your poor management, but that they are almost inevitable. And solvable.

Maintaining the drive and company values

No business can thrive beyond the point where the issues mentioned above are very evident without solving them. To do this, you need to replace your areas of expertise and zeal at lower levels, to ensure that the business can continue to serve customers as well as it did when it started, and which is what created the early success. Doing this will often take the skills of much higher calibre managers than growing companies tend to have on board to start with. But although more expensive, managers who have experienced how larger businesses succeed can apply that experience to creating systems appropriate for the growing business.

No matter how much you as founder might think that you are the only person who can do some things, the reality is, you aren't. And often you are not the best person. Once you accept that, it becomes a matter of thinking about what you should delegate at what stage, and how to find the right way to do so which will ensure that your quality standards are maintained.

> **No matter how much you as founder might think that you are the only person who can do some things, the reality is, you aren't**

EXPERT OPINION

TIPS ON THE BEST ROLE FOR A CEO

Are you the real barrier to growth in your business?

Did you know that almost two thirds of senior staff in small firms leave within two years of their appointment? This is mainly because their relationship with the CEO gets too frustrating.

Entrepreneurs, whether through a need for control, ego or pure enthusiasm, regularly become a bottleneck to progress. To grow your business beyond the constraints of your own time and energy, you need to step back from managing the day-to-day business and concentrate on the future.

First, it's important to take a hard, honest look at yourself. Most CEOs will change as their business moves from start-up to established company. I call these phases: **artisan, hero, meddler** and **strategist**.

For your business to achieve its real potential, you need to become a strategist. You need to find time to work *on* the business, as well as *in* it, looking outwards and forwards so that you can bring about the future you want for your business and for you.

Virtually all firms start as artisan businesses, set up by someone who has a particular skill, profession or trade. In the early days, artisan entrepreneurs spend most of their time producing a product or delivering a service.

Many CEOs then progress to heroes or meddlers; both are potentially limiting for a growing business. Heroes still believe that they perform most jobs in the business better than any one else. They probably still own the key customer relationships and they spend lots of time managing day-to-day operations and fire-fighting.

Eventually, heroes might start to delegate some responsibilities and create a management team. But some slip into the role of meddler. They find it hard to hand over routine management tasks and cannot resist getting involved with the team's work.

The key to becoming a strategist is to let go. The single biggest obstacle to the development of your business will be your inability to do this. You need to recognize that if you alone are the source of all power, decisions and leadership, then the business cannot grow beyond the limit of your resources. It's crucial to have a team in place to provide the launch pad for long-term growth.

To let go of power, you must trust your team. And before you transfer your powers to others, you must first have the confidence to let go emotionally.

Gerard Burke, director of the Business Growth and Development (BGP) Programme at Cranfield School of Management

Recognising staff limits

Usually implementing a solution to these issues will involve some very painful changes in personnel. Some of the people a business needs to say goodbye to will have been there from virtually the beginning, and will have worked extremely hard and helped make the business what it has become. It may feel wrong, cruel to even consider letting them go. Perhaps they continue to be significant personal stars even; yet if they stand in the way of the new systems working, they do need to go. It's far from unusual for some of these one-time heroes to tell you they support the moves, yet passively work to undermine them and prevent them succeeding.

The rest of company very often knows that these people need to move on – it's often the CEOs who are the last to see it. And although the CEOs will naturally dread the need to broach the subject with these staff who have probably become friends, the staff themselves may well know that the time has come for them to make way. They might well feel enormous relief that the battle they have probably been fighting to try to keep the business the way they liked is finally over; they can stop fighting. For instance, Steve Pankhurst, founder of the social networking site Friends Reunited, realised that his existing team needed retooling when the company began to get takeover offers from major companies.

'We quickly became aware of the true value of the company, but we were ideas people and developers who, all of a sudden, had this massive company on our hands,' he explains. 'We had a go at growing it ourselves and had taken on 10 people that were mostly friends and family, but we were struggling. We knew we were missing opportunities, such as global expansion, where we simply didn't have the experience.'

As a result of this moment of epiphany, the company appointed a chief operating officer who had previously worked for the *Financial Times* and a new marketing manager.

Reviewing your management set-up

So did the last section sound familiar? Do you know at what stage is your organisation?

Until you start to analyse the structural issues, you can't solve them

The best way to find answers is to talk with someone – preferably a person from outside the company. A member of staff may give biased answers. Try to find an independent person who understands the way organisations work and can help you assess your business. That person could be: a close friend or relative, a mentor, a coach or entrepreneurial support group, or a consultant, a non-executive director (NED) or even your accountant. You will need to look for someone you can trust, respect and feel at ease discussing these issues with.

Make finding someone a priority. If you are already experiencing some of the problems highlighted here, it will seem like you have no time to think about something as esoteric as this. But remember that until you start to analyse the structural issues, you can't solve them.

Revisiting your business's vision

A useful exercise you can do in very little time, on a train or plane or at home in the evening, is to channel your frustrations and anxiety into an analysis session. Write down everything that is bothering you about work at the moment:

- How you would ideally like to have the business run
- Which issues you would like not to have to deal with any more
- Which problems you would like to be solved
- How you would like those issues that you no longer like to deal with to be sorted out
- What structure you could imagine working which would accommodate those ideals.

From here you can work out what that structure might cost, and what size your business would need to be to sensibly afford it. That's

THE SUCCESSFUL FOUNDER VERSUS THE SUCCESSFUL CEO

The goal here is that you should end up with a business that is much less dependent on you, although that doesn't mean you have no role. Your role needs to change from being an operator, delivering to customers, to being a leader who inspires your staff with the passion they need to continue to serve your customers better than your competition. And you will need high-quality management around you sharing the burden of delivering and monitoring progress.

a first draft vision for the future. Sleep on it, and come back the next day to review those thoughts. Perhaps you will refine them a little after spending a day or two running the business again, viewing some of your key staff in a new light having had those thoughts.

Your vision document will show you which areas, and people, need changing. The next step is to work out what to do when, creating your action plan. It's wise to do things in stages, checking the plan constantly against new data as time moves on.

As stated above, it will help if you can find someone you trust and respect to discuss this document with.

Delegating effectively

When you have people you trust and respect in a role, it's easy to delegate. So the key to delegation is making sure you have the right people in the right roles. And once you have the right people, you need to let them get on with the job. But what does this mean? There are plenty of examples of where CEOs have delegated to ostensibly good people, and disaster has followed rapidly. There are a few things to do to help it work.

Clarifying the boundaries

First you need to make sure that whoever you delegate to understands where you come from, and that you still have a role to play. No good manager indeed would proceed to ignore the CEO in the belief that the latter had delegated total authority. Managers need to be aware that the business has been built up successfully on the CEO's methods, and that new hires need to buy into that ethos and those elements that have made the business successful thus far. Conversations with your new manager along the lines of 'You've delegated this to me, now get out and leave me to get on with it' are unlikely to be a good sign. The right new manager will understand your natural anxiety about delegating, and will help you by talking to you a lot about what is going on.

Second, you need to establish very clear objectives for the new manager, and parameters within which he or she can work. What would be okay, and what would be crossing the line? You need to be honest when you set these up, otherwise delegating won't work.

YES-MEN AND YES-WOMEN

Every organisation will have its share of people who want to impress their boss and believe that agreeing with them is the best way to achieve that. That is even more common in entrepreneur-led businesses since entrepreneurs are by nature strong personalities who fervently hold their opinions; it takes a brave new member of staff to suggest that the boss might not be right about something.

Having yes-people around you feels great initially – the team around you is affirming that what you are doing is right, so the world feels good. But that won't last long; unless you can get managers adding value, improving on your own ideas and adding new ones, your business will rapidly start to suffer.

To encourage this be careful not to strongly disagree with anyone who suggests an alternative to one of your ideas but rather make a point of praising the idea, whether you agree with it or not; have open, objective discussion which shows that other people's ideas get treated with respect and that you are a leader who is strong enough to be comfortable to be challenged.

Third, there needs to be a clear set of processes to monitor performance, and clear limits to authority. Ideally you should start by delegating small amounts of authority and gradually increasing this as the manager gains your trust by doing well with the early stuff you have delegated.

The power of teams

At some stage your growing business will need much more than one new manager. It will need a management team – which is more than simply a group of individual highly capable managers. Your team needs to be a group of people who behave cohesively as a team, understanding each other's roles, and each leaning on, respecting and helping the others, with you as their leader. For as long as you work with the business you will set the standards and working style of the business, whether you or your team likes it or not. So how you behave will make an enormous difference to how well the team works.

Recent years have seen the rise of the term 'joined-up thinking' which means that all involved in thinking about an issue are working well together, taking account of each other's points. All businesses, and especially growing businesses which are more susceptible to stresses and strains, need joined-up management. When an organisation first starts and is in its early successful stages this is easy and automatic. The management team will be just a handful of people who will naturally spend plenty of time together, understand and buy into the vision, and everyone will know all that is going on. As the numbers of staff grow that will change, initially without anyone noticing; typically management will already be pretty disjointed by the time the problems start to come to light.

As the leader you need to get some systems put in place to join everyone back together again. What it takes to do this will be quite different from what it took to start with; new managers with experience may well be what you need to craft the right systems for your business, otherwise you might find consultants helpful if you don't feel that you

REIGNITE THE PASSION

One main advantage of startups is the passion of the early staff. People feel almost on some sort of mission to improve the world at businesses like this, and fling themselves into their work with concentration, effort, energy and enthusiasm that is infectious and appealing, so helping win business and creating high levels of customer satisfaction. Without refuelling that fire in people's bellies, it inevitably will gradually dwindle.

As leader of the organisation one of your key roles is to reignite that passion – regularly. It's a good idea to get the whole company together twice a year or even more often if you can, to tell them what's going on, remind them of your ultimate objectives, and to let them see your continued belief and energy. You will need to let managers communicate much about day-to-day operational changes, but it's important that the business knows it still has a powerful leader driving things forward and with the same passion your staff felt when they first joined.

know quite how to do it yourself. The systems need to involve regular communication so all managers know what is going on and feel able to influence it the way they did in the early days, yet without slowing the organisation's decision-making ability down to a crawl.

Businesses in need of re-joining-up frequently implement less than a sufficient solution, perhaps for lack of knowledge, perhaps in order to try not to upset someone the CEOs feel loyalty to who wouldn't like the full system the business needs. And sometimes CEOs are simply not good at being unambiguous and crystal clear about how things need to work from here on, leaving grey areas which different managers are likely to interpret differently. The joined-up organisation is an extremely powerful thing, and an uplifting place to work for all your staff. Don't flinch from doing what is needed to make your business properly joined up.

Hiring senior managers

Some people are better than others at hiring great staff. It's a real skill, and arguably the most valuable of all for an CEO. Duncan Bannatyne

> **It's essential that the senior management you start to hire is right for your business**

and Richard Branson have grown so successful in large part because they have hired such good people and managed them well. But many growing business CEOs have not yet become great hirers. If you are experiencing some of the typical growing pains described at the start of this chapter, it may be that you haven't needed to become a great recruiter yet – perhaps you have been able to get by so far with hiring the right people.

It's essential that the senior management you start to hire is right for your business. The wrong hires can cause enormous damage, possibly even fatal. You may need to consider new methods for hiring this new senior management. That might include involving others to help with the process – perhaps NEDs or even a consultant. Venture capitalists should help substantially with this; some business angels will too.

Formulating the job description and person specification

The first step is to clearly define the role you are trying to fill, and what type of person you need to fill it. If the new position is a more senior version of an existing position, review the job description from scratch again; it's all too easy in today's time-pressured environment to presume that 'it'll be the same as before, with just one or two amendments'. But for all new hires it's worth taking the effort to go through the position thoroughly before using the new job description, to make sure you get what you really want.

You should try to hire someone who understands the business and its aims, and buys into those and who is good enough to take it on to at least the next level by evolving the business rather than revolutionising it – which almost certainly means paying more than you strictly need to for the size of business you are today. You don't want someone with too strong an agenda of their own, trying to steer the business in a different direction. The new hire should understand how your business feels – the work environment in smaller businesses is enormously different from that in than large multinationals; many people moving to smaller organisations love some aspects of their new employer but presume some support infrastructure will be there when it won't.

Finding the right people

Assuming that you aren't promoting from within for the new position(s), the best route is usually personal recommendation. Ask everyone you can think of who might know someone with the skills and experience you need. Recruitment consultants vary enormously, from the very poor who will try to squeeze anyone into a role just to earn a fee, to the excellent, who will work hard and add enormous value, and could find you precisely the person you need.

Many growing businesses are now turning to executive search agencies, known more commonly as headhunters, when it comes to hiring senior management. Headhunters will often network and use their own internal database to find suitable candidates. If you go down this route, ensure the agency takes the time to visit your business and has experience and knowledge of your sector.

Once you have a few candidates and come up with a shortlist, it's essential to check out their track records and consider how well they will contribute to your business's long-term objectives. Consult with your advisers and peers, and take up references both in writing and on the phone – people will often say things on the phone that they will never put in writing for fear of being sued. However, remember that you need to know more about your potential hire than just the dates they worked at their previous employers.

Payment

Senior staff are expensive – and the good ones are good value, it's worth remembering. When you bring in a new manager considerably more experienced than you have had before you might well need to

STOPGAP SOLUTIONS

Temporary staff and interim staff can be an excellent short-term solution. Available in most types of position, using someone on this basis can also be a great way to recruit permanent staff if the interim person turns out to be just right for you. There are a few specialist interim agencies that deal in this, otherwise you can network with your contacts or ask around at tradeshows or trade organisations.

break the invisible, subconscious payscale you have used up until now – may be even paying someone more than you currently pay yourself. Bear in mind that with people it's usually the case that the right person will be significantly better than someone who 'will do', and be far better value even if they cost a little more.

Hiring in haste or under pressure

Many growing businesses face the situation where they need someone but can't find a candidate they want to hire. At this point the pressure is on, and it's sorely tempting to hire someone quickly to get the job being done right now, even if you know they aren't right for the medium term. This is a bad idea. It's always worth waiting to get the right person, however painful that wait can be. The phrase *act in haste, repent at leisure* has never been more true, and the cost and stress of removing the wrong person from a role are simply not worth contemplating. Be patient and hold out for the right person.

A good FD will also help you make decisions based on rigorous financial analysis

Hiring directors
Financial director

One role within organisations is quite different from the rest, and is unlikely to be filled in young, fast-growing businesses early on. The

HIRING A CONSULTANT

You may be able to get all you need from an FD on a part-time basis. There are a few organisations which specialise in providing high-quality FDs to growing businesses. This enables a growing business to get the benefit of a very senior person, often with strong experience and contacts in your sector without breaking the bank. The going rate for part-timers is between £600 and £1,200 a day. This is still far from an insignificant sum, but it's certainly a lot cheaper than the full-time option. And it's not just a question of cash alone. By hiring on a consultancy basis, you can draw on the experience of FDs who have a track record in working on the boards of major public or private companies.

role of the financial director (FD) is often misrepresented. To the department head seeking an increase in resources, it's all too easy to characterise the finance chief as the man or woman who guards the company pursestrings rather too enthusiastically. If you can't get your project funded, blame the FD.

But a good FD is far from the beancounter of popular imagination. In fact, if your company needs to spend more money to grow, finding the cash will be much easier if you have got an experienced finance chief who can talk to banks and venture capitalists, prepare the business for investment and work on forward-looking financial plans. And if you aren't sure how much capital your business needs to grow, you do need an FD.

Responsibilities of an FD

Your FD should ensure that you have:

- Accurate and up-to-date management accounts so that you know how well your business is performing currently
- The right information to be able to make business decisions
- The right controls in place as your business grows to keep on the rails; all too many businesses don't, and suddenly get hit with expenses running wild, which can have a negative impact on both profitability and cashflow

- Up-to-date forecasts of both profit and cashflows (created by them) so that you don't get any surprises or run out of cash suddenly.

A good FD will also help you make decisions based on rigorous financial analysis, rather than simply functioning as a kind of uber-bookkeeper. Indeed, given that the majority of companies will already have a bookkeeper or management accountant handling the day-to-day number crunching, what you do want from your FD is someone who can take the numbers and add value. For instance, a bookkeeper will serve you and the board with historical numbers, but an experienced FD will interpret those figures and help you move the business forward.

Adding 'respectability'

Your FD should take on the burden of fundraising and managing your investors or lenders, freeing you up considerably if you are handling that yourself currently. The presence of a finance specialist can also have a positive impact on how your business is perceived from the outside. The truth is that investors, bankers and even major customers like to be reassured before they put money into a business or trade with a young company. If you can demonstrate that you have a good management team in place, a sound strategic plan and an experienced hand on the financial tiller, they will be very reassured indeed.

> **A good NED must challenge your opinions, question your decisions and bring an objective angle to bear on your business**

Non-executive directors

NEDs also offer a cost-effective means to bring a wealth of experience onto the board of your company. Essentially, an NED is someone who sits on the board, but doesn't play any part in the day-to-day running of the company. Instead, they are there to provide general or expert advice and guidance to you and your team and act as a sounding board for you. They will review your operational plans and budgets, and can often help you build the business by putting you in touch with key industry contacts and potential partners.

TAKING ON A PART-TIME FD

Company: IT Freedom
Managing director: Mick Sargeant

Founded in 2002, software company IT Freedom provides solutions to the insurance industry. In the early days, the focus was on research and development (R&D), but when the board conducted a review of the business in 2007, it was clear that the company had reached a watershed. 'We had done the development. Now we had to get our products out to the market,' says managing director Mick Sargeant. The review also underlined a potential weakness in the management team – there was no one with a professional accountancy qualification. Sargeant approached an organisation that supplies part-time FDs to companies.

'What I was looking for was advice on managing cashflow and possibly outside investment,' explained Sargeant. IT Freedom selected an FD with extensive experience in the software market, whose first task was reviewing the company's progress. 'His key observation was that we had to shift the focus from R&D to marketing,' says Sargeant.

As a result, IT Freedom hired more marketing staff, increased sales and set about selling its way out of its cashflow issues. The FD is still working with IT freedom, fulfilling a role between FD and management consultant and helping to plan the next phase for the company.

Although NEDs will typically attend meetings just once a month, they will usually be available for you to talk to by phone in between meetings. And they will take on the full duties and responsibilities of directors. That means they are as responsible as you if the company

DRAWING ON OLDER WISDOM

If your company is both youthful in terms of its own age and the demographic of the management team, then the arrival of a mature NED can be something of a culture shock. At first he or she may seem a little over-cautious with a tendency to explore the potential risks inherent in ambitious projects. But this is precisely the point. While they are there to add value, part of their role is to constructively challenge the executive team. What's more, an NED in their fifties or sixties will have steered companies through a number of recessions and will be thus be invaluable in helping younger board members make the decisions and set the strategies that will enable the company to weather hard times.

runs into financial trouble, and you can (and should) expect them to ask searching questions about the way the business is run. Indeed, a good NED must challenge your opinions, question your decisions and bring an objective angle to bear on your business. This means it's crucial to carefully select individuals with whom you can build a strong relationship. Ideally, they should also have complementary skill sets to your own.

Finding the right NED

The first step to hiring an NED is deciding why your business needs one. As with the hiring of an full-time or part-time FD, there may be a specific reason why you need to augment the board. It's also vital to identify the additional skills you need along with any weaknesses in the current board line-up that the NED could expect to fill. For instance, if you are chasing investment or planning a flotation, an NED with contacts in the venture capital world or the City of London could prove invaluable, especially if they have already been through the fundraising process. Alternatively, if you are planning to launch a new product line that addresses a previously untapped market, an NED with experience in that sector should be able to steer you in the right direction.

Once you have defined the role and the skills and characteristics required, the second step is to draw up a shortlist of suitable candidates. There are several ways to do this, including recommendations by business associates. However, if you want to cast the net as widely as possible, consider using a specialist search company. Those worth their salt will provide candidates that exactly match your specifications. As with all senior hires, use a formal interview process and make sure you and the candidates understand the scope of the role. It's important to get a good fit.

As with part time FDs, NEDs can be remarkably good value, bringing a wealth of experience, wisdom and contacts into your business. Typically NEDs at growing businesses will earn between £10,000 and £20,000 per year, possibly with some share options on top, for roughly one day per month.

Executive coaching

Although buying in talent is a tried-and-trusted approach to bolstering a management team, you shouldn't forget the importance of getting the most out of your existing executives – and indeed yourself.

Executive coaches are often useful when an individual is facing a major career change. Sometimes this will be directly related to a promotion – such as a department head receiving coaching ahead of an appointment to the board – or in response to upheaval within the company itself. For instance, a merger or takeover could result in a particular manager taking charge of the integration process and ultimately running a much larger and more complex operation. This will inevitably mean new operational and personal challenges, sometimes resulting in situations that are difficult to cope with. Coaching can help the manager successfully address those challenges.

Coaching is available from a wide range of business consultancies, ranging from one-person operations to larger specialist organisations, but it's vital to consider certain factors before taking the plunge.

- First, be clear about why you are considering going down this route. That means identifying managers or board members who are facing the kind of problems or issues that coaching might help them address. Then it's essential to get them to buy into the coaching concept. Working with a coach is an intense and occasionally difficult process, and because it's bespoke it's also costly, so you need to be sure that those taking part will commit to the programme.
- Second, you need to find a coach who will work well with the manager or managers you have identified as needing coaching. The chances are that any programme will touch on difficult or sensitive personal issues. It's never easy for anyone to admit to weaknesses and this is especially true of those who have done well in life. The coach, therefore, needs to have a rapport with the subject while being both tactful and authoritative. Above all, the coach should understand the needs of the company and be capable of delivering measurable change in the individual.

Stepping aside: hiring a chief executive officer

> **When the business grows to a certain size, CEOs often need to consider whether to step aside and let a professional CEO take on the business**

There may come a time when you want to or feel the need to bring in someone else to run the business from day to day – a chief executive officer (CEO). That is an enormous decision, and not one to take lightly.

When the business grows to a certain size, CEOs often need to consider whether to step aside and let a professional CEO take on the business and also whether they are the right person to take the business forwards. Sometimes the answer might be for them to step aside, other times it might be better to adjust the management team in some other way.

If you decide to bring in a CEO, it doesn't necessarily mean leaving the business altogether. A typical progression is a move from managing director to chairman, where you retain an involvement in the business, steering strategy and working with your CEO while he or she runs the business. As chairman you can continue to be the public face of the company, representing it to customers and investors.

Working together

Bear in mind though that an incoming CEO will want sufficient autonomy to make a difference. So before making the hire, you need to be as certain as possible that he or she will pursue the strategy you want, because it can go wrong. For instance, when Nick Wheeler, founder of clothing retailer Charles Tyrwhitt, decided it was time to hand over to a new man, he chose someone with a successful track record at Polo Ralph Lauren. It should have been a dream hire – with a senior manager from one of the world's pre-eminent luxury fashion brands coming in to supercharge a successful British company that also addressed high-end customers. However, Wheeler was unhappy with the strategy implemented by the new man and within months

245

he returned to the chief executive's role, blaming himself for stepping back too far and not working more closely with his new CEO.

Think it through

Be clear what your objectives are. If you are tired of running the business, perhaps it would be better to sell it than to take on a new CEO? That way you don't risk all the value you have built up if a new CEO works differently. If you don't want to sell yet but are worried that you don't have the right skills to take the business forward, consider training or coaching, or juggling the management board, rather than bringing in a new CEO.

There has been enough written on the benefit of delegation and hiring better people than yourself, and hiring a professional manager. But it's very hard to undo things when they go wrong, so be sure it really is what you want to do before you take the plunge. And if it really is what you want, then work very hard to find the right person, and have an extended handover period so you can get to know them while you are both working on the business before you hand over the reins altogether.

Staying on top

Business isn't necessarily a democracy, nor should it be. You as founder had the sixth sense to set up the business in the first place, and understand the make-up of your customers. Take time regularly to step back from the day-to-day role and think about your business and where it's going. What could go wrong with your current plans? Are you sure that the direction agreed by management recently is the right one? It's your job as leader to shake things up sometimes, to keep your business on its toes, fresh and keen to remain the leader in your field. The danger of a well-running management team is that you lose that sixth sense of originality, that spark which made your business really stand out originally.

Some Monday mornings you might still need to call your management team in for an unscheduled session to reveal some new thoughts you have had which adjust the direction of the business, leading it onto the next major growth path, just as Bill Gates famously did when he arrived one day committed to turning Microsoft into an internet business despite having previously written off that route. Whether it's a brand new thought or simply something the management team have agreed on which you are not comfortable about, work out why, then act. You are the founder, the leader. Dare to think dangerously sometimes.

HIRING A CHIEF EXECUTIVE

Company: Cobra Beer
Founder: Lord Karan Bilimoria

In 2007, Lord Karan Bilimoria stepped down from the role of chief executive at then £55m turnover company Cobra Beer and handed the job to a man he barely knew. That man was Adrian McKeon, a drinks industry veteran with experience at Beam Global Spirits and Wine and Allied Domecq. The aim of the appointment was to bring in someone who could build on Cobra's already phenomenal growth story, and during his first few months in the job McKeon undertook a top-to-tail review of the business that resulted in the acquisition of a brewery and plans to open up new sales channels in the UK and beyond.

Commenting on the change at the top, Bilimoria noted that when companies grow very rapidly, '90% of the time that has been down to a change at the top'. But he was very aware that when an CEO steps down and an outsider comes in to take on the chief executive role, there is a risk that things will go wrong and often this is down to the relationship between the outgoing chief executive and his successor.

'There are three ways that companies take on chief executives,' says Bilimoria. 'The first is that they bring a high-flying, top-notch person with a great track record in the industry and the founder hands over the keys, saying: "I'll see you when you need me and once a year I'll come to the AGM." At the other extreme, the founder brings in a chief executive and is constantly looking over his or her shoulder – second guessing and over-ruling.'

Bilimoria went for the third way, where 'the founder stays on, but it's so carefully managed that the new chief executive is given full leeway to run the company, bring in a new strategy and get buy in from the board.'

! TOP TIPS

GETTING THE RIGHT TEAM

! Hire the right managers – make sure you have the right managers, even if that means replacing people who have been with you for years but who are no longer right for the business.

! Delegate – it's all too easy for CEOs to feel that they have to take a hands-on interest in every part of the business, often doing things that senior managers ought to be taking responsibility for.

! Spend some time outside the business – if you spend your days fire fighting, that limits the time available to think strategically. Schedule in some time away from office with senior managers to discuss strategy.

! Assess your strengths and weaknesses – then focus on where you can add the most value, and what gaps need filling by other staff.

! Trust and monitor – ultimately growth will need you to allow others to do what you used to. The key is to set up systems to check they do it well, and fix any problems which might arise.

! Hire a financial director – rapid growth needs tight controls and systems, and a good FD will often add value far beyond the finance function.

! Take on a non-executive director or chairman – NEDs bring experience at a fraction of the cost of full-time directors.

! Develop your team – the right training or coaching could transform the performance of existing team members for considerably less expense and disruption than replacing them.

! Carry out a 'map and gap' exercise – look at your board and senior managerial team. What are its strengths and weaknesses. How can you fill the gaps?

! Invest in recruitment – if the company is coping with rapid change, take time to research the market and identify hires who would add value to your company.

INFORMATION AND CONTROL

THIS CHAPTER WILL DISCUSS:

- Creating an information and control framework for growth

- Keeping clear visibility of your finances

- Controlled delegation

- Reporting systems: keep track

- Using resources efficiently

Colin Mills, Founder and Chief Executive Officer of the FD Centre

As your business grows, you need to make sure you don't lose control of it. Many failed businesses have experienced rapid sales growth only to realise when it's too late that the growth didn't result in profit or cash flow. Relevant, accurate and timely information flow will help you control the growth of your business so that you can benefit from the profits and cash your business generates, and, most importantly, you can sleep at night along the way. This isn't difficult to do, as long as you are clear about what you need to monitor, and you allocate some resources to ensure you stay in control.

Creating an information and control framework for growth

Figure 4.2.1 The information and control framework.

Figure 4.2.1 illustrates the information and control processes your business needs both to help it grow and to keep it in control. Bear this in mind when you are considering spending any money on developing your information systems. Essentially, an efficient system will:

- Help you get a better view of your finances going forward
- Help you improve your confidence in delegating decisions to staff
- Improve promptness and accuracy of your reporting
- Produce useful information for you to make better decisions in your business.

A system that doesn't fulfil these criteria may be nice to have, but not essential, and when you are growing your business it's best to stick to essentials.

The next section discusses the information requirements at each stage in the control framework, so that you can decide what you need to do to keep your growth business in control.

Keeping clear visibility of your finances

A view three years forward on the 'shape' of your business finances will help you understand the finance you require to deliver your business plan

From a control perspective, your business plan needs to be supported by a financial plan. A view three years forward on the 'shape' of your business finances is an ideal starting point, and will help you understand the finance you require to deliver your business plan, whether this can be delivered via your own resources, or whether you will need to bring in funding from outside the business (see Chapters 4.3–4.6 for more details on funding).

The key information you will need to project for any external funder (including normal overdraft funding from banks) includes as a minimum:

- Profit and loss projections (by month)
- Cash flow – receipts and payments (by month)

THE BIG PICTURE

Planning is the start point in any control system. As mentioned previously in this book, an understanding of where you are going, what you are aiming at, and how you are going to get there is a key requirement of a successful growth business, as real-life experiences have shown time and again. A vision for your business, and a strategy to get there are the usual pre-requisites for any business CEO serious in growing a business. This is usually written down in a business plan. It's pretty much a fact that 'successful people write things down'. The written form tends to act as a business compass, so that although you may be off course for most of the journey, if you have some clear goals and a timeframe to deliver, chances are you will be more successful in achieving your aims than to just leave things to chance.

- Balance sheet (by month)
- Source and use of funds (by month) – this reconciles profit projections with cash flow.

A clear link to your business plan, with statements on the key assumptions you have made is also essential.

Even if you are in the fortunate position where you feel you are likely to have plenty of finance yourself without going outside the business, you should adopt the same approach in terms of producing forecast information. In this way you know how much you are likely to need and when. Examples of what these schedules look like are shown in Figure 4.2.2.

Budgets, regular updates and financial forecasts

Things change constantly so keeping your vision and business plan fresh, and having a strong management team and well thought through financial forecasts, will go a long way to raise any necessary funds for your business. This is also essential to keep in control.

FD Centre Template

PROFIT & LOSS FORECAST

	Jul 09 Proj. £	Aug 09 Proj. £	Sep 09 Proj. £	Oct 09 Proj. £	Nov 09 Proj. £	Dec 09 Proj. £	Jan 10 Proj. £	Feb 10 Proj. £	Mar 10 Proj. £	Apr 10 Proj. £	May 10 Proj. £	Jun 10 Proj. £	Total Act/Proj. £	%
SALES														
Sales	219,000	215,000	606,000	588,000	745,000	514,000	770,000	680,000	722,000	703,000	764,000	719,000	7,245,000	104.2%
Rebates	(8,760)	(8,600)	(24,240)	(23,520)	(29,800)	(20,560)	(30,800)	(27,200)	(28,880)	(28,120)	(30,560)	(28,760)	(289,800)	-4.2%
	210,240	206,400	581,760	564,480	715,200	493,440	739,200	652,800	693,120	674,880	733,440	690,240	6,955,200	100.0%
DIRECT COSTS														
Production costs	147,168	144,480	407,232	395,136	500,640	345,408	517,440	456,960	485,184	472,416	513,408	483,168	4,868,640	70.0%
Storage	5,256	5,160	14,544	14,112	17,880	12,336	18,480	16,320	17,328	16,872	18,336	17,256	173,880	2.5%
Distribution	5,256	5,160	14,544	14,112	17,880	12,336	18,480	16,320	17,328	16,872	18,336	17,256	173,880	2.5%
Carriage	631	619	1,746	1,693	2,146	1,480	2,217	1,959	2,079	2,025	2,200	2,071	20,866	0.3%
	158,311	155,419	438,066	425,053	538,546	371,560	556,617	491,559	521,919	508,185	552,280	519,751	5,237,266	75.3%
GROSS MARGIN	51,929	50,981	143,694	139,427	176,654	121,880	182,583	161,241	171,201	166,695	181,160	170,489	1,717,934	24.7%
OVERHEADS														
Salary	60,000	60,000	60,000	60,000	60,000	60,000	60,000	60,000	60,000	60,000	60,000	75,000	735,000	10.6%
Wages	7,333	7,334	7,333	7,334	7,333	7,334	7,333	7,334	7,333	7,334	7,333	7,334	88,002	1.3%
Rent & Rates	2,667	2,667	2,667	2,667	2,667	2,667	2,667	2,667	2,667	2,667	2,667	2,667	32,004	0.5%
Utilities	642	642	642	642	642	642	642	642	642	642	642	642	7,704	0.1%
Insurance	1,083	1,083	1,083	1,083	1,083	1,083	1,083	1,083	1,083	1,083	1,083	1,083	12,996	0.2%
Telephones	1,167	1,167	1,167	1,167	1,167	1,167	1,167	1,167	1,167	1,167	1,167	1,167	14,004	0.2%
Mileage Costs	3,800	3,800	3,800	3,800	3,800	3,800	3,800	3,800	3,800	3,800	3,800	3,800	45,600	0.7%
Travel & Subs: stence	3,333	3,333	3,333	3,333	3,333	3,333	3,333	3,333	3,333	3,333	3,333	3,333	39,996	0.6%
Entertaining	300	300	300	300	300	300	300	300	300	300	300	300	3,600	0.1%
Marketing & Stationery	8,500	8,500	8,500	8,500	8,500	8,500	8,500	8,500	8,500	8,500	8,500	8,500	102,000	1.5%
Product Development	1,000	1,000	1,000	1,000	1,000	1,000	1,000	1,000	1,000	1,000	1,000	1,000	12,000	0.2%
Personnel Costs	833	833	833	833	833	833	833	833	833	833	833	833	9,996	0.1%
Subscriptions	1,667	1,667	1,667	1,667	1,667	1,667	1,667	1,667	1,667	1,667	1,667	1,667	20,004	0.3%
Office/Site Costs	1,000	1,000	1,000	1,000	1,000	1,000	1,000	1,000	1,000	1,000	1,000	1,000	12,000	0.2%
Computer Costs	1,250	1,250	1,250	1,250	1,250	1,250	1,250	1,250	1,250	1,250	1,250	1,250	15,000	0.2%
Accountancy Fees	1,417	1,417	1,417	1,417	1,417	1,417	1,417	1,417	1,417	1,417	1,417	1,417	17,004	0.2%
Professional Fees	1,333	1,333	1,333	1,333	1,333	1,333	1,333	1,333	1,333	1,333	1,333	1,333	15,996	0.2%
Finance Charges	4,167	4,167	4,167	4,167	4,167	4,167	4,167	4,167	4,167	4,167	4,167	4,167	50,004	0.7%
Depreciation	9,531	9,409	5,777	5,777	5,777	5,778	5,777	5,777	5,777	5,777	5,777	5,777	76,711	1.1%
	111,023	110,902	107,269	107,270	107,271	107,269	107,270	107,270	107,269	107,269	107,269	122,270	1,309,621	18.8%
OPERATING PROFIT	(59,094)	(59,921)	36,425	32,157	69,385	14,609	75,314	53,971	63,932	59,425	73,891	48,219	408,313	5.9%
INTEREST EXPENSE	468	981	655	521	331	247	322	164	16	(341)	(770)	(1,149)	1,445	0.0%
NET PROFIT	(59,562)	(60,902)	35,770	31,636	69,054	14,362	74,992	53,807	63,916	59,766	74,661	49,368	406,868	5.8%
CORPORATION TAX	-	-	-	-	-	-	-	-	-	-	-	(100,000)	(100,000)	-1.4%
PROFIT AFTER TAX	(59,562)	(60,902)	35,770	31,636	69,054	14,362	74,992	53,807	63,916	59,766	74,661	(50,632)	306,868	4.4%
DIVIDEND ACCRUAL	(20,160)	-	(20,160)	-	(20,160)	-	(20,160)	-	(20,160)	-	(20,160)	-	(120,960)	-1.7%
RETAINED EARNINGS	(79,722)	(60,902)	15,610	31,636	48,894	14,362	54,832	53,807	43,756	59,766	54,501	(50,632)	185,908	2.7%
CUMULATIVE	(79,722)	(140,624)	(125,014)	(93,378)	(44,484)	(30,122)	24,710	78,517	122,273	182,039	236,540	185,908	185,908	

Figure 4.2.2 Example schedules

FD Centre
Template

CASH FLOW FORECAST

	Jul 09 Proj. £	Aug 09 Proj. £	Sep 09 Proj. £	Oct 09 Proj. £	Nov 09 Proj. £	Dec 09 Proj. £	Jan 10 Proj. £	Feb 10 Proj. £	Mar 10 Proj. £	Apr 10 Proj. £	May 10 Proj. £	Jun 10 Proj. £	Total Act/Proj. £
RECEIPTS													
Invoiced Sales	289,708	287,206	507,608	492,984	691,760	510,752	723,160	623,440	706,896	674,304	729,552	691,192	6,928,562
Interest Received	235	-	60	209	478	503	482	738	840	1,199	1,641	2,017	8,402
VAT	11,485	7,929	7,893	11,375	11,215	12,613	10,556	12,835	12,034	12,407	12,239	12,782	135,363
	301,428	295,135	515,561	504,568	703,453	523,868	734,198	637,013	719,770	687,910	743,432	705,991	7,072,327
PAYMENTS													
Invoiced Costs	495,724	202,277	247,490	481,762	470,511	584,581	517,360	602,408	538,175	568,288	554,672	598,934	5,862,182
Salary	40,000	40,000	40,000	40,000	40,000	40,000	40,000	40,000	40,000	40,000	40,000	50,000	490,000
Wages	4,889	4,889	4,889	4,889	4,889	4,889	4,889	4,889	4,889	4,889	4,889	4,889	58,668
Loan Payments	3,500	3,500	3,500	3,500	3,500	3,500	3,500	3,500	1,057	-	-	-	29,057
Overdraft Interest	189	736	223	-	-	-	-	-	-	-	-	-	1,148
Factoring Interest	514	245	492	730	809	750	804	902	856	858	871	868	8,699
Corporation Tax	-	-	-	-	-	-	-	-	20,000	-	-	-	20,000
PAYE/NI	26,407	22,444	22,445	22,444	22,445	22,444	22,445	22,444	22,445	22,444	22,445	22,444	273,296
Dividend Paid	20,160	-	20,160	-	20,160	-	20,160	-	20,160	-	20,160	-	120,960
	591,383	274,091	339,199	553,325	562,314	656,164	609,158	674,143	647,582	636,479	643,037	677,135	6,864,010
NET CASH FLOW	(289,955)	21,044	176,362	(48,757)	141,139	(132,296)	125,040	(37,130)	72,188	51,431	100,395	28,856	208,317
OPENING BANK	152,845	(137,110)	(116,066)	60,296	11,539	152,678	20,382	145,422	108,292	180,480	231,911	332,306	152,845
CLOSING BANK	(137,110)	(116,066)	60,296	11,539	152,678	20,382	145,422	108,292	180,480	231,911	332,306	361,162	361,162

Figure 4.2.2   cont.

FD Centre

BALANCE SHEET FORECAST

	Opening Actual £	Jul 09 Proj. £	Aug 09 Proj. £	Sep 09 Proj. £	Oct 09 Proj. £	Nov 09 Proj. £	Dec 09 Proj. £	Jan 10 Proj. £	Feb 10 Proj. £	Mar 10 Proj. £	Apr 10 Proj. £	May 10 Proj. £	Jun 10 Proj. £
FIXED ASSETS													
Leasehold Improvements	6,230	6,230	6,230	6,230	6,230	6,230	6,230	6,230	6,230	6,230	6,230	6,230	6,230
Plant & Equipment	381,413	381,413	381,413	381,413	381,413	381,413	381,413	381,413	381,413	381,413	381,413	381,413	381,413
Office Equipment	136,517	136,517	136,517	136,517	136,517	136,517	136,517	136,517	136,517	136,517	136,517	136,517	136,517
Motor Vehicles	108,240	108,240	108,240	108,240	108,240	108,240	108,240	108,240	108,240	108,240	108,240	108,240	108,240
Accumulated Depreciation	(503,964)	(513,495)	(522,904)	(528,681)	(534,458)	(540,235)	(546,013)	(551,790)	(557,567)	(563,344)	(569,121)	(574,898)	(580,675)
	128,436	118,905	109,496	103,719	97,942	92,165	86,387	80,610	74,833	69,056	63,279	57,502	51,725
CURRENT ASSETS													
Bank	152,845	137,110	116,066	60,296	11,539	152,678	20,382	145,422	108,292	180,480	231,911	332,306	361,162
Trade Debtors	1,168,520	771,179	367,149	737,909	1,095,389	1,212,589	1,126,029	1,206,229	1,353,029	1,284,149	1,287,029	1,306,469	1,301,709
Other Debtors													
VAT	11,485	7,929	7,893	11,375	11,215	12,613	10,556	12,835	12,034	12,407	12,239	12,782	12,381
Sub-Total	11,485	7,929	7,893	11,375	11,215	12,613	10,556	12,835	12,034	12,407	12,239	12,782	12,381
Stock On Hand													
Food & Production	450,000	450,000	500,000	500,000	500,000	500,000	600,000	600,000	600,000	600,000	600,000	600,000	600,000
Raw Material & Packaging Stock	250,000	250,000	250,000	250,000	250,000	250,000	250,000	250,000	250,000	250,000	250,000	250,000	250,000
Sub-Total	700,000	700,000	750,000	750,000	750,000	750,000	850,000	850,000	850,000	850,000	850,000	850,000	850,000
	2,032,850	1,479,108	1,125,042	1,559,580	1,868,143	2,127,880	2,006,967	2,214,486	2,323,355	2,327,036	2,381,179	2,501,557	2,525,252
CREDITORS DUE WITHIN ONE YEAR													
Bank													
Trade Creditors	487,870	192,545	237,739	473,849	462,514	577,321	509,015	595,266	530,610	560,920	547,215	591,764	559,121
Other Creditors													
PAYE/NI	26,407	22,444	22,445	22,445	22,445	22,444	22,445	22,444	22,445	22,444	22,445	22,444	27,445
Sub-Total	26,407	22,444	22,445	22,445	22,445	22,444	22,445	22,444	22,445	22,444	22,445	22,444	27,445
Invoice discounting	934,816	616,943	293,719	590,327	876,311	970,071	900,823	964,983	1,082,423	1,027,319	1,029,623	1,045,175	1,041,367
Provision for Tax	20,000	20,000	20,000	20,000	20,000	20,000	20,000	20,000	20,000				100,000
Hire Purchase	29,057	25,557	22,057	18,557	15,057	11,557	8,057	4,557	1,057				
Stock Provision	1,920	1,920	1,920	1,920	1,920	1,920	1,920	1,920	1,920	1,920	1,920	1,920	1,920
Provision for Sales Rebates	79,857	79,857	79,857	79,857	79,857	79,857	79,857	79,857	79,857	79,857	79,857	79,857	79,857
	1,579,927	1,096,376	793,803	1,206,954	1,478,104	1,683,170	1,542,117	1,689,027	1,738,312	1,692,460	1,681,060	1,741,160	1,809,710
NET CURRENT ASSETS	452,923	382,732	331,239	352,626	390,039	444,710	464,850	525,459	585,043	634,576	700,119	760,397	715,542
CREDITORS DUE AFTER ONE YEAR													
TOTAL NET ASSETS	581,359	501,637	440,735	456,345	487,981	536,875	551,237	606,069	659,876	703,632	763,398	817,899	767,267
CAPITAL & RESERVES													
Capital	10,067	10,067	10,067	10,067	10,067	10,067	10,067	10,067	10,067	10,067	10,067	10,067	10,067
Retained Earnings	571,292	491,570	430,668	446,278	477,914	526,808	541,170	596,002	649,809	693,565	753,331	807,832	757,200
	581,359	501,637	440,735	456,345	487,981	536,875	551,237	606,069	659,876	703,632	763,398	817,899	767,267

Figure 4.2.2 cont.

FD Centre
FUNDS FLOW FORECAST

	Jul 09 Proj. £	Aug 09 Proj. £	Sep 09 Proj. £	Oct 09 Proj. £	Nov 09 Proj. £	Dec 09 Proj. £	Jan 10 Proj. £	Feb 10 Proj. £	Mar 10 Proj. £	Apr 10 Proj. £	May 10 Proj. £	Jun 10 Proj. £	Total Act/Proj. £
PROFIT & LOSS													
Operating Profit	(59,094)	(59,921)	36,425	32,157	69,385	14,609	75,314	53,971	63,932	59,425	73,891	48,219	408,313
Plus Deprec'n/Grant Income	9,531	9,409	5,777	5,777	5,777	5,778	5,777	5,777	5,777	5,777	5,777	5,777	76,711
	(49,563)	(50,512)	42,202	37,934	75,162	20,387	81,091	59,748	69,709	65,202	79,668	53,996	485,024
WORKING CAPITAL CHANGES													
Trade Debtors	397,341	404,030	(370,760)	(357,480)	(117,200)	86,560	(80,200)	(146,800)	68,880	(2,880)	(19,440)	4,760	(133,189)
Trade Creditors	(295,325)	45,194	236,110	(11,335)	114,807	(68,306)	86,251	(64,656)	30,310	(13,705)	44,549	(32,643)	71,251
Other Creditors/Debtors	(407)	37	(3,483)	161	(1,399)	2,058	(2,280)	802	(374)	169	(544)	5,402	142
Stock On Hand	–	(50,000)	–	–	–	(100,000)	–	–	–	–	–	–	(150,000)
	101,609	399,261	(138,133)	(368,654)	(3,792)	(79,688)	3,771	(210,654)	98,816	(16,416)	24,565	(22,481)	(211,796)
CASH INFLOW FROM OPERATIONS	52,046	348,749	(95,931)	(330,720)	71,370	(59,301)	84,862	(150,906)	168,525	48,786	104,233	31,515	273,228
INVESTMENT RETURNS													
Interest Received/(Paid)	(468)	(981)	(655)	(521)	(331)	(247)	(322)	(164)	(16)	341	770	1,149	(1,445)
	(468)	(981)	(655)	(521)	(331)	(247)	(322)	(164)	(16)	341	770	1,149	(1,445)
CASH INFLOW BEFORE FINANCING	51,578	347,768	(96,586)	(331,241)	71,039	(59,548)	84,540	(151,070)	168,509	49,127	105,003	32,664	271,783
INVESTING ACTIVITIES	–	–	–	–	–	–	–	–	–	–	–	–	–
FINANCING & OTHER													
Invoice Discounting	(317,873)	(323,224)	296,608	285,984	93,760	(69,248)	64,160	117,440	(55,104)	2,304	15,552	(3,808)	106,551
Corporation Tax	–	–	–	–	–	–	–	–	(20,000)	–	–	–	(20,000)
Dividend Paid	(20,160)	–	(20,160)	–	(20,160)	–	(20,160)	–	(20,160)	–	(20,160)	–	(120,960)
Loans/Leases	(3,500)	(3,500)	(3,500)	(3,500)	(3,500)	(3,500)	(3,500)	(3,500)	(1,057)	–	–	–	(29,057)
	(341,533)	(326,724)	272,948	282,484	70,100	(72,748)	40,500	113,940	(96,321)	2,304	(4,608)	(3,808)	(63,466)
TOTAL CASH INFLOW	(289,955)	21,044	176,362	(48,757)	141,139	(132,296)	125,040	(37,130)	72,188	51,431	100,395	28,856	208,317

The annual budgeting process is the normal way to update your financial plans. However, you need to be careful that you don't make the annual planning process time consuming and rigid. In many large companies, this process has been known to turn into little more than a bargaining process for getting resources allocated to those managers who have the best negotiating skills.

As mentioned above the more effective method to keep control of your business is to regularly update your financial forecasts for:

- Profit and loss (by month)
- Cash flow – receipts and payment (by month)
- Balance sheet (by month)
- Source and use of funds (by month) – this reconciles profit projections with cash flow.

If you can do this at least once every quarter and, in times of constant change, ideally every month, you will know precisely where you are and importantly if you are relying on external funding (e.g. banks) to provide support, they will be much more comfortable and supportive if they also know what's happening financially.

If you have already set up your longer term financial planning from your 'big picture' (above), overwriting actual performance as you go

DO IT YOURSELF SOFTWARE FOR FINANCIAL FORECASTS

If you have strong financial skills yourself, you could set up these models in an Excel spreadsheet. The downside of using Excel is that mistakes can happen such as accidentally overwriting formulas, or balance sheets not balancing because the profit forecast has not been linked correctly to the balance sheet.

Sage (the accounting software supplier) also has some standard forecasting software, which comes in two versions – Sage Financial Forecasting for individual companies and Sage Winforecast and Winforecast Professional for small groups of companies, where there is a need to consolidate forecasts. The benefit of choosing a Sage option is that it can link to your actual reporting (if you also use Sage Accounting). The downside is that Sage Forecasting does take some time to learn, particularly if you haven't had any formal accounting training.

along and making any changes to forward forecasts puts you in a more solid control position.

You can either do the forecasting yourself (see box) or buy-in this expertise (see 'A finance director's skill set' below). Don't make the mistake of thinking you don't need this skill set. The more financial visibility you have, the more in control you will be and the more help you will get from banks or other funders.

Break even

'Break even' is the level of sales you need to achieve so that you are not losing money. The reason for understanding this is that if you monitor your sales you know at any point in time whether you are making a profit or loss. You don't want to be running a business at a loss for a sustained period, so having a clear focus to deliver sales over break even is important.

Break even is calculated by splitting your cost structure into fixed and variable costs. As mentioned in Chapter 2.1, fixed costs are those that don't vary with volumes sold. Typically fixed costs include things such as cost of renting offices, factory or warehouse space, cost of employing staff and related add-ons, e.g. cars, in fact anything you can't vary in the short term. Variable costs do vary with sales. Typical examples are distribution costs, costs of product sold, any labour costs directly related to production, in fact all the costs that vary as sales go up or down. Having a thorough understanding of your different types of costs is vital in understanding your break-even position. And a clear picture of break even will show you the benefits of increasing or losing sales volumes and the likely effect it will have on your business. Getting your break-even point as low as possible on the graph shown in Figure 4.2.3 will give your business flexibility.

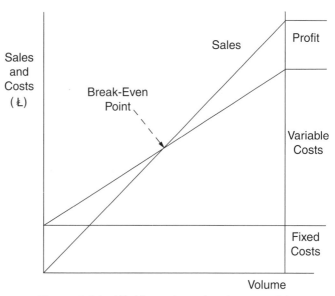

Figure 4.2.3   Working out your break-even point.

'NINE-WEEK' FORECASTS TO MAKE SURE YOU DON'T RUN OUT OF CASH

Regular forecast updates to your 'big picture' will give you great visibility and alert you to longer-term issues that you should be thinking about. For strong management of the cash line in the short term, a nine-week (two-month) forecast of receipts and payments will put you firmly in the driving seat and give you a chance to adjust things so your cash flow remains in control. This week-by-week view can usually be done without any external support as the money that you are likely to collect and pay will have already been entered to your accounting system. It's then just a case of figuring out which are the weeks you will receive or pay money. An example of what this looks like is shown in Figure 4.2.4. If you then commit to update it once per week, you will always have a picture of what your cash position is likely to be for the next nine weeks. If you can see at any future point you might be short of cash, you then have the opportunity to reschedule things to make it all fit. This simple tool has been the salvation for many small- and medium-sized business CEOs. If you expect your business to be under any form of cash pressure in the near future, start it today.

FD Centre Template - 9 Week Rolling Cash Flow Forecast

Week Commencing	11-Jul	18-Jul	25-Jul	1-Aug	8-Aug	15-Aug	22-Aug	22-Aug / 29-Aug	5-Sep
	£	£	£	£	£	£	£	£	£
Bank Account									
Receipts									
Customer Recipts - see detail	70,000	40,000	100,000		14,000	12,000	52,000	180,000	180,001
VAT Monthly Refund					10,000				
Other Income				6,000					
Total Receipts	70,000	40,000	100,000	6,000	24,000	12,000	52,000	180,000	180,001
Payments									
Suppliers - see detail	0	33,557	98,877	0	0	0	50,000	100,000	0
Weekly Expenses	1,000	1,000	1,000	3,000	1,000	1,000	1,000	1,000	1,000
Monthly Payroll	22,264				22,264				
Monthly PAYE / NHI	9,569					9,569			
Other: (Please List)									
Sundry Small Payments	500	500	500	500	500	500	500	500	500
Standing Orders - see detail	0	1,030	485	1,554	600	1,040	295	1,488	0
Dividend								75,000	
New Equipment		10,000							
Sales Rebate (Customer name)		12,000							
Total Payments	33,333	58,087	100,862	5,054	24,364	12,109	51,795	177,988	1,500
Bank Balance / (Overdraft) b/f	1,845	38,512	20,425	19,563	20,509	20,145	20,036	20,241	22,253
Bank Balance / (Overdraft) c/f	38,512	20,425	19,563	20,509	20,145	20,036	20,241	22,253	200,754

Figure 4.2.4 Working out your break-even point.

FINANCIAL VISIBILITY FOR CONTROL

Company: Green Gourmet
Owner and CEO: Adam Starkey

Adam Starkey, owner of Green Gourmet, decided to develop his foods business to provide high nutrition children's meals to schools after the Jamie Oliver-driven publicity of poor quality children's food in schools. This resulted in high business growth, and the need to plan and finance this growth. Adam implemented two key actions to enable the company's funders to provide the necessary finance to deliver his vision. With the help of his company's part-time finance director (FD; see 'Using resources efficiently' below), Adam created a three-year financial forecast to show funding needs. This consisted of a profit and loss forecast, balance sheet, cash flow and source and use of funds statement (produced from Sage Winforecast). This enabled the company to secure the funding structure to support the planned growth.

To keep a tight control of cash on a week-to-week basis, Adam then implemented (again with the help of his part-time FD) a rolling nine-week receipts and payment cash flow system (developed in Excel), to see exactly where he was, and manage cash flows within agreed funding facilities. Green Gourmet's business has doubled over the past few years to a turnover of £6m, with no restrictions from funders along the way.

Cash 'burn' and 'bleed'

> **Usually the best place to start is with simple things that take time, but that staff can be educated and trained in easily**

The next issue to look closely at when reviewing financial forecasts is the level at which your business uses or generates cash on a monthly basis. Fast-growing businesses tend to have an appetite for using or 'burning' cash. This is because sales growth usually requires working capital cash (i.e. more stocks, money outstanding from customers, less monies owed to suppliers). If your business is growing and 'burning' cash you need to understand how much it's burning per month and compare this to the funding you have available. This will tell you how long your business can last without any more finance, or alternatively how long you have got to make changes to stop cash 'burn'. Businesses that are not growing but are still using cash anyway are 'bleeding cash'. No business, or person, can tolerate 'bleeding' for too long, so if your forecast is showing this you will need to take action soon. The important thing is, of course, that you know.

Controlled delegation

To make progress in any business, you need to make decisions and take action. The more energy and resource that can be put behind those decisions and action, the more quickly you are likely to get the desired result. Necessarily therefore, as a business grows, more people will need to be involved in the decision-making process. This can be a difficult transition for the CEO who has done most things from the outset and made all the decisions.

Delegating actions and decision making effectively is therefore critical for the business to grow, and to make the business less dependent on you. Although this issue has been discussed in Chapter 4.1, this section will show you the way to achieve delegation without losing control.

The key is to ensure that the correct systems and procedures are put in place so that you are comfortable staff won't do things to damage the business, but equally your staff feel empowered and accountable to make decisions without fear that they will be punished.

Figure 4.2.5 shows how you can achieve controlled delegation. As a business grows, systems and procedures need to be developed that describe the way of doing things, and authority levels assigned, by way of an authority matrix to different managers and job holders in the business for making decisions. Don't start with everything at once – usually the best place to start is with simple things that take time, but that staff can be educated and trained in easily. First aim to get your staff to take responsibility and empowerment for the things you are happy that their skills are capable of delivering. Over time, the aim should be to build up systems and procedures for all key activities in the business. These should include, but not be restricted to, the legal requirements to hold employment policies, health and safety policies, etc.

The added benefit of such an approach is that when you come to prepare your business for sale, potential buyers of your business will be able to see how the business is run. If there's nothing written down and everything relies on you, the reality is you will find yourself either

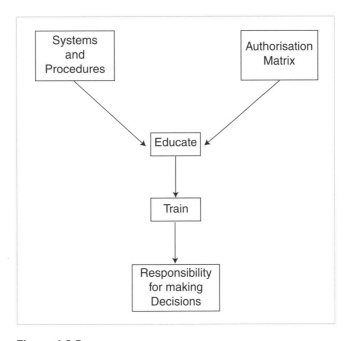

Figure 4.2.5

tied into the business for longer than you would want, or the chances of an earn-out will be increased because the buyer will perceive a higher level of risk in buying a business that is too dependent on the owner. The sale price is also likely to be lower for a business with poorly documented policies and procedures and weak systems. All business owners that have been through a sale process realise this, but as most CEOs only sell their business once, they don't realise it until it's too late.

A profit and loss account and balance sheet should be produced by at least the middle of the month following the month being reported

Reporting systems: keep track
The basics

Reporting is about knowing exactly where you are at any point in time, and a good reporting system is essential to keep control of a growing business. As mentioned above, as an absolute minimum you need your financial systems to be able to produce is a profit and loss account and balance sheet. This information should be produced in the same formats that you have used to forecast, ideally on a monthly basis. Certainly, don't leave it later than once a quarter to make sure you have this basic information.

Sage is the market leader when it comes to accounting systems, and over 80% of small- and medium-sized businesses use Sage for their accounting. However it is a product that requires some accounting knowledge to set up and use, so you need to make sure you have good expertise on board to set it up and use it. Many start-up and smaller businesses (typically those with less than £1m turnover per annum) start with cheaper systems, such as Quickbooks or MYOB (now part of Mamut). A quick search on Google for 'accounting systems' will bring up a vast array of software for you to choose from. Some start-up businesses just use an Excel spreadsheet to record income and expenditure, but if you are serious about growing your business get some proper systems on board early on.

A good accounting system won't produce accurate information without the necessary data input, so you need to have the necessary skills on board early to make sure that the basic financial information being produced is both accurate and timely (see 'A finance director's skill set' below). A profit and loss account and balance sheet should be produced by at least the middle of the month following the month being reported.

Another key aspect is that monthly numbers in themselves are only part of the picture. These numbers need to be put into context by comparing them with your budgets and forecasts, and how your business is performing over time. A good financial commentary on the numbers can also highlight any key concerns, trends or opportunities.

Trend information is also helpful, so you can see whether your business is performing better or worse over time. Graphing some of the key numbers can also reveal whether progress is being made. Budgets, forecasts and historic trends are all internal to the business. It makes sense, if you can, to check occasionally how this information compares with comparisons outside your business. Albeit competitor information is only filed at Companies House on an annual basis, a once-a-year comparison with how your competitors are doing can provide some useful insights into your own business.

Key financial numbers to track

Sales levels

Sales levels are the lifeblood of any business. You should be comparing how you have done versus last year, your budget, any revised sales forecast you have done and how this compares with your 'break-even' (see above for importance) level. Also check for trends over time.

Gross margin

The gross margin measures sales less the variable costs of producing those sales. The absolute level of money is important to monitor in the same way as sales above, but also check the percentage of gross margin to sales. The higher you can get this the better as it shows the profit benefit for each additional unit of sale made. For example, if you have a business that generates a gross margin of 40%, for each additional £1,000 of sales, you should expect an additional £400 of profit to flow directly through to your profit line, as other fixed costs shouldn't vary much in the short term. If the gross margin of your business is only 20%, obviously you have got to sell twice as much to get the same profit effect.

Fixed overhead levels

Monitoring the fixed overhead levels is important, as are ways to always be looking at how you can reduce these levels without harming the ability of your business to serve customers.

Net profits

As most businesses need to be making a profit to survive, comparisons with budget, forecast and history and inter-firm comparison are all important as is comparing your profit with sales percentage and with the funds you have invested in the business. The higher your profit per cent the higher return you are making. What you think this should be is all important when it comes to setting targets for your business to achieve. Rather than just taking your costs away from what you think sales will be to get a profit the business delivers, try turning this thinking around. Decide, based on research, what you think your profit percent to sales and funds invested should be, and then consider what you need to do with either your variable cost or fixed overheads to deliver your target profit. You may be surprised to see what this simple change in thinking can deliver.

Cash flow

There are a number of differences between the profit your business is making and the cash it's generating, or not, as the case may be. Make sure you understand those differences and keep monitoring your cash position. Most businesses go bust not because they make a profit or not, but simply because they run out of cash, particularly growing businesses. The absolute level of cash, or overdraft, you have is critical as well as the 'headroom' you have in your funding facilities. 'Headroom' is the difference between your cash balances and the maximum borrowing limits you have set up. A simple example to illustrate this point is shown in Table 4.2.1.

Table 4.2.1 Headroom calculation

You have a maximum borrowing facility with your bank of	£1,000,000
Your current borrowing facility is	£600,000
Headroom	£400,000

You will probably have a mix of funding facilities from different places in your business, and you need to list them all. Typical examples of funding facilities in a growing business are invoice discounting facilities, asset financing facilities, and bank overdrafts (see Chapter 4.3 for details). The mix of funding is critical to understand as not all of it may be available to use. For example you may be able to borrow money for some new equipment on hire purchase (an asset financing facility) but these funds won't be available if you want to invest £100,000 in more stock because your sales are going up and you need the stock to service your customer.

Working capital

Working capital includes debtors (monies your customers owe you), creditors (monies you owe suppliers) and stocks of some form (raw materials, work in progress or finished goods). Most growing businesses will need more working capital as they grow. Cash is required to finance this working capital growth, so ways to 'squeeze' working capital, i.e. reduce it, are important to understand (see Chapter 4.). Monitoring and measuring the amount you have across the different types is important. You need to:

- Review the absolute and amounts
- Check the age of debtors, creditors and stock (older usually indicates problems)
- Check in relation to sales (how long does it take to get paid from customers, how long are you taking to pay suppliers, how quickly are you turning over your stock).

In most businesses, there is the opportunity to release cash from working capital.

Monthly accounts

Figure 4.2.6 shows an example of the basic information you should be reviewing each month as a minimum, and key numbers to keep track of.

Weekly and daily reporting

Although most financial reporting is done monthly, if you can get more regular information, it may help to manage your business better. For example, in a fast-moving business reporting the sales numbers weekly or even daily can enable driving the business performance. Weekly updating of short-term cash projections and measuring performance is also essential for many businesses. The take-home message is – figure out the most important financial measures and track them, where you can, either weekly or daily.

FD Centre - Management Accounts Example
Profit Overview

Profit & Loss Account	Actual									YTD Total	YTD Budget	Forecast			Full Yr
	Oct-06 £000's	Nov-06 £000's	Dec-06 £000's	Jan-07 £000's	Feb-07 £000's	Mar-07 £000's	Apr-07 £000's	May-07 £000's	Jun-07 £000's	£000's	£000's	Jul-07 £000's	Aug-07 £000's	Sep-07 £000's	£000's
Sales	858	786	627	814	759	806	647	733	832	6,862	7,250	872	1,151	1,179	10,064
Gross Margin	351	272	261	339	293	325	231	259	273	2,604	2,828	348	461	471	3,884
GM %age	41%	35%	42%	42%	39%	40%	36%	35%	33%	38%	39%	40%	40%	40%	39%
Overheads	275	318	268	299	276	289	283	177	311	2,496	2,501	289	296	402	3,483
EBIT	76	-46	-7	40	17	36	-52	82	-38	108	327	59	165	69	401
Interest	13	14	14	15	15	15	17	19	19	141	160	20	24	22	207
Net Profit before Tax	63	-60	-21	25	2	21	-69	63	-57	-33	167	39	141	47	194

Highlights

June sales are starting to show increases forecast, but start up costs on project xxx continue to depress margins

Overheads continue in line with Original Budget

YTD small losses reported

Forecast / Risks

Sales Forecasts for the final quarter of the year include the new contract for xxx £650K

Sales Forecasts assume no delay on xxx works and contract forecasts as notified

Margins are assumed to revert to the longer term trend driven by better operational control and higher margins on xxx works

Sept o/heads inc dilaps cost and leasehold w/off for xxxreloca-tion, re-branding costs

Figure 4.2.6

FD Centre Management Accounts - Example

Sales and Profit Graphs

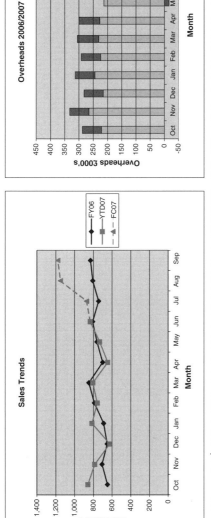

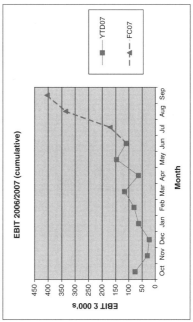

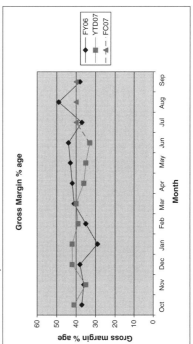

Figure 4.2.6 cont.

FD Centre - Management Accounts Example

Balance Sheet / Cash Overview

Balance Sheet £ 000's	Oct-06	Nov-06	Dec-06	Jan-07	Feb-07	Mar-07	Apr-07	May-07	Jun-07	Budget Jun-07	Jul-07	Aug-07	Sep-07
				Actual							Forecast		
Fixed Assets	3,187	3,233	3,190	3,153	3,141	3,350	3,312	3,558	3,544	3,703	3,596	3,547	3,618
Working Capital													
Stock and Sundries	159	86	155	144	152	198	202	151	402	250	280	280	280
Debtors	1,144	1,491	1,478	1,593	1,203	1,539	1,503	1,828	1,737	1,700	1,755	2,035	2,286
Work in Progress	1,166	1,211	787	978	1,063	846	834	815	969	950	872	1,151	1,179
	2,469	**2,788**	**2,420**	**2,715**	**2,418**	**2,583**	**2,539**	**2,794**	**3,108**	**2,900**	**2,907**	**3,466**	**3,745**
Creditors	691	644	680	531	645	875	764	651	767	651	866	670	894
Sundry Cred. & Acc	422	430	384	325	290	201	254	250	458	403	250	250	250
VAT/Payroll	177	267	358	193	254	288	161	300	291	320	189	330	412
Corp. & Def. Tax	239	239	239	239	567	567	567	567	567	550	427	427	427
	1,529	**1,580**	**1,661**	**1,288**	**1,756**	**1,931**	**1,746**	**1,768**	**2,083**	**1,924**	**1,732**	**1,677**	**1,983**
Working Capital	940	1,208	759	1,427	662	652	793	1,026	1,025	976	1,175	1,789	1,762
Total Assets Less Current Liabilities	**4,127**	**4,441**	**3,949**	**4,580**	**3,803**	**4,002**	**4,105**	**4,584**	**4,569**	**4,679**	**4,771**	**5,336**	**5,380**
Financed By													
Bank & HP Borrowing	2,413	2,790	2,313	2,918	2,468	2,647	2,819	3,235	3,276	3,186	3,437	3,861	3,904
Equity	1,714	1,651	1,636	1,662	1,335	1,355	1,286	1,349	1,293	1,493	1,334	1,475	1,476
Capital Employed	**4,127**	**4,441**	**3,949**	**4,580**	**3,803**	**4,002**	**4,105**	**4,584**	**4,569**	**4,679**	**4,771**	**5,336**	**5,380**

Highlights

Gearing levels increasing on back of asset investment not supported by profit growth

Total borrowing position remains within £100k of budget

Working Capital Control remains a priority

Forecast / Risks

Refer Forecast paper

Consideration needs to be given to alternative funding approaches for 2007/8

Figure 4.2.6   cont.

FD Centre - Management Accounts Example
Working Capital Graphs and Capital Expenditure

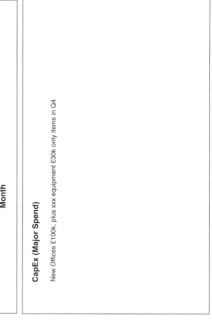

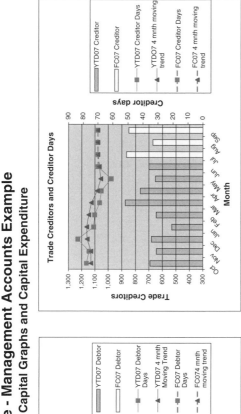

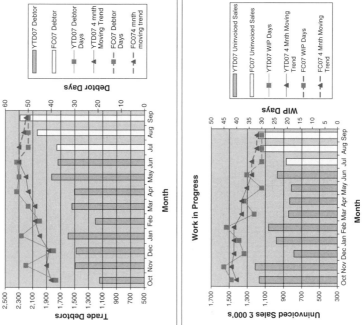

Figure 4.2.6 cont.

Non-financial numbers to track

As well as financial indicators that you should keep track of, all businesses will have many non-financial measures that will be critically important to monitor. Many of these are forward indicators of financial performance. They can be measured monthly, but often weekly or even daily. These measures or indicators are often referred to as key performance indicators or 'KPIs'.

Here are some ideas of what you might consider as KPIs for your business:

Sales
- Sales orders in the 'pipeline' – forward indicator of sales
- New enquiries received – even more forward indicator of sales
- Sales conversation levels – how many sales enquiries the business is converting to sales.

Operations
- Utilisation of key equipment or people – forward indicator of cost and efficiency
- Reject/waste per cent – how efficient you are being in producing goods.

Delivery
- On time in full delivery – measures how well you are delivering what the customer wants.

Safety
- Safety incident rates.

Staff
- Staff turnover – how well you are retaining staff.

SYSTEMS FOR EFFECTIVE DELEGATION

Company: DBI Group
Part-owner and CEO: Matthew Byrne

Matthew Byrne, together with his partner Nick Handover, embarked in 2001 on a major growth pro-gramme for their £6m turnover business, DBI Group. Matthew and Nick had been hands-on managers, but to achieve their aims they recognised they needed to step back from the business a bit, and start working on the business, rather than in the business, and recruit professional managers to run day-to-day operations. They also didn't want to risk losing control of the business as it grew.

Using their part-time FD (see 'Using resources efficiently' below) they set up a series of systems and controls that provided them with weekly and monthly information, where they were able if they wished to drill down to detailed levels of profitability on individual customer contracts, but allowed their manag-ers to run these contracts day to day, only intervening where they could see there were some major problems.

This approach gave them the comfort to spend more time working on the business, and via organic growth and a series of acquisitions they achieved a sale of 2/3 of the then DBI group to Cape plc for £20m in 2006.

Using resources efficiently

You can hire an FD from the growing band of part-time FDs in the market-place

You may have the financial skills and experience required in applying some of the ideas in this chapter to your business. However, if you don't, and even if you do, your time will probably be better spent doing the things that are going to really drive growth in your business. Growth should come first, followed by correct information production, so that you keep control.

To set up, run and manage the information and control systems described above, you need a person with appropriate knowledge and experience. If you run a larger business (about +£25m turnover), you will probably have your own finance director (FD), who has the knowledge and experience to do all this work. If you are a smaller business CEO (a turnover under £1m) you can probably run the business with a bit less information. However, if you are the CEO of a growing business in the middle (turnover between £1m and £25m), on the one hand you do need the information described here to control your business growth, and allow you to concentrate on the things to drive growth, but on the other hand you probably can't afford a full-time FD who has the experience and knowledge to set up, run and manage these systems.

The benefit these days is that you can hire an FD from the growing band of part-time FDs in the marketplace. The FD Centre (www. thefdcentre.co.uk) is the UK market leader in this area, and has a rigorous selection process to make sure it provides only the very best FDs. A quick Google search of 'part time finance directors' will

A FINANCE DIRECTOR'S SKILL SET

- Preparation of budgets and regular financial forecast updates, creating forward visibility of likely performance to check the business is on track against the business model and business strategy developed.
- From these financial forecasts, recommend best use and get best rates in terms of any finance required or how to make best use of cash balances.
- Development of business performance reporting: development of a monthly management accounting pack of information that can be produced quickly, accurately with relevant information, including KPIs, graphical representation, trend information and commentary. This can provide a major benefit in understanding how the business is performing against plan, highlighting issues that required speedy action to resolve.
- Provide direction and guidance to existing accounts team in production of monthly management accounts and the day-to-day operational activities.
- Financial evaluation of business development ideas to quantify any investment, assess risk, report financial returns and recommend action.
- Provide constant support for development of business strategy, sounding board, models and methods to aid business growth and help develop the most effective business plans.
- Liaise with corporate financial advisers as required in terms of merger and acquisition activity, flotation or restructuring possibilities, providing confidence about the business, its professionalism and management capability.
- Support implementation of new business software, advising on accounting issues and best set-up of accounting software to generate meaningful management information.

highlight others that operate in this marketplace. If you think you need a part-time FD, check them out thoroughly and be convinced you can work with them and they understand you and your business and what makes it tick.

In the next chapters, we look at difference ways of external funding available for growing your business, starting with the most familiar one – the banks.

! TOP TIPS

! Make sure you have got an up-to-date 12-month forecast (by month) for profit, cash and balance sheets.

! For tight management of cash flow set up a nine-week rolling receipts and payments Excel spreadsheet, and get it updated every week.

! Know your break-even sales level.

! Set up systems and processes so that the business is less dependent on you. Use authority matrices to enforce this.

! Make sure monthly management accounts are produced so you know where you are.

! Monitor your gross margin per cent and think of ways to improve.

! Always know what your cash headroom is.

! Graph your debtor collection days, supplier payment days and stock holding days. Look for ways to 'squeeze' the business.

! Decide on the most important KPIs for your business, and review them regularly (they should be non-financial as well as financial).

! Get a part-time FD.

GROWTH FUNDING: HOW MUCH WILL YOUR GROWTH NEED?

THIS CHAPTER WILL DISCUSS:

- Accurately calculating your ingoings and outgoings

- How much do you need?

- Creating capital internally through adjusting your business

Gerard Burke, Director, Business Growth and Development Programme (BGP) Cranfield School of Management

Whatever strategic direction you propose to pursue to grow your business, it is almost certain to require money. The constant search for funds is not in itself necessarily a cause for concern. It usually takes a while for the business cycle to move from strategic ideas to profit and from profit to positive cash generation and so, as long as you are growing, more money will be needed.

What should concern you, however, is where that money comes from. There are two main sources of money: internal and external. Getting the right balance of funds from these different sources is one of the keys to profitable growth – and perhaps even to survival itself.

This chapter will help you identify how much cash you will need to grow your business, through simple calculations that allow you to pin down accurately the money coming in and going out of your company. Understanding where your money is going will give you a handle on which areas of the business you can tighten up to encourage growth and how much finance you need to expand further. You will also find out about internal sources of funds, including squeezing working capital and ways of making more profit.

Accurately calculating your ingoings and outgoings

You need cash to do two things:

- Fund working capital – debtors, stock, suppliers, etc.
- Fund any capital investment – new plant, equipment, factory, etc.

Funding working capital is the most challenging because you have to understand the way cash comes in and goes out of your business. So let us start with the most difficult area – calculating working capital.

By changing the way your business is run, you can create additional funds, reducing the amount needed for further expansion or allowing you to borrow more to accelerate growth if necessary

Calculating the working capital requirement

Some businesses will have no real working capital requirement: a window cleaner, for example, where there is no physical product. But most businesses do buy-in some materials to sell on later, either as a product or together with a service. Probably, if they are selling to another business, they will have to give credit and, with a bit of luck, they will get some credit from their suppliers.

Let us look at an example to see how the requirement for working capital can become sizeable. Ashcroft Engineering buys in raw materials which it marks up and sells on to its customers. Table 4.3.1 shows: sales, cost of sales, gross profit (all figures are shown excluding VAT and come from the profit and loss account).

Table 4.3.1 Ashcroft Engineering sales and gross profit		
Sales	100%	£2,500,000
Cost of sales	60%	£1,500,000
Gross profit	**40%**	**£1,000,000**

The business holds a lot of stock to make sure it can satisfy its customers. When the management looked at the balance sheet, they found that they had stock at the year end that was worth £430,000, or around 105 days worth. The figures used to calculate this are shown in Table 4.3.2. The number of stock days (105) is arrived at by dividing the cost of sales by value of remaining stock (3.49), which is then divided into the number of days in a year (365).

Table 4.3.2 Ashcroft Engineering stock	
Value of remaining stock	£430,000
Cost of sales	£1,500,000
Stock days	105

There were further surprises in store when management looked at who owed them money (the company's debtors). The balance sheet showed that they were owed £482,877 (including VAT). Knowing that

Ashcroft's sales were £2,500,000, or £2,937,500 including VAT, a quick sum revealed that it was giving its customers an average 60 days' credit. The figures used to calculate this are shown in Table 4.3.3. The number of debtor days is arrived at by dividing sales by debtors and then dividing this figure (6.08) into the number of days in a year.

Table 4.3.3 Debtor days

Debtors (including VAT)	£482,877
Sales (including VAT)	£2,937,500
Debtor days	60

Next, they converted their cost of sales figure to a VAT inclusive figure, which was £1,762,500, and compared this to the outstanding trade creditors figure in the balance sheet, which was £265,582 (including VAT). They found they were taking on average 55 days to pay their suppliers. The figures used to calculate this are shown in Table 4.3.4. As before, the creditor days figure is arrived at by dividing cost of sales including VAT by trade creditors including VAT, and then dividing this number (6.62) into the 365 days. This again came as slight shock as Ashcroft's standard suppliers' terms were 30 days. No wonder some suppliers were always chasing them and sometimes refusing to supply them.

Table 4.3.4 Creditor days

Trade creditors (including VAT)	£265,582
Cost of sales (including VAT)	£1,762,500
Creditor days	55

When all this was put together, it gave a very good picture of Ashcroft's working capital requirement, revealed in Table 4.3.5. In addition to showing each figure in days, which had already been calculated, the figures were displayed as a percentage of sales (excluding VAT). The reason for this is that, since most profit forecasts show sales excluding VAT, it makes sense to have a working capital requirement model that reflects this. The management was surprised to find that for each pound of sales about £0.25 would be needed to finance working capital. Table 4.3.5 shows how this is made up.

Table 4.3.5 Current working capital

Working capital requirement	Days	% of sales
Current assets:		
Debtors	60	19
Stock	105	17
		36
Less creditors:		
Trade	55	11
Net current assets (working capital)		**25**

It's now clear how the business is run: customers pay in 60 days, suppliers are paid in 55 days, and 105 days' worth of stock are held. And there is a very good measure of how much working capital the business needs to fund the level of business. Assuming there are no changes, Ashcroft's managers could predict the working capital requirement for the business if they decided to grow sales by 35% to £3,375,000. If the business does this, it will need to find an additional £226,553 cash. This is calculated by taking 25% of current sales of £2,500,000 away from 25% of proposed sales of £3,375,500 (£873,848 – £647,295 = £226,553) – see the summary in Table 4.3.6. It's just as well to know this kind of information before you start off on a rapid growth plan.

Table 4.3.6 Working capital required for growth

Working capital requirement	Days	% of sales	Current sales (£)	Proposed sales (£)
Current assets:			2,500,000	3,375,000
Debtors	60	19	482,877	651,884
Stock	105	17	430,000	580,500
		36	**912,877**	**1,232,384**
Less creditors:				
Trade	55	11	265,582	358,536
Net current assets (working capital)		**25**	**647,295**	**873,848**

So now we have a dynamic model of the working capital requirement for this business if it grows but does not change. But what if you want to grow and improve your business at the same time? What effect would this have on the working capital requirement?

Let us look at Ashcroft Engineering again. It has decided as a prelude to growth that it is going to improve its business. Its managers have proposed to put up prices by 15%, chase customers faster and harder to get debtor days down to 40 days (its terms are 30 days), and reduce stock to 70 days. They anticipate that the business will lose customers and sales will fall by 5% as a result. At the same time, they plan to pay their suppliers within 40 days. How will the new Ashcroft Engineering look alongside the old? The figures in Table 4.3.7 summarise the before and after picture.

Table 4.3.7 Effect on working capital of improving business

	Current position		Proposed position		Benefit from action	
Sales (£)	12,500,000		2,375,000		−125,000	
Margin (%)		40		55		15
Gross profit (£)		1,000,000		1,306,250		306,250
Working capital:	Days	%	Days	%		
Debtors	60	19	40	13		
Stock	105	17	70	11		
Less creditors:	55	−11	40	−8		
Working capital/ sales ratio (%)		25		16		−9
Working capital (£)		647,295		380,000		−267,295
Other benefits:						
Interest costs						Reduced
Asset investment						Reduced
Fixed costs						Held/reduced
Gearing						Reduced

Working capital – before and after

Looking at these figures, you would hardly recognise Ashcroft Engineering as the same business – the financial transformation is almost too good to be true. Despite reducing sales, each sale made has much better margin and gross profit contribution – up £306,250. And assuming fixed costs (overheads) remain the same, net profit will also be improved by the same amount. The reduced volume of business and improved working capital requirement (just 16% of sales as opposed to 25%) means some £267,295 less working capital is required. That will ease the overdraft position, which will cut interest costs and reduce gearing. Reduced sales will ease the pressure on the need for new capital investment and help keep the lid on fixed costs.

A working capital model like this one for Ashcroft Engineering can be used to grow and improve your business. To get the complete picture, all you need is to add the cash required for any fixed asset investment. There is no need to make it any more complex than that. It shows that by changing the way your business is run, you can create additional funds, reducing the amount you need to raise for further expansion or allowing you to borrow more to accelerate growth if necessary.

How much do you need?

To calculate the complete funding picture, follow these steps:

1. Calculate the working capital requirement (NCA) – done
2. Calculate the net fixed asset required (NFA) – done
3. Add NCA and NFA to get the total funding requirement
4. Deduct what the shareholders can provide
5. What is left is the actual borrowing requirement.

Let us see how this works with Ashcroft Engineering, which has decided to grow sales from the current £2,5000,000 to £3,375,000, but without making any of the improvements shown above. To achieve this, its managers will need £226,553 extra cash (as calculated earlier) to meet their working capital (NCA) requirement. Let us also assume that they have decided to invest another £200,000 in fixed assets (NFA) to help make sure they can meet the extra business. In total, they will need £426,553 to meet their total funding requirement. This should be met first from shareholders' funds and then from borrowing.

If sales do grow from £2,500,000 to £3,375,000, this is an increase in sales of £875,000. If they achieve the gross profit of 40%, these sales will produce an additional £350,000 of net profit (40% of £875,000 assuming no extra overheads. If the shareholders leave this profit in the business, the managers still need to find an additional £76,553 (£426,553–£350,000). That's a reasonable sum to negotiate with their bankers, making this a bankable deal. These figures are shown in Table 4.3.8.

Table 4.3.8 Calculating the funding requirement

1. NCA requirement	£226,553
2. NFA requirement	£200,000
3. Total funding requirement	£426,553
4. Less shareholders (improved profit)	£350,000
5. Additional borrowing (balance)	**£76,553**

Now let us look at a more extreme situation. Assume that Ashcroft Engineering is struggling. Its managers are contemplating growing sales, but the business was going to make a loss of £75,000 in each of the two growth scenarios we are going to look at. The figures in Table 4.3.9 assume gearing of 50% (i.e. matched funding between the bank and shareholders). Sales grow, but the business incurs losses and makes asset investments. The total funding requirement becomes astronomical and the additional investment by both shareholders and the bank becomes unrealistic.

In the base year where sales are £2,500,000, the shareholders are funding the business to the tune of £323,648 (see Table 4.3.10), which we assume is being matched by the bank. However, as the ambitious sales growth plan escalates through £4,000,000 and up to

Table 4.3.9 Funding growth when loss making 1

Sales		£2,500,000		£4,000,000		£5,000,000
1. Ratio of NCA to sales	25%	£647,295		£1,000,000		£1,250,000
2. Additional fixed asset investment		£0		£200,000		£200,000
3. Proposed loss		£0		£75,000		£750,000
4. Total funding requirement		**£647,295**		**£1,275,000**		**£2,200,000**
Shareholders funding	50%	£323,648		£637,500		£1,100,000
Borrowing requirement	50%	£323,648		£637,500		£1,100,000
Total funding		**£647,295**		**£1,275,000**		**£2,200,000**

£5,000,000, we can see that, as a result of the proposed loss and fixed asset investment, both the shareholders and the bank would have to more than triple their support of the business. Since the business is not making any profit for the shareholders to reinvest, this would represent a real investment of extra cash. On the face of things, this plan is not fundable.

What the figures in Table 4.3.10 demonstrate quite clearly is that growth and losses are, by and large, unfundable. Assuming that the shareholders could not make the further investment to support the gearing of 50% at sales of £2,500,000, it would have to move to

Table 4.3.10 Funding growth when loss making 2

Sales		£2,500,000		£4,000,000		£5,000,000
1. Ratio of NCA to sales	25%	£647,295		£1,000,000		£1,250,000
2. Additional fixed asset investment		£0		£200,000		£200,000
3. Proposed loss		£0		£75,000		£750,000
4. Total funding requirement		**£647,295**		**£1,275,000**		**£2,200,000**
Shareholders funding	50%	£323,648	25%	£323,648	15%	£323,648
Borrowing requirement	50%	£323,648	75%	£951,352	85%	£1,876,352
Total funding		**£647,295**		**£1,275,000**		**£2,200,000**

75% at £4,000,000 and 85% at £5,000,000. This just is not going to happen. Banks, while usually happy to match 50% gearing, are most unlikely to go to 85%.

Creating capital internally through adjusting your business

Surprisingly enough, many businesses have much of the money they need to finance growth already tied up in the firm. It may require a little imagination and some analysis to uncover it, but it can be done.

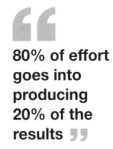

80% of effort goes into producing 20% of the results

Squeeze working capital

Working capital is an area rich in possibilities to release cash for expansion. Debtors and stock control are perhaps the most fertile areas to start.

Debtors

According to research at Cranfield School of Management ('Business finance in today's challenging environment', an independent business finance study, 2003), collecting money from customers is still a major problem for most owner-managed businesses. The difference between the best and worst collection periods across Europe is an extra 48 days of credit. It is salutary to remember that the total cost of providing customers with this extra credit is equivalent to 5.7% of the average business's turnover, and, assuming a net profit margin of 10%, more than half its net profit. Instead of businesses being able to borrow to grow the business, they often need to borrow just to fund their sales ledger.

MAKING BETTER USE OF YOUR WORKING CAPITAL

Here are some things you can do to manage your debtors more closely:

- Consider your terms of trade. Can you ask for part payments up front, or for staged payment? Do you need to allow credit?
- If you are going to give credit, always take trade references and look at the customers' own accounts to see how sound they are
- Make sure that your invoices are accurate so your customers can't query them
- Send out invoices promptly, if possible on delivery
- If you sell on credit, set out when you expect to be paid clearly on your invoices
- Find out when your biggest customers have their monthly cheque run and make sure your bills reach them in time
- Send out statements promptly to chase up late payers, and always follow up with a phone call
- Bank cheques and cash promptly.

Stock control

Stock of all types (raw materials, work-in-progress and finished goods) ties up capital. Minimising the amount of stock, and maximising the speed with which stock flows through the business, are key levers to release working capital.

On the other hand, you need enough stock to meet demand. So, it's important to have detailed and accurate forecasts of demand, and then to match your stock requirements to them. Growing businesses can achieve considerable improvements in stock management by relatively simple changes in the way they purchase and monitor their stocks:

- Have accurate stock records for each item. Regularly review for any slow-moving items
- Regularly forecast your sales for each item. Review forecasts against actual sales to improve forecasts. Match stock and work-in-progress to these forecasts
- Where possible, buy from suppliers with short delivery times

INTRODUCING TIGHT STOCK CONTROL

For businesses that have failed to monitor stock levels closely, the introduction of tight controls can prove daunting. A quick way of making improvements is to grade stock as A, B or C, according to the value of individual items or of the total number held. Items in the A category can provide the greatest savings so subject them to regular stock-takes and study patterns of demand. B and C items can be brought into this programme once it is well established.

- Buy more frequently but in smaller quantities
- Much of the cost of many products is incurred in the final stages of manufacture. Potentially big stock savings can be made by holding stocks of semi-finished items
- Re-examine any automatic stock re-order points to see if lower levels can be set.

Other ways to squeeze working capital

You can also improve your working capital management by managing your own credit and cash better. For instance:

- Take the maximum credit from your suppliers. Once you have a good track record, try to negotiate extended terms with major suppliers
- Make any cash you have work harder. Overnight money markets, now more easily accessible through internet banks, could allow you to get interest on cash
- Work out if it makes sense to pay bills quickly to take advantage of early settlement discounts.

Make more profit and plough it back

Another internal source of finance is to make your present business more profitable and plough that profit back to grow your business.

There are several steps you can take to unlock the extra profit potential in your business.

Recognise the iceberg

Just as the small tip of the iceberg showing above water conceals an enormous mass below, the small(ish) percentage of profits the average business makes (typically under 10% of sales), conceals a great volume of money being used to arrive at that profit. It requires only a few percentage points reduction in costs to dramatically improve profits, as Table 4.3.11 illustrates. In the example in this table, the last profit margin was 5%. Costs – the 'below the water line' mass – are 95% of sales. By reducing those costs by a mere 2%, bottom line profits have been increased by a massive 40% (this is a simplified example from a real life case). This extra profitability can then be used to finance extra investments, saved as a reserve for bad times, or be used to compensate for lower sales.

Table 4.3.11 The effects of cost savings on profits

	Before		After 2% cost saving		Extra profit		But if sales drop...	
	>£000	%	£000	%	£000	%	£000	%
Sales	1,000	100	1,000	100	–	–	714	100
Costs	950	95	930	93	–	–	664	93
Profit	50	5	70	7	20	40	50	7

Use the 80/20 rule

This rule states that 80% of effort goes into producing 20% of the results. Look at Table 4.3.12, which was prepared for a company where 18% of customers account for 78% of sales. A quick glance at figures in your own business will, in all probability, confirm that 20% of your customers account for 80% of your sales, and yet your costs are probably spread evenly across all your customers.

The 80/20 rule can be used across the business to uncover areas where costs are being incurred that are unwarranted by the benefits. Consider the way that sales staff spend their time. A salesman in the company used in the above example was asked where he thought his sales in two years' time would be coming from (see column 3, in the table below). He thought that his top 18% of customers would account for 88% of sales (up from 78% of actual sales this year). And yet, he spent over 60% of his time calling on his bottom 68 accounts, and planned to continue doing so. This activity-based – rather than results-based – outlook was being used to make out a case for an additional salesperson. What was actually needed was a call grading system to lower the call rate on accounts with the least sales potential. This grading process would save costs, eliminate the need for an additional salesperson, and even free up time so the salesman could prospect for new, high-potential accounts.

Table 4.3.12 The 80/20 rule in action

Number of customers		Value of sales		Value of potential sales	
	%	£000	%	£000	%
4	3	710	69	1,200	71
21	18	800	78	1,500	88
47	41	918	90	1,600	94
116	100	1,025	100	1,700	100

Zero-based budgeting

The 80/20 rule is helpful in getting costs back into line – but what if the line was completely wrong in the first place?

When you sit down with your team and discuss budgets, the starting point is usually this year's costs. So, for example, if you spent £25,000 on advertising last year and achieved sales of £1 million, the expense would have been 2.5% of sales. If the sales budget for next year is £1.5 million, then it seems logical to spend £37,500 next year. That, however, presupposes last year's sum was wisely and effectively spent in the first place, which it almost certainly was not.

Popularised by Robert McNamara, zero-based budgeting turns the cost argument on its head. It assumes that each year every cost centre starts from zero spending and, based on the goals of the business and the resources available, arguments are presented for every penny spent, *not just for the increase proposed*.

Cut out mistakes through training

According to a former chief executive of a major bank, basic mistakes by employees account for between 25% and 40% of the total costs of any service business – and not just in banking. Training your people, on a regular basis, in all aspects of their jobs, is a surefire way to reduce mistakes, and get costs down and customer satisfaction up. Training can be one of the fastest payback routes to cost reduction.

Incentivise everyone around profit

Lots of businesses have incentive schemes, but most end up rewarding the wrong achievement. There are always hundreds of reasons for giving people intermediate incentives, such as sales commission. But, unless you build profit targets into your goals and incentives, nine times out of 10 you will end up with the wrong result. Building incentives for everyone around the profit you make focuses the whole business around customers and costs, and that has to be good. It will make everyone look for ways to do things cheaper; to eliminate waste; to spend their time (and your money) more effectively; and to get more money out of more satisfied customers.

Increasing margins

Increasing margins has the double effect of increasing the flow of cash into a business by increasing profits, while at the same time reducing the amount of money tied up in producing low or even no profit items.

To achieve increased margins, you need first to review the mix of your sales. This requires accurate costs and gross margins for each of your products or services. Armed with that information, you can select particular product groups or market segments that are less price sensitive and potentially more profitable.

Pricing

Pricing is one of the biggest decisions your business has to make, and one that it needs to keep constantly under review. It is certainly the decision that has the biggest impact on company profitability. Try comparing the impact on profits of:

- A 5% cut in your overheads
- A 5% increase in volume sales
- A 5% cut in materials purchased
- A 5% price increase.

Almost invariably, the 5% price increase scores the highest, as it passes straight to the net profit, bottom line. Even if volume falls,

WHEELER-DEALER

Company: Strida
Founder: Mark Saunders

Mark Saunders set up a company to sell his innovative folding bicycle, the Strida. When he launched it into the mature 100-year-old bicycle market, he recognised two things: his manufacturer's capacity was strictly limited and his target market was 'well-to-do, city commuters' or 'life-style weekenders'.

He set his price accordingly at nearly £300 per bike. This was well above established competitive models, but gave good margins to dealers in taking up the product and left room for manoeuvre later in the product lifecycle when competition would react to the Strida's unusual features. By selecting a less price sensitive market segment, Strida's margins were maintained at a much higher level than they might otherwise have been had they gone for a blanket approach to the market.

because of the effect price has on gross margin, it is usually more profitable to sell fewer items at a higher price. For example, at a constant gross margin of 30% with a 5% price increase, profits would be unchanged even if sales declined 14%. Yet, if prices were cut 5%, an extra 21% increase in sales would be needed to stand still.

Frequently, resistance to increasing prices, even in the face of inflationary cost rises, can come from your own team members. In these instances, it is important to make detailed price comparisons with competitors.

Working smarter

Making more of your own money rather than having to raise money outside doesn't always have to mean working longer hours. You could just work smarter, and who knows you may even end up working fewer hours than you do now and still make more money.

One way to get everyone's grey matter working overtime is to create smart circles (and smart rewards). You could formalise the process of encouraging employees to rethink the way they work, and reward them in such a way as to make their working environment better still. For example, at Dairyborn Foods, the cheese component business, management decided to develop a culture of working 'smarter not harder'. Any employee can arrange a meeting with other staff members to discuss a new idea or operational change. Every quarter, the managing director presents an award for any outstanding ideas, which is published in the company's newsletter. The award is a sum of money, which has to be spent on things of value to the team, such as an evening out or a photocopier.

As ever, it is important to find the right funding structure for your business, with a balance of profit, equity and debt funding which allows your business to grow at the rate you want it to without bearing too much strain. The next chapter is the first of three chapters that look at how you can fund your growth business, starting with borrowing from banks or taking out a government guaranteed loan.

SAY CHEESE

Company: Dairyborn Foods
Managing director: Robert Segesser

Robert Segesser, managing director of Dairyborn Foods, a cheese component business, spent his first five years in business building sales – £3 million a year's worth – without making much profit. Then he made the company's principal objectives to raise its profit margin from 16% to 25%. This moved the business into what he likes to refer to as 'margin-protected' business. In other words, things that only Dairyborn can do, that certain groups of customers want badly and will pay for. Segesser believed that, if his customers get to the future before he does, they would leave him behind. He had to create solutions for customers' problems before they even realised they had one.

Refocusing on solving problems rather than selling cheese, and aiming for profit margin growth rather than turnover growth alone, has transformed the business into a £15 million sales and £2 million a year profit business. From being worth little, within two years the company had turned away a potential suitor with £20 million on the table.

! TOP TIPS

PREDICTING FINANCIAL NEEDS

! Calculate how much money you can squeeze out of your business.

! Calculate the extra capital required to fund any planned growth in sales.

! Calculate the new funding required to meet your growth objectives.

! Decide which sources of funds would be most appropriate for you.

HOW TO UNLOCK YOUR EXTRA PROFIT POTENTIAL

! Recognise the iceberg – cut back on spending a lot of money for a small amount of profit.

! Use the 80/20 rule – uncover areas where the benefits don't justify the investment.

! Use zero-based budgeting – assume each year that every cost centre starts from zero spending and review every penny spent as well as any forecast spend.

! Train your staff – well-trained staff make fewer mistakes and keep costs low.

! Incentivise round profit – build incentives for everyone around the profit the business makes.

! Increase margins – review your product portfolio and identify products that could make more profit.

! Get your prices right – a 5% price hike can pass straight to your bottom line.

! Work smarter – work more efficiently and keep your workforce motivated.

FUNDING GROWTH 1: DEBT

THIS CHAPTER WILL DISCUSS:

- Types of debt

- Other options for finance

- The importance of being flexible

- How much you can borrow

- The new debt environment

The vast majority of business funding comes from banks. Banks have always had a mixed reputation, and you will find as many business people full of praise for how their bank has helped them as you will critics. Bank funding for growing businesses is attractive in two ways compared with private equity funding: banks usually look for a much lower rate of interest on their money, and they don't take a stake in your company, leaving you in charge of running your business. On the other hand, banks want their money back regardless of how well your business performs – and having too much debt to pay interest on or pay back can sink an otherwise successful business.

Banks have inevitably and appropriately come under an immense spotlight given the near collapse of the world banking system in late 2008. But they continue to provide significant lending to business, and should be the first place you should look for certain sorts of funding. The recent credit crunch does mean that borrowing is no longer as easy as it was, and you might pay a bit more over base rate than you would have done before the downturn – but with interests at an all-time low, it is still likely to be very cheap money.

> **Banks avoid negative publicity, and they are in business to help clients**

Before we go through the different forms of bank debt, it is important to understand the role bank loans can play. Fundamentally, banks aren't set up to provide what they call 'risk capital', which should instead be provided by share capital. A bank is usually keen to lend against specific assets where it can see an existing business that is capable of repaying it. But the price it charges doesn't come even close enough to the rates charged by venture capitalists, so a bank can't take the risk that it will lose all its money. So a brand new company will find it hard to borrow much money, and this is appropriate. It would be rash for banks to take big risks, and any startup is a big risk.

Let's also make clear that by 'banks' here we really mean 'lenders', which includes invoice finance and leasing firms. Leasing and invoice finance are both ways to borrow money, and both can be powerful sources of growth finance. Most banks have subsidiaries that offer these services but there are also many other independent leasing and invoice finance companies.

Types of debt

There are several types of bank debt: overdraft facilities; term loans; mortgages; invoice finance; and leasing and asset-based lending.

Overdraft

An overdraft is a 'facility' that gives you the right to spend more money than you have. It shows up as a negative balance in your bank statement. Banks will charge an arrangement fee to set it up, often 1% of the facility, and then will charge a margin over the base rate that you pay on the amount you actually borrow, typically 3% or 4% for medium-sized businesses. This is more than it used to be in previous years.

Disadvantages: The biggest drawback with overdrafts is that the bank has the right to demand you repay it with as little as 24-hour notice, so you can't rely on it. Overdrafts are supposed to be facilities you dip in and out of, perhaps to pay your staff at the end of the month before your customers pay you. If your overdraft is almost always at full capacity, you aren't using it as it was designed to be used, and you run the risk that the bank might request you to switch to a more appropriate form of borrowing. Overdrafts typically need to be rearranged every year, with a fee for the bank every time.

Term loan

A term loan is a more secure form of borrowing. You borrow a set sum and agree to repay it over a fixed time period, usually two to five years.

Advantages: This money is put into your bank account so you have positive cash balance rather than an overdraft. You will again pay an arrangement fee, as with the overdraft, but you just do that once, when you set up the loan, rather than every year. You also then have the comfort that the bank can't ask for the money back so long as you

> Banks are often helpful, and can build in delays after you take out the loan and before you need to start repaying it

stick to the terms of the agreement. These terms include 'covenants', which are promises your business makes, such as your level of profitability or other borrowings. Covenants assure the bank that you will not do anything so risky as to put the bank's chances of being repaid at risk.

A bank will usually want some form of security for term loans (see below).

Mortgage

A mortgage sounds much more substantial but is basically another way of describing a term loan with a very specific form of security for the bank. The word mortgage simply means a registered charge over one or more assets – often freehold property, but the word mortgage could apply to other assets, too.

Security

The 'S word' for most CEOs – some years ago CEOs used to avoid giving personal guarantees or any other security for loans. Today, especially since the banking issues of late 2008, a bank will usually expect you to provide a strong level of security for their loan.

Disadvantages: If you can't repay the loan according to the terms agreed, the bank will call in the agreed security and use that to repay the money it is owed. The most common types of security will be assets within the business, especially freehold property (expect the

REPAYMENT HOLIDAY

Banks are often helpful, and can build in delays after you take out the loan and before you need to start repaying it. 'Repayment holidays' as these are known, can be for a year or even more if that is what the business needs.

GETTING AROUND SECURITY AGREEMENTS

If you can provide strong evidence of a trading record with consistent, growing cashflow, then you might just avoid the requirement to put up security in the conventional sense (although you will probably still be asked for a personal guarantee). For instance, if your business has sustained cash flow of £1m a year, your bank may be willing to advance credit on the basis of that performance. The principle is straightforward: if your business has performed well over a certain number of years and the bank concludes that you will be able to maintain or improve on that performance, then it may lend against those projections.

bank to lend up to 60% of a recent value for the property), a personal guarantee from several of the directors, or a 'fixed and floating charge over all business assets'. This last form is common and all-encompassing – basically meaning that the bank can take anything from company that it can lay its hands on; usually this will be cash, stock and debtors, though this charge would give the bank the right to take anything else of value also.

Many directors feel concerned about giving personal guarantees. But why should the bank take a risk which you aren't willing to take with your business? Banks don't take major risks; so if you are unwilling to back your request for a bank loan with a personal guarantee, you should consider other forms of growth finance.

Invoice finance

> If invoice financing suits your business, it could revolutionise it

Invoice finance is when a lender pays you in advance a percentage of money owed to you by your customers. The lender gets its money back when your customer pays you. Three decades ago, businesses that used invoice finance were sometimes presumed to be in trouble – this form of borrowing was called 'lending of last resort'. This has changed completely, and many highly successful businesses have grown dramatically on the back of this form of borrowing. If it suits your business, it could revolutionise it.

There are two forms of invoice finance: factoring is where the lender actually collects the debts for you, while invoice discounting is where you continue to collect the money yourself. Factoring is usually more expensive, because it provides credit collection services as well as just lending money, but is widely available for smaller businesses as the lender feels in far better control of the risks than with invoice discounting. Invoice discounting is usually available only to profitable businesses turning over more than £1 million and which have been trading for several years.

Lenders charge in two ways: there is a fee based on a percentage of turnover, to cover the processing and handling of every invoice your business puts through the lender's system. Then there is a lending charge calculated in the same way as an overdraft. When you set up the facility you negotiate what fees and interest rates you will pay. To qualify for factoring and invoice finance, you will need to demonstrate a good spread of clients, with respect to size and number, ideally with no single one dominating, as well as a healthy order book. Typically, banks will also want evidence that you have already done work and issued invoices.

Advantages: Invoice finance is specifically designed to help fund growth. Typically businesses that sell on credit have a substantial working capital need, as they have to pay for raw materials, staff time and overheads before they sell a product or service, and then wait even longer before they get paid. As a business grows, it needs to spend more on stock, staff and so on, while the amount it is owed grows. This working capital need can make a profitable, otherwise successful company insolvent if it is not careful. Invoice finance can help fill this gap. Invoice finance can grow automatically with the business – as the amount your customers owe you grows, so can the amount you can borrow, without you needing to go back to the bank for a larger overdraft or an extra loan. Lenders will usually lend between 75% and 90% of the value of your invoices (including any VAT you charge).

Disadvantages: Invoice finance is not suitable to every business. Retailers, for example, wouldn't have enough invoiced debt to be

WHICH LENDER?

If you are seriously considering invoice finance, do shop around. There are a number of different lenders in this sector, and some might be more suitable for your business than others: some are better at collecting debts than others; some might not want to lend to your business sector while others might; some might take a different view as to how risky your customers are; some will happily lend against export debtors, while others won't; and some offer credit insurance, some will insist on it, whereas others won't mind.

Do ask for references from other bosses of current clients of any lender you are considering. There are a number of business finance brokers who can advise you on which lender might be most suitable for you. The Growing Business website has details of lenders and advisers.

able to use it. And the cost might be too high for some low margin businesses. If your business is not growing, invoice finance is a bad idea because you will be dragging forward the cash that you are owed. A business with even a small drop in revenue will be able to borrow less tomorrow than today, and if it has already spent the money, it could create cashflow problems to repay the difference.

Many businesses sell on terms that allow customers to return some proportion of the goods being sold. Invoice firms understandably don't like 'sale or return' or 'consignment' sales. Some lenders won't touch a business which has even a small element of sale or return, while others will try to understand your business to find a way to provide you with some funding. If you have been trading long enough to establish clear patterns, some lenders will rely on these patterns. You might not be able to borrow quite as much as a company that has no sale or return risk, but what you can borrow might still enable your business to grow, and therefore be worthwhile.

Leasing and asset-based lending

To secure more funding from a bank, you can borrow money against any assets your company may have. This reduces the risk for the lender, because if you can't make the necessary payments, they can seize the asset or assets as compensation.

Before seeking to secure a loan against assets, you need to bear in mind that lenders are looking for something more than an office full of computers. They want goods with a clear second-hand value, such as cars, forklifts, plant or property. These are known as tangible assets, but if you don't have any of these, you may be able to borrow against the value of your intellectual property. Lenders are wary of this because its value can plummet, but if the intellectual property rights are strong enough you might find someone to lend against them. But if you have signed deals with third parties who are using your intellectual property or brand, you can point to measurable value.

Equally, you could sell your equipment to a finance company and then lease it back. The result will be a lump sum that can be used as working capital, with the repayment taking the form of monthly rental payment to the leasing company over an agreed period.

Technically when you lease assets they won't be 'yours' but will belong to the lender, who will rent them to you. This shouldn't make any difference – so long as you get the equipment you want to grow your business, at a sensible price, who owns them shouldn't matter. *Disadvantages*: You should expect to pay slightly more to lease assets than you would for an overdraft as there is more work involved for the lender in enforcing their security should they need to. Most banks have leasing arms and there are also several independent firms. Some specialise in leasing certain sorts of asset, such as planes, motor vehicles, or even shop fittings. GE Capital is one of the larger specialist leasing companies.

EASIER LEASING

Leasing assets at the time when you buy them is easier than leasing used assets. Often manufacturers will provide help with finding a leasing company happy to lease their assets. And other finance companies find the newer assets much easier to value and use as security than used assets.

Other options for finance
Mezzanine finance

As stated above, the usual difference between debt and equity finance is that the bank doesn't take a stake in your company when it advances money. However, mezzanine finance is the exception. It is used most commonly in management buyout (MBO) situations, where the funds offered by banks on a straightforward repayment loan basis (generally referred to as senior debt) and the investment of shareholders is insufficient to get the business off the ground. Mezzanine finance (also known as a subordinated loan) can be used to bridge the gap, providing perhaps 20%–30% of the total required. These days, mezzanine is also used for acquisition finance and in some cases to boost working capital.

The additional sum put forward by the lender to bridge the gap in financing is offered at a higher rate of interest to reflect the additional risk, and in many cases, the deal will involve the bank taking an equity stake in the business or receiving a bonus payment if the company performs particularly well.

Advantages: Repayment is often on an 'interest-only' basis until an agreed percentage of the senior debt (the conventional loan) has been paid off, and although the bank may have a stake in your company, it is a cheaper option than ceding more equity to a venture capitalist.

Disadvantages: Interest rates are considerably higher than those associated with senior debt.

In theory, you can arrange a mezzanine loan independently from the senior debt supplier, but in this era of structured finance, banks tend to offer it as part of an overall package.

Acquisition finance

Although acquiring another company is one of the fastest ways to achieve growth (see Part Three), it's also a strategy that is cash hungry.

MIXING INVOICE AND ASSET FINANCE

Company: Livingston
Financial director: Tom Flynn

Livingston, a pan-European technology-leasing business headquartered in Scotland, used asset finance to fund growth following an MBO in March 2004. The investment bank that backed the MBO wouldn't provide an additional €21m (£14m) required by Livingston to invest in new equipment, such as laptops and telecommunications testing machines, so Livingston's financial director, Tom Flynn, looked to refinance the business. 'We presented to lenders such as GMAC, GE and Lombard, and were looking to secure a deal within six months,' he recalls. The process was complicated by Livingston's international outlook, its high-tech, quick-burn stock and the company's size, which positioned it between small and big business lenders. After some toing and froing between prospective lenders, a broker approached Livingston offering to source a financier.

'They put us in touch with a smaller bank, which was like a breath of fresh air,' said Flynn. 'It understood our business immediately and asked a lot of very pertinent questions, which put us at ease.' With a debtor book worth €14m and rental assets priced at €25m, Livingston opted for a combined invoice discounting and asset-backed borrowing facility. The new bank used specialists to value Livingston's assets and regularly recalculated their worth after the deal.

Meanwhile, Livingston brought in the same trusted law firm that dealt with the MBO to oversee the drawing up of contracts. 'All in all, it was a positive experience,' says Flynn. 'We provide detailed information on a regular basis, but you'd expect that from a complex arrangement.'

In addition to finding the money to make the purchase, you may need funding to develop the enlarged business while taking steps to ensure that you don't run into cashflow bottlenecks. In terms of debt finance, that could mean a term loan, backed by mezzanine finance, as explained earlier, with an invoice discounting facility, where you are advanced money on invoices as soon as they are raised, allowing you to borrow money from the bank as soon as you have billed a client.

An acquisition finance team of a major bank can put together a package based on your needs, but it will look closely at the risks involved and that will mean a degree of due diligence on both companies involved. In addition, the bank will want to look at the business plan for the merged entity to make an assessment on

WHAT BANKS LOOK FOR

Your bank will be less concerned about your growth potential than your ability to repay the loan within the term agreed. Depending on the complexity of the funding package and the perceived risk, it may also carry out due diligence to assure itself that your company has the ability to service the debt. So you should expect a lender to look carefully at your business plan and they may also take an active interest in whether you have the right mix of skills in your management team to meet your objectives. It's not just the quality of the directors that the bank will be assessing, but also their commitment.

Generally speaking, bankers feel reassured if borrowers are also putting up some money, as your friendly business bank manager is keen to know that you also have something to lose, so they can be sure that the interests of lender and borrower are aligned.

whether it's likely to deliver a cashflow that is commensurate with the proposed loan. Human elements, such as the impact of directors leaving, will also be taken into consideration.

Some sectors lend themselves to acquisitions. For instance, in healthcare many small nursing home businesses in themselves make very little money, have little room for organic expansion and suffer from high administration costs against revenue. Join them together, however, and the revenues rise while the administration costs remain relatively static. By and large bankers smile on these kind of deals.

Disadvantages: Loans for acquisitions tend be relatively short term, as business plans tend to foresee a rapid return. However, you should ensure that the bank is inclined to be flexible should things not work out as planned.

The importance of being flexible

When looking to borrow for growth, aim to build flexibility into your agreement with the lender where possible. As circumstances change, the loan or overdraft you agree today may not be enough in two years' time. This may be easier than you think, as banks tend to use their stated commitment to the ongoing support of businesses as a selling point. This means they are usually open to debts being renegotiated or restructured and can be refreshingly flexible – but allow plenty of time to arrange any change as your bank won't always be able to give you what you are after.

The 2008 crisis in the financial sector does mean that banks have become far more risk averse, and you can't assume that an overdraft

PREPARE FOR SCRUTINY

Company: Metropolis AV & FX
Chief executive: Simon Harris

'We see it in terms of a relationship rather than a deal,' says Simon Harris, chief executive of Metropolis AV & FX, a supplier of lighting and audio equipment to the entertainment and hospitality industries. The company – which counts theme parks, nightclubs, pubs and fitness centres among its clients – has recently secured a package of restructuring finance that will enable it to invest in the relatively new technology of LED lighting, currently one of the hot buttons of the electronics sector. Agreed with HSBC, the package included three main elements: invoice discounting, asset finance and a long-term loan to provide cash.

According to Harris, the company was not necessarily sold on the idea of bank finance before it began discussions with HSBC. But it quickly became apparent that the bank had experts on hand who could not only draw up a comprehensive finance package, but who also took an informed interest in the business itself and the market it was seeking to address. 'They wanted to understand the electronics market and the likely impact of LED technology. And their level of understanding was pretty high,' recalls Harris. But it wasn't only the market that was assessed by the lender. With the cash element of the package coming in the form of an unsecured loan, the bank was at pains to assure itself that it was backing a viable business. That meant that the quality of the company's management came under scrutiny, as did its trading record. Harris believes this third-party involvement with the company did have a positive effect.

'It did mean that we had to look at the strengths and weaknesses of the management team,' he says. 'We took on a new director as a result.' While Harris described the due diligence process undertaken by the bank as 'arm's length' when compared to the hurdles that his company might have been required to jump had it gone to a venture capitalist, the Metropolis experience illustrates that anyone seeking a significant amount of bank finance should be prepared to see the lender take a long look at all aspects of the company before it puts any cash on the table.

you have today will be either extended or renewed when the current deal runs out. What's more, on larger funding packages banks have been imposing much more onerous terms and conditions – the so-called banking covenants – and are more likely to pull the plugs if the agreed rules are breached. This shouldn't worry you unduly, especially if you take the time and effort to gain your bank's confidence in your operation. The key is not to take the bank's largesse for granted. Bankers don't like shocks. So talk to them well in advance about possible problems, and if your business is basically sound, the chances are they will support you with additional cash. Ask for additional funds if you are just days or weeks away from a financial crisis and your plea is likely to fall on deaf ears. Keep the lines of communication open and they are far more likely to receptive to any funding requests.

It is far cheaper and better for banks to allow businesses facing difficulty to trade on and have a chance to repay the loans in due course than to shut a business down at the first sign of trouble. Banks avoid negative publicity, and they are in business to help clients – they genuinely do want to help. They all also have divisions which can help businesses facing tough times. It is natural to try to hide bad news from your bank manager, but the best policy is to be open and honest, so that your bank manager can help.

To secure more funding from a bank, you can borrow money against any assets your company may have

How much you can borrow

The amount of funding a bank will offer you largely depends on your company – the nature of the business, the assets it possesses (as these provide something the loan can be secured against), how it is performing and its previous borrowing record – along with what you want the money for. So, ultimately, this is decided on a case-by-case basis.

The amount you are offered can also depend on the bank. Some have particular expertise in certain sectors or business strategies, such as acquisitions or MBOs, and their understanding of what you need the money for will influence their willingness to lend and the amount they are prepared to put on the table.

You may even get different decisions within a bank depending on who you talk to, so it's worth taking time to make sure you are dealing with the right individual and department. If you are getting answers you are unhappy with from one bank manager, ask another – possibly in a different department of the same bank, or at a different bank altogether. If you get on well with your bank manager, and he or she can't lend you what you need, they might introduce you to a different part of the same bank that could help. Your accountant or lawyer might well know someone at another bank who might be keen to lend to businesses like yours – it's always worth asking.

The answer to how much you can borrow is how much a lender thinks you can comfortably afford to repay, and how much security can you offer. You stand to be offered more if your business is sound, you have a good track record and have assets that you are prepared to secure.

The new debt environment

The key reason behind the credit crunch that plunged the world into a global economic crisis in 2008 was banks and finance houses being more than a little too free and easy with their lending. Too many people unable to pay put many institutions on the verge of collapse, and it will take a long time for confidence to build.

All this means that there have been easier times to borrow money, but as stated previously, companies that are performing well with strong teams and assets should be able to find a lender willing to advance sensible funds they need for growth. But, yes, banks are cautious, will charge a higher margin, though interest rates have fallen to unprecedented low rates, meaning that debt is still about as cheap as it has been since the second world war. Banks have also committed to the government that they will continue to lend to business.

If your business growth needs more money than you can borrow, you will need to either take on an investor who will buy new shares in your company, or adjust your growth plans. Read the next the chapter to find out more about this approach to funding.

THE SMALL FIRMS LOAN GUARANTEE SCHEME

One manifestation of government attempts to make life easier for Britain's entrepreneurs is the Small Firms Loan Guarantee Scheme. Primarily aimed at businesses that have previously tried and failed to secure bank support, the scheme applies to loans of between £5,000 and £50,000 for new ventures, with the maximum rising to £250,000 if your business has been up and running for two years or longer. To be eligible, your company's turnover must be between £3m and £5m, so criteria are quite tight.

Under the rules of the scheme, the business borrows from a bank, with the Department for Business Enterprise and Regulatory Reform guaranteeing the loan in return for payment of 2% per annum on the outstanding debt. However, the department doesn't intervene in negotiations about the cost of the loan itself or the term, as these details are a matter for the lender in its client. Although the government remains committed to the scheme, it is undertaking a review of its effectiveness, as one particular perceived problem is insufficient attention to the quality of the businesses that benefit from the initiative.

! TOP TIPS

! There are several types of bank debt: overdraft facilities; term loans; mortgages; invoice finance; and leasing and asset-based lending.

! Other options for finance include mezzanine funding and acquisition finance.

! When looking to borrow for growth, aim to build flexibility into your agreement with the lender where possible.

! Talk to banks well in advance about possible problems, and if your business is basically sound, the chances are they will support you with additional cash.

! The amount of funding a bank will lend depends on your company: the nature of the business, the assets it possesses, how it is performing and its previous borrowing record – along with what you want the money for.

! Although lenders are more cautious now, companies that are performing well with strong teams and assets should be able to find a lender willing to advance funds they need for growth.

FUNDING GROWTH 2: INVESTORS

THIS CHAPTER WILL DISCUSS:

- The role of investors in growth businesses

- What investors are looking for

- Finding potential investors for your business

- Successfully pitching to potential investors

- Due diligence

- Negotiating with investors: understanding the small print

- Living with investors

- The exit

Like anything, there are pros and cons of taking on investors, which we will discuss in this chapter. Some CEOs decide they don't want to take on investors because of the cons, instead preferring to grow more slowly. Others do take on investors – some find it was the best decision they made while others may have regrets. You should think long and hard about what you want – would you prefer to have a larger stake in a smaller business, or a smaller stake in a larger business? While reading this chapter, bear in mind that it's much easier not to take on investors than it is to buy them out once you have taken them on.

The role of investors in growth businesses

If your business growth needs more money than you can borrow, you can either take on an investor who will buy new shares in your company, or adjust your growth plans. Investors fall into two broad types: business angels and venture capitalists (VCs). These differ in some ways, but both are looking for the same sort of businesses to invest in, and will have broadly the same impact on the companies they back. And both will buy shares in your company – which they will want to sell for a substantial profit some time later.

A business angel is someone like the 'dragons' on *Dragons Den* – a wealthy individual who invests money and time in other people's businesses, usually as a sideline. Business angels are mostly successful business people in their own right, and are mostly far lower profile than the dragons. There are so many business angels that, collectively, they invest far more money every year in small businesses than VCs. They will often also invest in earlier stage businesses than VCs.

A VC is a business that exists just to invest money (often other people's money, which it raises in discrete chunks called 'funds') in fast growth businesses. Many people use the terms venture capitalist

Both angels and VCs will get a little involved in your business, providing help, advice and contacts

and private equity (see box below) interchangeably, though, so it can sometimes be a bit confusing.

In the UK, much of the venture capital money available is channelled through venture capital trusts (VCTs). A VCT is a capital fund quoted on the AIM, which VCs set up to attract money from individual investors and institutions, and which they then invest in a portfolio of companies.

Both angels and VCs will:

- Get a little involved in your business, providing help, advice and contacts. Typically they will also put a non-executive director (see Chapter 4.1) on the board to represent their interests. You should expect to have the right to approve who this is
- Prefer to back businesses that are likely to grow fast, and which will make it easy to get their money back – usually three to five years after the investment (this is called an 'exit'). This means that the investors will sell their shares in your company, and this usually happens when the whole company gets sold (which means you would probably need to sell your shares, too) or when the company floats on the stock market. If your company is unlikely to be large enough to float on the stock market, then you would need to be willing to sell the business.

PRIVATE EQUITY VS VCs AND ANGELS

The term 'private equity' has received much negative press in recent years; it's a phrase that has come to be associated with very large funds that have bought some of Britain's better known businesses, such as Debenhams, the AA and Saga. Although VCs and business angels are technically in the same broad category as 'private equity', they have very different characteristics from the large buyout firms written about so much in the press. The main difference is that private equity firms invest considerably more in a business than a VC – typically hundreds of millions of pounds or more; they will often also want to buy a majority stake in a business, whereas a VC or business angel will usually invest considerably smaller sums and will not want a majority stake.

Many businesses have taken on outside investors and thrived because of it. Innocent Drinks, Green & Blacks, Federal Express, Google, Boden, and Cobra are just some of the success stories that have been made possible by outside investors. If you want to grow to £50 million in revenue or more, reasonably rapidly, it may well be the only way.

How much money will investors put in your business?

Typically business angels will invest amounts between £10,000 and £100,000 each in a business – the average is £25,000 per angel. Angels often invest alongside other angels so a group of angels could fund a few hundred thousand pounds. There are some who have invested over £1m in a single business, although this is rare. Because angels usually invest as part of a group (which they often call a syndicate), the amounts typically raised from angels range between £50,000 and £250,000 in total.

> **It is probably easier to raise between £1m and £5m than to raise £750,000**

Most VCs invest more than this – they vary considerably, but many won't invest less than £1m. There is no real upper limit to how much money you can raise if your plan is good enough. Ocado, the home delivery grocery retailer, has raised several hundred million pounds from its investors, for example. That is unusual, but shows what can be done, and several companies have raised more than £10m from investors.

REGIONAL VENTURE CAPITAL FUNDS

Regional Venture Capital Funds are government-initiated VC funds that are available in every region of England, which invest between £50,000 and £250,000 in businesses. They work very well and are well worth considering on their own or in perhaps alongside some angel funding.

It is probably easier to raise between £1m and £5m than to raise £750,000. This is because there are more VCs that want to invest more than £1 million than those that want to invest less than that – the costs of making an investment and managing that investment are no different whether the investor has put in £10,000, £100,000, or £5m. All those investments need finding, negotiating, researching, and ongoing monitoring. So the profit for the investor is much greater if they can invest more money in each company they back.

Non-financial help from investors

Experienced investors also bring a huge amount of expertise to the table

The right investor should make a demonstrable difference to your business's growth. As your company grows, the value of an investor's holding rises and they profit when the shares are sold. For many companies, third-party investment is the catalyst that kicks the business to a higher level, and not just because of the money. Experienced investors also bring a huge amount of expertise to the table. They advise on strategy, open doors to new opportunities and, often most important of all, provide invaluable contacts. If you want to break into a new market, scale up through acquisition or simply make the business more efficient, private equity investors often have the skills available to help you to do just that.

Sometimes the mere fact of being associated with an investor can help. Think about Levi Roots's business, Reggae Reggae Sauce. When Dragon Peter Jones agreed to invest in the business on television, it gave the brand instant credibility and appeal. And Peter Jones spoke to a few people he knew, and persuaded major supermarkets to stock the product, which then took off.

Some businesses like the idea of having a large group of angel investors in order to directly grow income. The Cinnamon Club is one of London's top restaurants, and deliberately sought investment from a wide group of London investors as it wanted them to treat it as 'their own' restaurant, which worked well, providing a steady base of business and a team of unpaid 'evangelists' telling their friends about the great new restaurant. Meetingzone is a highly successful telephone conference call business; it raised money from business angels who introduced it to a number of contacts at large businesses, significantly reducing the time it would have taken to build up its sales without those introductions.

What investors are looking for
Capital growth

Above all, business angels and VCs are looking for capital growth – they want to find businesses which will make their money worth far more in a few years' time. But how much is far more? Certainly more than many CEOs expect. Each investor will have their own criteria, but you should expect that investors will want to grow the value of their investment by between 25% and over 50% per year. Typically, VCs will want a higher return than angels. Although that is clearly more than the cost of a bank loan, bear in mind that loans get repaid regularly whereas money used to buy new shares in your company never gets repaid. And every good investment has to fund several poor ones that don't work.

The question is whether or not it represents value for you – is it worth it? For the many CEOs who have no other way to achieve their ambitions, it is.

Business plan

As evidence of the potential of your business, investors will need to see a well-researched and thought out business plan. There are several books available explaining how to produce a business plan; Business Plan Services, in association with London Business School, has written probably the best – *Successful Business Plans*.

WHERE INVESTORS ADD VALUE

The received wisdom is that bringing in private investors adds value to a company, but how does that work out in practice?

First and foremost they are likely to have a network of influential contacts, whether potential clients, suppliers or even other investors. They can also help mould management teams and offer sound commercial business advice. Many also act as mentors, working with board members to improve their performance.

Second, in some cases the presence of investors provides reassurance for those who come in at a later stage. For instance, David Kilpatrick, founder of technology company Eden Brook, found that his VC investors relied on the company's angels to tacitly rubber-stamp key decisions and cites one example where, having networked at a senior level with no luck, the angel brokered an introduction with the prospect's managing director. 'For the client it removed the risk of engaging with a relatively young business,' he says. They can also bring structure. One of Extreme Group founder Al Gosling's angels helped establish much more professional investor relations practices within the business. According to Gosling, this proved invaluable as the company expanded rapidly.

FreshMinds co-founder Caroline Plumb points to a third area of value. She had received valuable advice from investors when her company was negotiating a contract with an FTSE 100 customer. 'They made sure we didn't expose ourselves on the contract,' she says. 'They pushed us to negotiate on areas such as liabilities, which we would have given more ground to in client negotiation. We were worried we'd lose the whole thing and were so excited we would have let them get away with more than they should have.' Similarly, Innocent Drinks' angel played devil's advocate and challenged their thinking, says co-founder Adam Balon, and also encouragingly pushed for international expansion.

Fourth, sector knowledge can also be invaluable. Gemma Lewis, founder of clinic Preventicum, cites an example of an investor with experience in the property sector. He helped her business secure premises and agreed the lease. Meanwhile, another investor, from the hospitality sector, helped source staff uniforms and crockery.

The management team

The single most important aspect of your business for potential investors is your management team. Investors know that a great management

---

TEAM MAKE-UP

Investors generally don't like businesses where there is just one member of the management team (you!) or husband and wife or other partner teams, as there are too many things which can go wrong.

---

team will usually produce better results from an average idea than an average management team will produce from a great idea. The quality of your team is more important than the idea itself. This doesn't mean that you have to have every member of the management team you will eventually need in place already – rather, it means that there is a strong base already, and that you demonstrate a willingness to build the team over time. Your investors will probably want to help you with that, and it's one of the areas they can often add the most value. A good management team will be one which has good experience of the areas most critical to your business, and which can demonstrate successful business management in the past.

Enthusiasm to succeed

Investors will also want to ensure that you and your management team are sufficiently hungry for success. They know just how much hard work it takes to build a business, and will want to be satisfied that you will all be willing and able to put that effort in.

Investors will also want to see that you will 'hurt' if the business goes wrong. Usually this means that they expect you all to have invested your own money in the business. This doesn't necessarily mean hundreds of thousands of pounds, rather, they want to make sure that you will be significantly financially hurt if the business fails. They don't want it to be easy for you to walk away when the going gets tough (which is fair enough if given that they are putting up serious money to back your plans).

Niche markets

Investors like ambitious companies working in markets that have a high barrier to competitor entry. Often they will also expect candidates for investment to have an international outlook. This is particularly true in the technology sector, where it's unlikely that a UK company would have a sufficiently large home market for, say, a specialist business software product, to generate sufficient growth.

Most investors have very strong sector guidelines. A small number will invest in most general businesses, but most specialise in a small number of sectors. This makes it easier for them to know what is going on and decide which businesses are worth backing, and also for them to add value to you.

Finding potential investors for your business

At an early stage, we let them know what we were doing, even if it was too early for them to come aboard

The vast majority of angel investment is by people known to the CEO raising money, or to friends of friends. Suppliers can be a useful place to consider, too. There are also several organisations that aim to match businesses seeking funding to angels looking to invest. These are typically regionally focused, as most angels don't like to invest in a business more than an hour's travelling time away from them. Some useful contacts to start with are:

- London Business Angels Network (ADD URL) – one of the biggest and oldest established networks
- Beer and Partners (ADD URL) – this company has one of the best track records in recent years of raising money for businesses
- British Business Angel Association (www.bbaa.co.uk) – provides advice for UK companies in search of angel finance and also provides an online directory of individual investors and syndicates
- Your local Business Link office – this will also provide advice and contacts

---

HOW LONG WILL IT TAKE?

You should expect to get lots of rejections before you find someone to invest in your business, and you will need to devote considerable time to the process of raising the money. It would be rare to raise money in much less than six months, which can seem an eternity to a hungry CEO, so start looking early!

- Your accountant, lawyer or bank manager – they might also know of angels or networks near you.

  Finding venture capitalists is a similar process:

- Online directories – check these out, such as Venture Capital Reports
- The VCs trade association website (www.bvca.co.uk)
- Networking – this is invaluable, especially within certain industry sectors such as technology
- Accountants – some accountants are well connected with the venture capital community, and an introduction to a VC from an accountant they know will help open the door. If your current accountant doesn't have good VC contacts it might be worth finding a new firm which does; the medium-sized firms are probably your best bet.

Successfully pitching to potential investors

It's possible to go through the funding process on your own, but many companies hire the services of a corporate financier. Financiers can be expensive, but a third-party expert on the books can make the process of securing finance on favourable terms considerably easier.

Good advisers can help your company address the investment-readiness issues that could make or break a deal. So if your business

> **It is worth rehearsing the pitch in the comfort of your offices to iron out any flaws and identify weaknesses**

DOING THE GROUNDWORK

Company: Video Island
Founder: Saul Klein

Saul Klein discovered the benefits of making an early start looking for funding. His online DVD-rental service Video Island is a great example of a business that should light the imaginations of potential investors. In September 2003, Klein picked up £2.1m from VC's Index Ventures and Benchmark Capital, which specialised in dot com companies and had backed online success stories such as eBay and Betfair. As the co-founder of The Electronic Telegraph, the world's first daily newspaper on the internet, and Fantasy Football, Klein's online credentials were impressive, to say the least. But when he started his latest venture, he still made a point of putting in the groundwork to make raising funding as smooth a process as possible.

'Starting up a company like this is easy, it's carrying on that's hard because you need a lot of growing capital,' says Klein. 'We talked to individuals in the VC and private equity world right from the off. At an early stage, we let them know what we were doing, even if it was too early for them to come aboard. Then, when the timing was right, we would have a much better idea of who our ideal partners would be.' But even with all his connections and experience, Klein had to make sure he could demonstrate an acute market awareness and show his business would operate differently to US market leader Netflix, rather than cutting-and-pasting its strategy. Instead, he impressed them by going the partnership route, linking Video Island's service through major players such as MSN.

'The clever ones recognised that the UK and European markets are different, and we would have to do something to compete with the large national brands,' he says. So thorough research, business credentials and market knowledge worked for Klein. 'It was critically important to have investors who shared my vision,' he concludes.

plan isn't investible, the management team is weak or you need more time to improve your software systems, they will tell you and, if possible, help you put those problems right. Once the basics are in place, they will introduce you to the investors most likely to back your company, including those who might not have let you through the door unless professional help had been at hand to make the connection. A non-executive director or chairman may also provide similar contacts. Last but not least, they will help you prepare your pitch.

Most investors will expect to see a business plan before agreeing to see you, but you will also need to put together a presentation for the meeting itself. Key areas to cover include:

- The market size
- Growth potential opportunities
- Your company's position in that market (including information about competitors)
- Revenue streams
- The history and qualities of the management team
- The growth plan
- Your company's attitude to working in partnership with the funder.

Although the product or service that is core to your offering is important, remember that the investor will want to know exactly how you bring it to market.

Even if you are accustomed to extolling the merits of your company, it is worth rehearsing the pitch in the comfort of your offices to iron out any flaws and identify weaknesses. If you don't have an adviser, find an independent third party to act as a sounding board. Again, a non-executive executive or chairman can prove invaluable here – after all, most of them will have been there, seen it and done it – or a financial public relations company.

For better or worse, PowerPoint presentations tend to be the order of the day, but there are pitfalls that you should be aware of. A common mistake is cramming too much information onto the screen – three bullet points per slide is probably more than enough. Technology can fail so have paper versions ready as well in case your electronic presentation doesn't work for various reasons. Your technology worries will probably be lessened if you make the presentation at your own offices, and this will also help you to feel more confident and less nervous. But remember you will also have to consider your office environment and the impression it will give to potential investors.

Your presentation should be about 20 minutes, covering all the relevant detail but avoiding overkill. Be prepared, though, for a meeting that will last about two hours. Much of that will be taken up by questions, although the overall structure will vary. Some investors will prefer you to kick off with a formal presentation before a question-and-answer session. Others expect to ask questions as you go through the pitch.

THE IMPORTANCE OF BEING HONEST

It may be tempting to field projections that show you will be as big as Microsoft by 2015, but remember that savvy investors aren't going to be impressed with unreliable statistics. Instead, be honest and point out the potential obstacles as well as the opportunities. Rather than deterring investors, pointing out the risks and challenges is likely to impress them, especially if you can show that you have the vision to address and overcome them. Equally, weaknesses on the board may not be deal breaker. If you are in need of a strong sales director and say so, the investor may be in position to help.

Some CEOs pitch single-handedly, but by and large investors want to meet your management team, so that they can get a better feel for the dynamics of the people who might be spending their money. This will mean making sure that the key players are available, and that they

DEVELOPMENT FUNDING
Company: Prevx
Founder: Nick Ray

When Nick Ray started Prevx back in 2001, with a view to developing a market-leading intruder prevention product, finding funding was difficult. 'To start off, it was a bit bewildering,' he recalls. 'We did have corporate finance advice in terms of identifying where to go, but we ended up speaking to around 70 sources of funding. It was a long and laborious process as 2001 was not a great time for new tech firms. It was very difficult for a pre-revenue and pre-product company to get anywhere with VCs. The trouble was we couldn't possibly get there without their help.'

After getting close to a deal with two investors before the deal finally fell through, Ray was forced to continue developing Prevx's product with the company's own financial resources. The breakthrough came when he eventually sat round the table with the South East Growth Fund, convincing those behind it to invest £500,000 in the company. 'Their willingness to listen and understand our business was great,' he says. 'They were very supportive and introduced us to other opportunities, while not really interfering with the day-to-day running of the business.'

However, as is often the case with a fast-growth business, by the time Ray had his hands on the money, he realised it wasn't enough and another round of funding lay ahead. No longer private equity novices, Prvex gravitated towards Hotbed, a company that has created a network of private investors. 'As they began to promote it to their investors, we developed our products, and in the end we were three times oversubscribed,' explains Ray.

have been briefed thoroughly on how to present themselves and what to say.

When the meeting comes to an end, don't expect an instant answer, but be certain about what happens next. Always get a timetable for getting back an answer.

If your pitch fails, you can expect to get some comments on the reasons why, which you should use to sharpen future pitches. However, don't be tempted to argue or try to convince the funder that a mistake has been made. Instead, take on board any criticism or feedback from the last presentation before moving on to the next prospect. Often an investor will say that your business is not quite right for them – at which point do ask whom they suggest might be more suitable. Investors may well know others who would be a better fit for your business.

Due diligence

Although private equity investors can be hard nuts to crack, if you approach the pitch professionally and your reason for requesting the funding is sound, there's a good chance that they will say: 'Yes'. So always be prepared for what happens next.

First, remember that a positive response to your pitch is only provisional. Once a deal is agreed in principle, the investor will send you a 'term sheet'. This is in important document, as it will detail the agreed terms and conditions of the deal, providing a template for the more detailed contractual negotiations to come later.

Second, your company will have to undergo an intense verification process known as due diligence before the deal is signed. This is where the investor carries out a thorough check of your business, so be prepared to answer a myriad of questions about your company's past, present and future status. There are several different types of due diligence – you may have come across references to technical, insurance and even human resource due diligence, but the most common are commercial and legal. Essentially, you will hand over accounts details, management CVs, legal documents and information concerning clients, suppliers and even competitors on top of any other data your investors feel they need to see.

Investors want to be sure you can achieve your expansion plans with the money they're offering, so they will look into your IT systems, office space and production facilities. They will talk to your clients, customers and suppliers to find out whether you have a good relationship with them, and if they plan to work with you or buy more of your product in the future. VCs also insist on checking the work history of the company's senior executives. Be warned, these personal checks can be exhaustive, so be prepared to explain any career gaps. Investors will always want you to account for past business failures too.

To get the clearest possible impression of your business, a VC will most probably hire a specialist commercial due diligence company to assess your operation against your competitors. Add the various lawyers, bankers and advisers on both sides of the transaction, and you are right in thinking that you will be faced with several interested parties, all of whom want access to your business. Unfortunately, all of these advisers must be paid. And while VCs will want to establish a good rapport with management teams, they will not pick up the bill.

Financial aspects of due diligence

Altogether you should expect to pay approximately 10% of the value of the investment in costs. This money comes from what the investors give you, so if you are looking for £1m you should ask for around £1.1m to help settle up afterwards. But be aware you might end up footing the fees if something is discovered which leads to the investor pulling out. Check your term sheet carefully, and make sure you are comfortable with it – the VC will want you to write back confirming you are satisfied before due diligence begins.

Timescale for due diligence

You can speed up the due diligence process in two ways. First, be as honest as possible about the business ahead of the process beginning, and second, try to ensure that you agree as much as possible about the parameters of the deal before the due diligence process even begins. For instance, if the company is using a vital piece of equipment or property that is owned by you rather than the business as an entity, you need to be clear in advance whether it is included in the deal. Having done that, liaise with your advisers and ask what kind of information will be required, thereby having it ready when called upon. Remember also there are several different groups involved in the process and which may ask for the same information at once. So it pays to sort out copies of key documents and arrange with your lawyers to have them distributed as soon as they are needed.

Although due diligence is wearing, it won't last for ever. In fact, it's relatively brief, taking, on average, between three and six weeks. To minimise risk, investors look at likely problems first and then move on to the finer details once they are happy the business has nothing obviously wrong with it. At the end, the lawyers will draw up a shareholder's agreement – which should mirror the term sheet, although it will be legally binding and with more detail. Then you are ready for the money.

Negotiating with investors: understanding the small print
Shareholders' agreement

Investors shouldn't seek to manage the business, but they will typically have a power of veto in key areas

Your investors will almost certainly insist on a shareholders' agreement. This include warranties – statements made by you confirming that everything you have told the investor about the business is factually correct – and confirmation of everything that is 'in' the business. For instance, the agreement will list the business's assets, contractual arrangements, unforeseen liabilities (such as litigation round the corner) and warranties on the business plan you presented.

A shareholders' agreement will also put down a marker on management performers, stipulating what the investor expects. This needs to be based on reasonable assumptions.

Covenants

Shareholder agreements typically contain two types of covenant – the rules under which you, the management team and indeed the investors are required to operate:

- Corporate covenants define what the company can and can't do. This may include the investors' rights to monitor the investment, receive management accounts four weeks from month end, take a seat on the board and attend 12 board meetings a year. Corporate covenants also lay down the law on actions for which consent is required. These consents typically cover borrowing money, issuing new shares, capital expenditure not in the budget, changes to the business plan, senior appointments or removals and contractual obligations affecting profit and performance in the medium term.
- Management covenants are aimed at securing a level of commitment from the business owners. For instance, a typical management covenant agreement will commit you to the business full time and prevent you from launching a competitor.

Articles of association

The degree of control that their soon-to-be-acquired equity stake bestows on the investor is defined by the 'articles of association'. Investors may insist on separate classes of shares, such as A or B, giving them a preferential dividend linked to profits, meaning the more your company makes, the higher the dividend payment. Equally, they may demand stronger voting rights, allowing them to step in and override your decisions, even if the stake they hold in the company is less than 50%.

If investors – particularly angels – are looking to recoup their outlay over the course of the investment, it can be achieved through:

- Dividends, usually paid at the end of each financial year in the same way as those paid to company directors
- Straight capital, simply taking money out of the business
- Monitoring fees or directors' fees, submitted as invoices in the same way as a supplier would.

The issue of shares

Investors may also expect to be able to transfer shares more freely than management. This could be concerning from a management point of view as you could end up with an investor you don't want. To avoid this you need to have the right of first refusal – pre-emption rights – enabling you to buy out the investors' shareholding before they sell to a third party.

Equally, management would not have rights to sell shares at all initially, as you are the ones the investor has backed. This restriction tends to last for two years and is negotiable. If you do leave, a 'good leaver, bad leaver' clause will enforce further restrictions on you. This may include placing limits on the value of a leaver's equity stake, potentially leaving the departee with no return for his or her effort.

One other tricky area is provisions agreeing terms of dilution of your investor's stake in your company at the next round of funding. A lot of private investors insist on anti-dilution caveat which protect an investor's stake in the company against further investment that may dilute their holding. This can make it difficult to plug a funding gap if your existing investors are not in a position to put in more cash. Make sure you ask what would happen if you require further rounds of investment – it could shift the power base if you relinquish more equity.

Other powers

Investors shouldn't seek to manage the business, but they will typically have a power of veto in key areas, notably:

- Decisions to sell the business
- The appointment of new directors
- Remuneration packages
- Decisions to make acquisitions
- Significant new borrowing.

Living with investors

> **Try to ensure an investor's ability to exercise their rights are linked to the monthly reporting of the company**

Once an investment has been made, it is important to recognise that you are answerable to some other people. Although they are investing primarily for financial return, because most business angels have a good track record building and running companies themselves (many being serial entrepreneurs), they also tend to have a genuine interest in getting involved with businesses. Those who provide business finance as individuals, rather than through a syndicate, will almost certainly want a seat on the board.

Try to ensure an investor's ability to exercise their rights are linked to the monthly reporting of the company. Take communication seriously. Your investors may expect to attend board meetings, and the minimum you should provide is a monthly set of accounts. Some CEOs provide larger board packs, covering company performance, key issues and targets, a discussion of sales and challenges, in addition to accounts. Passive and minority shareholder investors deserve to receive quarterly reports.

To benefit from their wealth and expertise, you need to face up to surrendering not only a percentage of your company, but also a degree of independence. An investor's return is based on the performance of your business, which means they are likely to want a say in how you run it. If this benefits your company, then everyone wins, but you are unlikely to be used to sharing the decision-making process with an outside influence, and it's something you need to come to terms with before looking for equity investment. That's because, to make the most of the situation, you are likely to have to work well with the investor.

If the relationship works out, the result should be the kind of growth that makes your remaining stake in the business much more valuable than the original holding. If it doesn't, and the company doesn't expand as planned, you will be left with a diluted stake and a potentially difficult relationship with your backer. So it's vital to seek investment at the appropriate time and from the right type of private investor.

Private investors can ride you and your management team pretty hard – not surprising given that your company is now part of their investment portfolio, and how it performs has a direct impact on their return – and you will undoubtedly want to benefit from their expertise. But what is it like to live with an angel investor or VC on board?

Taking the back seat

You may be surprised to find that they are not around as much as you would expect. Angels and VCs invest in a portfolio of companies. They want them all to do well, but they won't necessarily be planning on spending a lot of time with your or any other business. For instance, Extreme Media Group's Al Gosling took on two angels five years after starting up, receiving £3m for 17% equity, and in November 2007 he was able to buy them out. He wanted proactive investors who could open doors and drive things forward. It half worked out. One helped implement board-level discipline, but the other proved particularly busy with a vast array of other projects. This is something you should think about before signing the deal and you should ask yourself a number of key questions. Will they really commit enough time? Will my business be a significant part of their portfolio? What access to their contacts will I have? How credible are they in the industry?

Taking control of the steering wheel

Some investors will take an overly active approach – to the point of seeking to micro-manage the business. The golden rule is that day-to-day operations should be sacrosanct, unless your angel or VC agrees to an executive role. So watch out for interference. You may not have a problem dealing with a more hands-on investor, but again you should think long and hard about the relationship in advance. If you suspect that the investors will seek to play a closer role than you would find comfortable, you may find it better to look elsewhere.

You need to remember that once the deal is done, you will be living with the investor for some time and they will be inextricably linked with your business. This makes it vital that you are happy with their level of input, and that you can enjoy a strong and healthy relationship with them.

The exit

Angels and VCs won't usually invest without an exit plan. Angels will usually want to move on after three or four years, perhaps taking advantage of a further funding round to sell up. When VCs are involved, the exit is more likely to be trade sale, flotation or even a sale to private equity fund. At that point, the chances are that your association with the business will also end. You sell up, cash in and look ahead to new business challenges or a well-earned retirement.

If things have gone well, you will be passing on a healthy company to enthusiastic new owners knowing that its managers and employees can look forward to a secure future. Even so, selling the business you have built can be a difficult thing to cope with. So before taking on a VC investment, ask yourself if an exit at a time of someone else's choosing is something that you will be comfortable with.

The last chapter of this book deals with floating on the stock markets – read on to find out if that is the way forward for your company.

! TOP TIPS

- ! Investors fall into two broad types: business angels and venture capitalists

- ! A business angel is a wealthy individual who invests money and time in other people's businesses, usually as a sideline

- ! A VC is a business that exists just to invest money in fast growth businesses.

- ! Investors can advise on strategy, open doors to new opportunities and provide invaluable contacts.

- ! Investors are looking for capital growth, typically between 25% and 50% per year.

- ! Your own networks as well as suppliers, accountants and business angel organisations are a good place to look for investors.

- ! When dealing with an investor, seek good advice – lawyers and accountants are vital, especially if a significant amount of money is involved.

- ! Take up references on your investors – don't venture into the unknown. Once the deal has been done, it will be too late.

- ! Know your numbers – when talking to potential investors, make sure you are confident talking about not only your historical revenue, cash flow, profit and key performance indicator statistics, but also your future projections.

- ! Rehearse your pitch – it's easy to stumble in an unfamiliar situation.

- ! Be prepared to answer a myriad of questions about your company's past, present and future status for the due diligence process.

- ! A shareholders' agreement will set out the fine print of the investment, including how much power the investor will have.

- ! An investor will usually want to move on after three or four years so consider if an exit at a time of someone else's choosing is something with which you will be comfortable.

FUNDING GROWTH 3:
STOCK MARKET FLOTATION

THIS CHAPTER WILL DISCUSS:

- Reasons to consider going public
- Is AIM right for your company?
- Preparing to float on AIM
- Life on AIM
- PLUS as an alternative

Stock markets channel money from investors wanting to earn more than they will get from a bank to companies that need capital to grow. Until a few decades ago stock markets were for 'Big Business' – going public on a stock market was a sign that a company had arrived. Then stock markets for smaller businesses appeared. Initially there was Nasdaq in the USA, which focused on raising growth capital for high tech companies. The London Stock Exchange (LSE) set up AIM a little over 10 years ago, with the aim of helping companies too young to float on the main market raise money. AIM has proved a great success, helping thousands of companies raise money since its launch. Today the UK also has PLUS Markets, which is a slightly smaller, independent stock exchange primarily targeting slightly younger or smaller companies than AIM.

A company raises money on a stock market by issuing new shares, which investors buy – just as with angel or venture capital (VC) investment. But there are several significant differences between the 'private' equity of angels and VC, and the 'public' equity of stock markets such as AIM. Unlike large public companies, most companies that float on AIM or PLUS actually have remarkably few private individuals as shareholders. Most of the money raised comes from a handful of institutions that invest in smaller companies. Some venture capital trusts (VCTs) are set up just to invest in new shares of companies launching on AIM, for example.

Going public is, indeed, very public. In order to list a company's shares on a stock market a vast amount of information needs to be published initially, and from then on public companies need to make their accounts public every three to six months so that investors can see how the company is performing.

FURTHER INFORMATION

- The London Stock Exchange: www.londonstockexchange.com
- PLUS Market: www.plusmarketsgroup.com

Reasons to consider going public

"Typically a company going public will raise considerably more than businesses raising money from private equity "

The main reason most companies go public is to raise money. This is usually new money to help the company grow, but occasionally existing shareholders can sell some shares to new investors, which can be one way to provide an exit for angel or VC investors.

Typically a company going public will raise considerably more than businesses raising money from private equity – £2m would be a small sum to raise, £5m probably a more typical amount, and companies have raised as much as several hundred million pounds on AIM in the past. The amount you can raise depends primarily on market sentiment – if the markets are feeling bullish, tiny companies have been known to raise significant amounts of money; when markets are depressed, even good companies can struggle to raise modest sums. The impact of market sentiment is much higher for AIM than for private equity.

Advantages of going public

Depending on sentiment when you first go public, you may well be able to achieve a much higher market value from AIM than you would get from a VC or business angel. This can mean that you need to give up much less equity than you would raising the same amount of capital privately – though the cost of going public is higher than that of raising funds privately (see below).

Remaining independent

For CEOs, probably the biggest single difference between going public on AIM and raising money from angels or VCs is independence. Both VCs and most business angels will require a shareholders' agreement (see Chapter 4.5) when they invest, which will give the investor considerable power over how the company is run. When you float, there is nothing like that at all – so you and your management team remain very much in charge, for better or worse. You will need to appoint one or two non-executive directors (NEDs) to your board, but that will still represent much less of a change to the independence of your management than a normal VC investment approach.

Raising more cash

Once you have joined a market – in the case of AIM through an 'initial public offering' – those shares can be traded in a secondary market. Essentially this means that shareholders will trade your shares and, depending on the laws of supply and demand, the price will go up and down accordingly. Although this won't effect the money you have at your disposal, a rising or stable share price will engender confidence in your company and make it easier to raise more cash in future. Conversely, a fall will hit confidence and make it harder to raise cash.

Once you have been on a market for a while, if you need more money to grow, you can turn to the market for additional finance through a 'secondary offering'. This can be an important facility, allowing you to address new funding requirements as your business grows. Entering the secondary market means that your share price can change every day, and can be shown in the tables in newspapers alongside other public companies. This can be useful for staff motivation, especially if you opt for share option or staff share purchase schemes.

Mergers and acquisitions

Public companies can also use their shares to make acquisitions. Instead of paying cash when you buy a business, you could issue new shares to the selling shareholders, which means that you can grow by acquisition for much less cash than a private company. This is a reason many companies choose to go public. AIM is extremely good for raising money, but has so far been less good for selling large values of shares. One effect of this is that some companies you want to acquire might not be willing to accept shares in your quoted company, and might insist on cash. (Plenty of companies have done both.) AIM can help here, too, though, as frequently a company's institutional investors will be willing to invest more money specifically to fund an acquisition.

Dominic Berger, founder of £5.8m turnover business Venue Solutions Holdings, bought an American-based business, Your Day, following his company's flotation in December 2005. He felt that being on the market made it easier to buy. 'AIM makes you more attractive to other companies looking for mergers and acquisitions,' he says. 'We now see opportunities in the market we wouldn't otherwise have seen. There's a perception that you have the financial muscle to make acquisitions.'

Choice of exit strategy

Another benefit of flotation is that exiting your company isn't an inevitable by-product of listing, as it is if you take investment from a

ABOUT AIM

AIM has been one of the City of London's success stories. It was originally intended as a stepping stone to the LSE main list. The idea was that young companies could get a taste of public life on a junior market before moving on to the LSE. The bar was set accordingly. Costs were lower than on the main list, there was no requirement to show a trading record and the regulatory regime was (and still is) one that would protect investors without putting an unworkable burden on listed companies.

Today, however, AIM has established itself as a destination in its own right, and has recently attracted more flotations than the LSE itself. This is because it is cheaper, quicker, and more tax efficient than the main list, yet offers most of the same advantages. AIM has even succeeded in attracting institutional investors, which traditionally have not wanted to go near investments in smaller companies. Indeed, these days most of the UK's institutions invest in AIM, which means that for the right companies there is a huge amount of capital available.

One reason that the institutions have been prepared to invest is that AIM has pulled off a remarkable trick. Although regulation is handled with a lighter touch than on the LSE's main list, making life for listed businesses much less onerous, it is also deemed robust enough to assure the investment community that companies on AIM are fit for public status.

VC or angel, who will ultimately want to realise their return. Flotation provides a means to raise large amounts of capital without having to sign up to an exit timetable. It also tends to be cheaper in terms of the equity you will be required to surrender in exchange for the capital you need to grow.

Disadvantages of going public

The financial cost

It's very expensive to go public. It can be hard to bring the total cost of going public in below £500,000, for example. If you only want to raise £1m, clearly this is hard to see making sense. But plenty of companies do spend £500,000 to raise £2m; and raising £3m or £4m brings the cost down considerably as a percentage of the sum being raised.

There are also a number of other costs to stay being public. You need to pay annual fees to the LSE, and pay your AIM adviser an annual retainer even if you don't do any new transactions. Most companies find that their legal and accounting bills are also higher, and also use a financial public relations (PR) firm to promote their company to the investment community. You should expect annual costs for all this to be at least £100,000, and probably closer to £200,000.

Non-financial costs

We have already mentioned that you need to make your accounts public faster and more frequently than private companies, giving your competitors access to that information. In addition you will need to declare any major events, such as possible takeover bids, which again is a slight disadvantage compared with being private. When business goes well, disclosing your performance might attract potential competitors; when your business goes badly, you should expect that most of your industry, including your suppliers, will know about it.

BUSINESS AS USUAL WHILE GETTING LISTED

Company: Qonnectis
Managing director: Mike Tapia

Technology company Qonnectis listed on AIM in February 2005, raising £1.2m. 'It helps to remember that floating is just a means to an end, not an end in itself,' says the company's managing direct Mike Tapia. 'The greatest challenge was coordinating the flotation while making sure the business continued to grow and develop at the same time.'

Tapia found the process of getting listed time consuming and distracting, and says he was very conscious about ensuring the business was not affected. 'We solved this problem by creating a small, dedicated flotation team and made sure that the rest of the management team were allowed to get on with the day-to-day management of Qonnectis,' he explains.

Since listing, Qonnectis has found investor relations crucial. 'We have a lot of contact with shareholders, who often call or email us directly asking for information,' says Tapia. 'But we've realised it's important to be pro-active, too, and we're currently in the process of updating our website to add a number of features specifically designed for investors.'

Time costs

The process of going public is very time-consuming. And once you go public, you need considerable time to deal with all the announcements that need to be made and for preparing the extra accounts, speaking to shareholders, and so on. You can delegate part of this to a non-executive chairman or financial director, but some of it will still have an impact on your management team's ability to run the business.

By listing, you should have plenty of people to turn to for advice who have an active interest in your company performing well. So use your shareholders and other key contacts wisely, and warn the right people in advance of any potential problem so that you have time to deal with it. Shareholders are often sympathetic when profits aren't huge and will usually offer constructive advice rather than calling for heads to roll at the first opportunity.

BEING AWARE OF THE RISKS

There are two major risks during flotation for which you need to be prepared:

- First, you may fail to gain backing for the float and so can't actually list. Although brokers often work on a no-list-no-fee basis, you will still be liable to pay most of the other fees, not to mention the amount of your time the process has occupied. However, dealing honestly and openly with all parties from the outset is the key to avoiding such a problem. You can also sound people out a long time before a float. Advisers are often happy to hold a meeting, even if you are still just considering flotation.
- Second, the process of floating can be so time consuming that management takes its eyes away from the core business, and results suffer (see 'Time costs' and the accompanying case study). Once you are listed, this can lead to your share price falling, which would be a poor start to life as a listed company. Good reputations take time to build, but can be wiped out fast. Public markets don't like surprises – be as conservatively honest as you can when setting expectations.

Is AIM right for your company?

General requirements for floating on AIM

Although AIM isn't focused on a particular industry sector, companies listed on the market tend to have some common characteristics. This mainly reflects the preferences of investors, and before you embark on the lengthy process of preparing for flotation, you need to ensure your company will appeal to them. The key to floating successfully on AIM is to prove to investors that your business is worthy of investment. Investors generally look for businesses that have the potential to deliver a higher return on their investment than they would usually get from LSE main list stock, which tend to be FTSE 350 companies offering security, but not a huge amount of growth in share value. AIM investors will usually expect slightly lower growth in share values than VC or business angel investors. This means AIM investors have a preference for companies that:

> **Investors tend to look for companies that have demonstrated their ability to compete for business and make money**

- Operate in clearly defined markets that are either growing or where there is scope to increase share value through mergers or acquisitions
- Work in markets where there is a high barrier to entry that will prevent competitors moving in with 'me too' products
- Have a strong management team and sound business plan.

If you can offer the above, then in theory you can float on AIM with nothing more than a brilliant idea, as there is no requirement to have a trading track record. In practice, though, investors tend to look for companies that have demonstrated their ability to compete for business and make money. So typically, they like to see a few years of audited accounts, healthy order books, growing revenues and profits.

Exceptions

However, there are exceptions to these general requirements. Some of the companies on AIM are huge, with market capitalisations in excess of £100m. At first sight these would seem likely candidates for the LSE main list, but as some had a trading history of less than three years when they sought a listing, AIM was the market of choice.

Although a good trading history is clearly a big plus when you are pitching to the City, there are some companies on AIM that have yet to generate revenue. However, these are usually raising money for 'discoveries', be it technological or natural resources. In such cases, the credentials of the board will come under scrutiny, because investors will be putting their faith in the management team. So if you are confident that your idea has high growth potential – whether it's a technological innovation or it's targeting an as yet untapped or up-and-coming market – there is no reason why you shouldn't float even though you haven't started trading. However, this is a higher risk strategy and you do need to tread carefully.

Preparing to float on AIM

You may need to make several changes to your company in preparation for its flotation on AIM. Although the process will be a challenge, particularly to CEOs used to being in absolute control, your company should emerge from the changes in a stronger position, not simply from the perspective of appealing to investors, but also from a trading point of view. For instance, AIM investors expect to see strong and accountable boards, with an experienced finance director, chairman and NEDs.

> **In the run up to flotation, you will need to introduce much more rigorous systems**

Typically procedures will have to be formalised. For instance, in a young entrepreneurial company, the information flow often centres around the CEO. In the run up to flotation, you will need to introduce much more rigorous systems to provide the new board members with timely, high-quality management information. You will also need to have your accounts and all relevant information in excellent shape, ready to prepare your admission document. Don't underestimate how much time this will take. Ideally, you would start six to 12 months before your planned flotation date, and, therefore, give yourself plenty of time to deal with any problems that may arise.

There are three main ways to become an AIM-listed company – one whose shares can be bought, traded and 'listed' among other AIM companies. The traditional route is via an initial public offering. However, increasingly companies are opting for a slightly cheaper route of a placing and introduction, whereby a company places shares with a group of investors and then immediately lists its shares on AIM. Most of the details (costs, information needs and process) are similar for both processes.

If you are seriously considering floating on AIM as a growth option for your business, you will need a minimum of five advisers: an official AIM-nominated adviser (or NOMAD), an auditor, a stockbroker, a law firm and a financial PR company. All are essential and don't come cheap, so you have to make sure you have the necessary financial resources in place. Here's what you can expect to be charged for their work:

- NOMAD: £100,000 or more
- Brokers: 3% to 5% of the money raised
- Law firm: £50,000 to £500,000
- Accountants: £40,000 to £100,000
- Financial PR: £30,000 or more.

So who are these people and what do you get for your money?

Nomads

Without a NOMAD you can't list on the market

These are the AIM gatekeepers and have all been pre-vetted and approved by the LSE. Their first task is assessing the suitability of new candidates for AIM. Without a NOMAD you can't list on the market and if for some reason your particular NOMAD firm resigns post-flotation, your company's shares will be suspended until a replacement is found.

Once you decide to float, you select a NOMAD. They look at your business and tell you whether an initial public offering is feasible. Getting a negative response doesn't necessarily imply you have got a bad company. It may simply mean that your management team isn't yet strong enough or that the business plan doesn't match the expectations of the investment community. If the NOMAD does advise against flotation, you can try to find another adviser. NOMADs do vary a little, and some might be a much better fit for your business than others. Your accountancy firm should be able to steer you to a good one for your company.

If you get a positive response from a NOMAD's initial assessment, they will take on the role of managing the flotation process, act as financial advisers and liaise with the other advisers, such as the legal team and the accountants. Post-flotation, their role changes again, becoming an ongoing advisory role, in particular counselling clients about AIM regulation. A list of approved nominated advisers is available from the LSE.

The accountancy firm

Although you almost certainly already have an accountant, once a flotation is on the cards it is essential to work with one that has credibility in the City, even if that means switching firms. Everyone involved in the flotation needs to be able to rely absolutely on the numbers, so it's advisable to work with a firm that has handled flotations successfully before. That doesn't necessarily mean paying for the services of one of the Big Four accountancy firms, as a lot of other firms also have AIM experience. Mid-tier firms such as Grant Thornton, Baker Tilly, Smith & Williamson do a lot of AIM flotations.

> **It's advisable to work with a firm that has handled flotations successfully before**

The role of the accountant is to report to the directors and the NOMAD, providing audited figures for the prospectus – the admission document that needs to be prepared as part of the pre-flotation process. Along with the legal team, the accountants carry out much of the due diligence work – the detailed background checks that need to be carried out for your business to make sure it meets the necessary criteria – that takes place ahead of flotation. They will also advise on tax, share options, company structure and governance.

The legal team

You need good legal advice throughout the flotation process. Lawyers will advise you on your contracts with your NOMAD and broker, and help ensure compliance with the regulations associated with an AIM listing. In particular they will brief you on the legal implications of the information submitted in the prospectus and the liabilities and responsibilities of being an AIM director.

In addition, lawyers work closely with the NOMAD on the preparation of the prospectus, casting a legal eye over the statements made. In terms of the due diligence process, the lawyers' work includes checking director and employee contracts, verifying ownership of intellectual property and reporting on any outstanding or impending litigation.

The stockbroker

Brokers are effectively the sales people, City insiders who connect your business with investors. Their role is to promote the shares, generate interest and attempt to ensure the widest possible distribution of the stock when the company comes to the market. In the run up to the flotation, they will organise roadshows – meetings at which the financial director, chief executive and chairman pitch the business to institutions.

Financial PR firms

As there are now several thousand AIM companies, getting your message out to investors has never been more important and challenging. A financial PR firm will help you to refine your story to give your pitch maximum investor appeal, and will be responsible for relaying and publicising key announcements, such as results, appointments and new contracts.

 ADVICE IS KEY

Company: Servocell
Chief financial officer: Steven Wever

Despite not having begun trading, technology company Servocell raised £5.5m to fund growth when it listed on AIM in April 2006. One of the main reasons for Servocell's successful flotation was getting the right advisers on board. 'The key ones are the NOMAD and broker,' says Wever, 'When we spoke to the press and to private clients without brokers present, they all said that the reputation of the advisers was very important.

'Our nominated adviser and broker Bell Lawrie built a shareholder list that exceeded our expectations, and ran a very tightly targeted marketing campaign, so that we saw very few people who weren't genuinely interested in investing,' Wever continues. 'We only had two bad meetings out of around 30. If you do prove yourself to the investors, there is plenty of finance available for AIM companies to continue to invest in growth.'

Choosing advisers

When looking for any of the advisers discussed here, check out their track record, experience in your sector and contacts; be prepared to check out several before making your choice. Seek recommendations and take up references with other clients and find out how they have reacted when a client has encountered difficulty.

It's also a good idea to meet the executives who will handle your account, and look at their individual track records. Some firms grow fast and a company with a great name might not be the best one for you if you get one of their less experienced or able staff.

Whether you go for a small or large firm is a matter of personal taste. What is more important is that you have a good relationship with them, so take time and effort to build a rapport – and make sure they are doing the same.

Board structure

To float on AIM, you should have separate people in the roles of chairman and chief executive. You will also need a finance director, company secretary, and several NEDs.

There are no definitive rules on how many NEDs an AIM company should have on its board, but two is considered the minimum. Use the appointment of NEDs as an opportunity to boost your company's expertise or contacts. Some CEOs will mix their NEDs, so one, say, has a particular skill-set while another has City of London experience.

NEDs will question your ideas, so it is important to make sure you get on well. They should be challenging, but not disruptive nor destructive. Having a board with strong credentials will help in the City, so if your current team doesn't look great on paper, a few older and wiser heads added to the mix might allay investors' fears.

> **If your current team doesn't look great on paper, a few older and wiser heads added to the mix might allay investors' fears**

Fundraising

You have 40 days from the date you make your application to raise the minimum investment set by your NOMAD and broker. If you can't generate enough in time, any cash you have raised will have to be returned.

The broker will help put together a presentation and arrange an investment roadshow where you will pitch to backers who will hopefully agree to invest, at which point you will sign a contract with the broker agreeing the funding. However, even getting in front of the right investors with the right presentation is no guarantee of winning investment, as the market fluctuates throughout the year.

Cash shells

Some companies choose a much less common route to market, that is they choose to do a reverse takeover of a cash shell. This means that you sell all the shares in your company to an AIM-listed company in return for shares in that company, such that your shareholders would end up being majority shareholders in the AIM company. Usually you would then change the name of the AIM company to your brand.

This can be much faster than a normal AIM flotation, and has the advantage that you know in advance exactly how much cash will be raised. Against that, it can prove more expensive than floating normally, since the original shareholders of the AIM cash shell will remain shareholders in 'your' company after the deal has gone through.

One concern is also what nasties there could be lurking within the cash shell. A cash shell is merely a phrase used to describe a company listed on AIM which no longer trades. 'Clean shells' are companies which have never traded, and simply list in order to raise funds and then seek companies to acquire – just as Clapham House did (see Chapter 1.3). 'Dirty shells' are companies that are floated doing one activity, and then for whatever reason cease that, and look around for something else to do.

The AIM rules about cash shells changed some years ago, limiting the time a cash shell can remain on AIM, which has reduced the number of cash shells somewhat. It is well worth asking your accountant whether the cash shell route might be suitable for your business.

Life on AIM

Once you have successfully negotiated the listing process and you have finally arrived on AIM, your company can start to reap the rewards of flotation, from a higher profile and all the benefits that brings, to easier access to funds and acquisitions. You will probably feel relief and euphoria at what you have achieved, but you also need to prepare yourself for somewhat of a culture shock. Once listed, you are suddenly answerable to shareholders and the public at large, and you are obliged to announce profits, losses and intentions to buy or sell.

> **Aside from addressing corporate governance, you should also be prepared to promote your business to the media and investors**

Complying with corporate governance and the Combined Code

One of the biggest changes you will face is the formalising of corporate governance, which, as an CEO, you will need to take time to understand thoroughly. This involves having the necessary systems and procedures in place to ensure that you are acting in the best interests of your shareholders at all times. Issues you will need to address include making sure you have the right number of NEDs on the board, that they're spending enough time scrutinising the work of the executive team, and that risk is being properly managed.

The 'Combined Code' is a document that defines best practice across a range of boardroom issues. Compliance with the code isn't compulsory, but companies on the LSE main list must provide shareholders with an explanation if they contravene its principles.

Strictly speaking, AIM-listed companies are not required to do this, but you need to bear in mind that as your market capitalisation grows, investors will expect to see a greater degree of compliance with the code.

One key area that will need attention is the roles of chairman and chief executive, which, according to the code, should be separate. On joining AIM it makes sense to make sure the roles are split, or investors may want to know why. Another issue is part-paying NEDs in shares rather than cash. Although normal practice in private companies, the code requires that NEDs should be independent of the boards on which they sit, which share ownership compromises, so you are supposed to pay NEDs just wish cash.

However, institutions tend to be more flexible with AIM-listed companies and often fall well short of demanding that the full rigours of the Combined Code be applied. But it's still of benefit to get to know the Combined Code and to implement as many of its requirements as you can into your newly listed company. Aside from addressing corporate governance, you should also be prepared to promote your business to the media and investors.

Promoting your business

'I probably spend about one day a month talking to journalists and about two weeks each year on face-to-face meetings with investors,' says Elizabeth Gooch of AIM-listed operations management company eg Solutions. Although you may be unaccustomed to the PR machine, Gooch sees it as an essential part of being listed on AIM. 'PR is something you have to do,' she asserts, so you will need to get used to talking up your business.

There are also certain rules you need to follow when listed. For example, you can't reveal all details of your company all of the time – there are non-reporting periods when you can't speak to the media. In addition, you can only disclose details to investors that are 'material' and not tell them about speculative deals, no matter how tempting this may be. 'It can be really frustrating taking criticism from investors when you know you are waiting for a deal to come through, but you aren't allowed to say so,' Gooch warns.

Carefully managing the relationship with your AIM investors is important. They need to be confident that your company is being run well and like the direction it's taking. This will encourage them to retain their shares. They can make their feelings known at your annual general meeting or simply sell their shares if they are unhappy. Although that won't affect the amount of money that your company has at its disposal, a sell off will certainly push down your share price, making it difficult to raise further cash and reducing your ability to make paper acquisitions.

The more of your investors that sell their shares, the greater the likelihood that they will end up in the hands of a relatively small group of shareholders, with the wider investment community having little interest in the stock. In this situation, any individual shareholder who decides to sell will have a disproportionate effect on the share price as a whole.

Although the costs and challenges of listing on AIM are by no means insignificant, the benefits can far exceed them if you handle your company appropriately once listed. The higher profile, better access to capital and the ability to use shares to buy other companies mean that once listed on AIM, companies seldom wish to return to the private arena.

PLUS as an alternative

Originally set up as OFEX, PLUS Markets Group has been working hard over the past few years to establish itself as a viable alternative to AIM. To support its ambitions, PLUS has now been granted Recognised Investment Exchange (RIE) status by the Financial Services Authority, making it a fully-fledged stock exchange with the same rights and privileges. And as AIM attracts ever larger companies, there is an argument that PLUS is ideally placed to cater for businesses that need low-cost access to public markets – the very audience that AIM was originally set up to appeal to.

PLUS Markets Group has two sides. On one hand, it provides a platform that enables investors to trade stocks that are already listed on any UK public market, including the LSE and AIM. Companies taking advantage of this equity market service are 'PLUS traded' stocks. At the same time, it also operates as an independent stock exchange, providing small- to medium-sized businesses with a means to raise up to £10m through flotation. Companies that list on the market are known as 'PLUS quoted'.

PLUS versus AIM

The big advantage of PLUS over AIM is that it is considerably cheaper both to join through an initial public offering and then to maintain a listing on. This makes it viable to raise smaller sums using it than with AIM. The regulatory burden is also lighter.

Both AIM and the PLUS Market are seeking to attract fast-growth companies, but there are some key differences between the two. PLUS primarily attracts individual investors (with very few institutions), whereas AIM has increasingly become a forum for institutions seeking to add high-risk/high-return shares to their portfolios. This is changing to an extent, but may take some time. Institutions are beginning to recognise the potential of PLUS for clients looking to raise profile by going public on a market not as crowded as AIM, whereas RIE status will certainly assist the elevation of PLUS in institutional fund managers' minds.

PLUS provides many of the benefits common to public markets. You can raise cash, boost your profile and use shares to buy other companies. However, without the same degree of institutional investment, shares are less actively traded on PLUS compared with AIM. This means it's easier to buy and sell shares on AIM, as trading is more active. Poor liquidity – a lack of available funds – can be a problem in a poor economic climate, and AIM arguably offers more in terms of profile, if you can succeed in your battle for air space with other listed companies.

Floating on PLUS

To undertake an initial public offering on PLUS, you have to appoint a corporate adviser approved by the market. You will also need audited accounts and working capital for 12 months. The adviser will help you prepare a prospectus if you are planning to raise more than €2.5m, or an admission document in the case of smaller sums.

The average cost of listing (including adviser fees) comes in at around £150,000 compared with £500,000 to £1m for a place on AIM. As with AIM, it is also possible to join PLUS through an issue of shares to a limited number of investors, rather than the public at large, in a private placing. And if you don't need to raise cash, you can enter the market via an introduction, enabling you to enjoy the benefits of listed status – including tradable shares – without first issuing new equity to the marketplace.

! TOP TIPS

! A company going public will generally raise much more money than businesses raising money from private equity.

! Advantages include the ability to achieve a much higher market value for your company, as well as the ability to remain independent and to choose your exit strategy.

! However, going public is expensive, time consuming, and means you disclose your accounts faster and more frequently.

! The key to floating successfully on AIM is to prove to investors that your business is worthy of investment.

! You will need the right management team, a strong offering, an impressive trading record, robust business systems and the appropriate paperwork.

! Be prepared for a culture shock when you experience life as a public company - you are suddenly answerable to shareholders and the public at large.

! Expect constructive criticism from directors – they should add value to the business, but investors expect non-executives to represent their interests in scrutinising the work of the executive team.

! Watch what you say – the Financial Services Authority enforces strict rules on public statements and you should be aware of the guidelines

! Be prepared to dedicate time to investors and journalists – this is part of the process of managing share price.

! Work on corporate governance – as an AIM-listed company, you don't have to comply with the Combined Code, but it provides a good template for governance standards

! Plus is an alternative to AIM, providing small- to medium sized businesses with a means to raise up to £10m through flotation.

ABOUT THE AUTHORS

Colin Mills is the Founder and Chief Executive Officer of The FD Centre Limited (www.thefdcentre.co.uk), and has over 20 years of financial director experience in UK, USA and European businesses with turnovers of £2 million to £500 million. A member of the Chartered Institute of Management Accountants and Institute Prize Winner, Colin also has an MBA from Henley. His industry experience covers construction, FMCG, retail, food, IT, contracting services, building products, paper, printing and property development in major UK & global companies in both FD and CEO roles

Clive Sanford has been involved in the mid-market mergers and acquisitions (M&A) marketplace since 1985. He was a partner and head of M&A at a major professional firm until 1990, and since then he has run his own specialist corporate finance advisory firm. He also has M&A experience as a principal, having been the financial director of an acquisitive £20m group. Clive has been involved in over 200 private company transactions and now combines the transaction-related advisory activities of Magus Partners (www.maguspartners.com) with his private investments and acting as a non-executive director or adviser to the boards of growing companies.

David Lester started his first business aged 22 and sold it for millions before he was 30. He has since started several other successful businesses and invested in many more. He is the founder of Startups. co.uk, the UK's most popular website for starting a business and Growing Business magazine, the UK's most popular magazine for entrepreneurs.

Gerard Burke is the founder and managing director of Business Growth Partnership Ltd, a business whose purpose is to help owner managers create the future they want for their businesses and themselves. In particular, Business Growth Partnership runs the world renowned Business Growth and Development Programme (BGP), the UK's leading programme for ambitious owner managers, on behalf of Cranfield School of Management. Gerard is the lead designer and programme director of the BGP programme. In this role, he leads the programme, co-ordinates the overall delivery ensuring that it meets the objectives of all the participants and leads the team of business counsellors who work with participants on a one-to-one basis and in small groups.

Previously, Gerard worked for 12 years as a management consultant with Price Waterhouse. He joined the faculty of Cranfield School of Management in 1992 and left to set up Business Growth Partnership in 2004.

Gerard is highly entrepreneurial and is also the founder of Cranfield Creates, which started life as a technology business incubator, providing management services to early stage technology ventures, and then became the technology transfer and commercialisation unit for Cranfield University.

Trevor Clawson is a business journalist, specialising in fast growth companies, corporate finance, new media marketing and technology. His work has appeared in a broad range of publications, including the Times, Sunday Times, the Guardian, Growing Business and Revolution. Trevor acted as a research editor on this project while contributed material for The Net Effect, Going Global, Extending Your Brand and Doing the deal.

INDEX